What Others Say . . .

"*Powering Up!* synthesizes much of the latest thinking on women's advancement into an inspirational and easy read. Anne Doyle provides a motivational look at how women can build on their strengths to fulfill their true leadership potential."

– BETH BROOKE, Global Vice Chair, Ernst & Young

"Anne Doyle's debut book is

eading for aspiring women of all ages."

thor of *Overexposed*
...ly as Good as Your Word

"Anne Doyle has been breaking barriers and shattering stereotypes all her life. Her advice is honest, hard-earned, and comes from the heart."

–ALEX TAYLOR, III, Senior Editor-at-large, *Fortune* magazine.

"When Anne Doyle broke into sports reporting, the glass ceiling for women in that profession was made of steel–and so was the door, which was often locked. With good grace, common sense and unrelenting professionalism, Doyle and other pioneers changed the demographics of the craft for the better. She is exceptionally qualified to author a book on female leadership. She knows the turf.

– JOE LAPOINTE, Sports journalist, *FanHouse, New York Times, Huffington Post*

"Anne Doyle shines an up-to-date spotlight on the unique talents and experiences that forge women leaders today. Her own unusual leadership pathway–from journalist and sportscaster to auto industry executive and now elected office–offers rich insight into how far women have come and what's next for those who dare to want more. Read this book."

– BETSY BERKHEMER, President, Berkhemer Clayton Executive Search
& Former California President, National Association Women Business Owners

"In the 1980s, when I began working with Ford, I was the only woman race car driver supported by an auto company. I quickly learned there were very few women in high level positions in the auto industry—and the ones who were there did not always support other women. Anne Doyle was different and immediately celebrated my efforts. She has continued to be an advocate and ally for all women who dare to test their limits and lead."

– LYN ST. JAMES, 1992 Indy 500 Rookie of the Year,
Author, Automotive Expert, Mentor

POWERING UP!

How America's Women Achievers Become Leaders

Anne Doyle

Library of Congress Control Number: 2010916598

ISBN:	Hardcover	978-1-4568-1175-4
	Softcover	978-1-4568-1174-7
	Ebook	978-1-4568-1176-1

Cover and interior design by Nancy Cohen, www.NancyCohenDesign.com

To contact author or engage with her blog community:
poweringupwomen@gmail.com
www.annedoylestrategies.com
Facebook: poweringupwomen

This book was printed in the United States of America.

To order additional copies of this book, contact:
Xlibris Corporation
1-888-795-4274
www.Xlibris.com
Orders@Xlibris.com
83646

PROLOGUE

Just a few days before I signed off on the final galleys for this book, our nation experienced something we had never faced before: a national female leader targeted by an assassin and shot down in cold blood. Arizona Congresswoman Gabrielle Giffords was the primary target of a mentally-ill, 22-year-old who shot her in the head at close range. Within a matter of seconds, Jared Loughner wounded 19 people, killing six, including a federal judge and a 9-year-old girl. They were all participating in a "Congress on the Corner" event that Rep. Giffords was hosting. If it hadn't been for courageous citizens who tackled and disarmed the madman while he was reloading, he would have killed or injured many more.

There is always danger in stepping forward as a leader. The more visible you are and the more willing to take stands, particularly on controversial issues, the greater your exposure. As a nation, we have learned that lesson the hard way. I'm old enough to remember the stunned horror that gripped America when John Kennedy, Martin Luther King and Robert Kennedy were murdered before our eyes. They were each courageous men who left tremendous legacies before being silenced by lone gunmen.

The pre-mediated attack on Congresswoman Giffords, as well as the death and injury of the citizens and staff who were with her, are stunning reminders of the dark side of leading. As the number of women stepping up to high-profile public positions increases, so will the risks. In modern history, three women heads of state have been assassinated. India's first Prime Minister, Indira Gandhi, was murdered by her own bodyguards in 1984. Agathe Uwillingiyimana had served as prime minister of Rwanda for one year when Hutu soldiers killed her in 1994. Most recently, the first female prime minister of Pakistan, Benazir Bhutto was assassinated in 2007 while campaigning for a second term. Congresswoman Giffords was well aware of the dangers of leadership. Hundreds of shouting, angry protestors routinely gathered on the street corner near her Tucson office. She had received multiple death threats, as many public officials do. And several times, after she cast particularly controversial votes, the glass-paneled door of her Arizona office was shattered with bricks or gunfire.

Leadership is never an easy path and not for everyone. But when Gabby Giffords recovers, which we all pray she will, I believe she will be the first to urge other women to join her and dare to lead.

Auburn Hills, Michigan, January 2011

For my sister, Mary, who gave up on herself before she discovered how magical she was.

And for my son, Kevin, whose possibilities all await.

The day will come when man will recognize woman as his peer, not only at the fireside but in councils of the nation. Then, and not until then, will there be the perfect comradeship, the ideal union between the sexes that shall result in the highest development of the race.

— SUSAN B. ANTHONY
American Civil Rights Leader, 1820-1906

CONTENTS

INTRODUCTION

Size Matters

It was in the most prestigious hotel in Madrid, in the spring of 2006, surrounded by more than six hundred highly accomplished women from all over the world, that I first sensed an emerging global force field of women. I have never forgotten the passion and strength in the voice of a leader from South America who spontaneously walked to the open microphone, looked around the ballroom at her peers from twenty-four countries and challenged her global sisters with these words: "Men are not the norm. Women are 51 percent of the world's population. It's time we give ourselves permission to be the leaders we were born to be and start to lift one another to positions of power." I felt chills and a sense of unprecedented possibility as I stood, along with every other woman in the room, to applaud.

That unforgettable moment occurred at a conference of the International Women's Forum (IWF), one of the preeminent global networks of women leaders. Since then, I have attended four other IWF conferences: in Chicago; Amman, Jordan; Pittsburgh; and Montreal. Each has enabled me to meet and begin building friendships with educated, evolved, aspiring female leaders from all over the planet. Women who are able and eager to travel to meet and learn from other women thinkers. Those gatherings and the women I have met from every corner of the globe were catalysts, inspirations and sources of wisdom for this book.

It was during my trip to the Mideast, for the 2007 IWF conference, that I first began asking women leaders from countries as diverse as Cameroon, Russia, Ecuador, Israel, Mexico, Canada, China, and Jordan, "What would you like to say to American women about leadership?" Their words differed, but the message they asked me to convey was nearly always this: "American women underestimate the ability and responsibility they have to help lift their global sisters throughout the world. When you rise, it helps us all rise." They are asking and waiting for American women *Achievers* to become *Leaders.*

It's Not That We're Ahead, We're Not

It's not that women in other parts of the world look to the United States as a model of gender equity or that we're more accomplished than our global sisters. We're not. The reality is that the United States slipped from twenty-third (in 2006) to thirty-first (in 2009) on the Global Gender Gap Index of 155 countries. Published annually by the World Economic Forum, the Index determines a country's ranking by measuring the differences between men and women in four key areas: economic participation and opportunity, political empowerment, education and health. The good news is that the U.S. jumped 12 places in 2010, cracking the top 20 for the first time in the five years that the Global Gender Gap Index has been published.[1] But we still trail 18 other countries. Most recently, Iceland moved into the number one position, with the other Nordic nations—Norway, Finland and Sweden—close behind. However, there is still not a country on the globe that has achieved equity for its female citizens.

Two factors, however, make American women unique: (1) we are citizens of the most influential nation in the world and (2) there are so many of us: 155.8 million (U.S. Census Bureau), compared with 151.8 million American men, with over 72 million American women in the workforce.[2]

At the beginning of the 21st Century, the United States is home to the largest critical mass of educated, accomplished, and politically active women *Achievers* in the history of the world. So why then is a country that is ranked first for women's education levels lagging behind 39 other countries when it comes to the political empowerment of our female citizens? Why has the number of women on our corporate boards barely budged for more than a decade?[3] With unprecedented numbers of women earning MBAs from Harvard, Booth, Wharton and other top business schools for several decades, why is it that female CEOs and executive-suite officers are still so rare? When women consistently vote in higher numbers than men, why, in 2011 are only 93 (18 Senators & 75 Representatives) of our 535 members of Congress female?[4] And how long must we wait until a woman sits at the desk in the Oval Office? What does it take for women *Achievers* to make the leap to leadership?

Those were the questions I pondered on the long plane ride home from the Mideast leadership conference. Those were the answers I sought as I put on my journalist's hat and began searching for fresh insight on what it takes to become a skilled leader—from the perspective and experience of *women* who have been there. What lessons learned could they pass along that could speed the journey of other women who hear the call to leadership? As Joan Anderson, author of several of my favorite books, including *A Walk on the Beach,* told me from her Cape Cod home, "Wisdom isn't worth a damn, Anne, unless you share it with others."

I began by interviewing my peers, women 50 and over, who had dynamited the tunnels, macheted the trails, and poured the pavement for the superhighways of opportunity that so many women are traveling on today. Then I started thinking about the generation of women who came after us. They have more medical degrees, law degrees, and MBAs; many played competitive sports and entered the military. And they often moved faster into higher positions of authority than we dreamed possible. What do all those "I'm no feminist but . . ." women know that my Gloria Steinem generation didn't? And how could I ignore the tsunami of social networking and web-savvy New Millennials who are oozing with confidence and itching to prove themselves? What could they teach us?

I started thinking deeply about the similarities and differences among the three generations of skilled, ambitious American women *Achievers* who are steadily re-shaping the workforce. We are quite different, molded and influenced by very distinct cultural values and work environments that were changing rapidly as each of our generations came of age and moved into the professional world. By the time I finished my original field research, I had interviewed more than 125 women of different generations, professions and economic, ethnic, and cultural backgrounds. As I reviewed transcripts of over 100 hours of interviews, I saw clear themes emerging—qualities and skills that women from all corners of the country repeatedly mentioned as being essential for their evolution into leaders. The same pattern occurred with specific weaknesses and gender-related behavior that came up over and over when I asked, "Why are women still so rare at the top?" In addition, I also spoke with several dozen global women leaders to explore their observations on American women. I began this project with a deep conviction that there was undiscovered leadership gold to be mined. I was right. The good news is that I could have gone on interviewing highly accomplished women for years. There are so many. But the time came when I realized that I had *the story*. I didn't need more evidence of what women *Achievers* need to do—and stop doing—to make the leap to leadership. I had discovered rich veins of insight about becoming effective leaders that women can only learn from one another. My mission became to share it.

Why Another Book on Leadership?

Yes, I know, there have been hundreds of books written on leadership. I've read nearly all of the best ones. So, why another one? Because most have been written by men, based on men's experiences and values. Very few draw upon the rich experience of growing numbers of women who have been developing a new leadership style and tapping the strengths of our own gender for decades.

A recent trip to a large Borders bookstore in an affluent Midwest suburb provided a revealing snapshot of the present marketplace for books on leadership. When I asked the 20-something young woman working at the information desk, “What book or author comes to mind when you think about women’s leadership?” she paused, thought for a minute, and then responded, “I don’t know. I’ve never really heard of a book about women’s leadership.” She then directed me to two departments: the women’s studies section and the leadership shelves of the business section. Of the 139 distinct titles related to leadership on Borders’ shelves that day, only nine were written by women. And those books were primarily guides to individual professional and personal success or academic dissections of gender inequity. The other 130 leadership books were written by men and based, nearly exclusively, on male experience and work environments. Most of the authors were business executives, sports stars, or military leaders. One was the leader of a motorcycle gang.

Men and women have plenty to teach one another. Part of the same human nation, we are still different tribes with fundamental and important differences, including, as we now know, how our brains process information or react to stress and stimulation. Because of our genders, we see and experience the world through very different lenses. Women will never learn to tap our full leadership potential by modeling ourselves after men.

Size Matters

Of course, there have always been extraordinary, gutsy women who slipped their gender chains, bucked cultural pressure, and pushed the edges of feminine possibility: Cleopatra, Marie Curie, Golda Meir, Queen Victoria, Sojourner Truth, Susan B. Anthony, Rosa Parks, Amelia Earhart,

Annie Oakley, Eleanor Roosevelt, Indira Gandhi, Coretta Scott King and Margaret Thatcher, to name a few. I'd be the last person to minimize the distance we've covered, even in my working lifetime. Every time I turn on the TV in my kitchen and see network news anchors Katie Couric and Diane Sawyer reporting from Mideast hot spots or Haiti, Rhodes Scholar Rachel Maddow anchoring her own political show on MSNBC, and Whoopi Goldberg or Ellen DeGeneres hosting the Oscars, I flash back to my loneliest and most difficult days as one of the first female TV sports broadcasters in the nation. As I stood outside locker rooms, trying to find the courage to walk in, or faced a roomful of mocking businessmen, I could hardly imagine a day when over 1,000 women would be professional sports journalists, as they are today.

Don't kid yourself: size matters. Not just because it's nice to have company when you're sticking your neck out and leading, but because sustainable cultural change requires collective power. An abundance of recent research shows that a few lone women, no matter how exceptional they are, have little impact on the conversation of a nearly all-male group, let alone its decisions. It takes critical mass to shift group dynamics. It isn't until minority voices reach a "tipping point" of one-third representation in groups that they begin to significantly influence outcomes.

Groundbreakers, a comprehensive 2009 report on harnessing the global power of women, published by Ernst & Young, cites research on the correlation between bottom line corporate performance and the number of women in senior leadership positions. For management teams and boards averaging ten members, the magic number is three: one-third. "Performance increased significantly once a certain critical mass was attained—namely, at least three women on management committees," the study reported. "Below this threshold, there was no significant difference in company performance."[5]

On a ten-member corporate board, critical mass means at least three. Yet fewer than 20 percent of Fortune 500 companies have three or more women board members serving together, according to Catalyst,[6] the leading non-profit research and consulting organization working to advance women in business and the professions. In the 100-member U.S. Senate, critical mass would be 33. Yet, in 2011, with only 18 women senators, we need to nearly double those numbers to reach the influence tipping point. Whether it's an executive leadership team or scriptwriters for Jon Stewart's *The Daily Show,* lone, diverse voices—with a different perspective than the dominant majority—have little power. Think about it. What size stake does a Warren Buffett-size investor or a company need to own in a business in order to make sure that its voice is heard? And listened to? The magic number is thirty-three and one-third percent. While I was working as a communications and governmental affairs executive at Ford Motor Company, that was exactly the percentage of Mazda stock that Ford owned—just enough to influence outcomes—anything lower than that, and you're truly a minority stockholder.

The Wind Is Changing

When I started my research, I was discouraged about women's progress. For all of our individual accomplishments, we seemed to be idling in place—stalled just below all those nearly impenetrable glass ceilings. But women are on the move again. This time, the wind is at our back. In its June/July 2010 issue, *Atlantic* magazine published an article entitled "The End of Men." The headline was a controversial but catchy way to make a serious point. "Man has been the dominant sex since, well, the dawn of mankind. But for the first time in human history, that is changing—and with shocking speed," author Hanna Rosin reported.[7] A few weeks later, *Newsweek* magazine followed with an article entitled "Women Will Rule the World." It called the 2007 recession a "man-cession" and predicted that women would lead the global economic recovery.[8] And when Elena Kagan was sworn in on August 7, 2010, as the 112th justice on the highest court in our land, it opened a new era in American justice: for the first time in U.S. history, three of the nine justices—one-third (remember the tipping point?)—on the Supreme Court are women. That's an unprecedented breakthrough.

Powering Up Is Full of Stories

"A story is a container for memory." I'm not sure who said that or when I first heard the quote, but I've always understood that we humans learn best through stories. You'll hear my own. And I have some doozies from my years on the front lines of some of the toughest leadership laboratories for women: sports broadcasting, the global auto industry, politics, and parenting. (Yes, parenting is most definitely a leadership laboratory!) But this isn't a memoir. I'm just one example of millions of American women who are leading a deep cultural change in our country that continues to ripple throughout the world. That's why I've drawn upon the stories and lessons learned from many exceptional women.

In Part One ("Who Are We?"), you'll meet the groups I call the *Pioneering Interlopers, Influential Insiders, and I'll-Do-It-My-Way Innovators.* These high-achieving females are subsets of Baby Boomers, Gen Xs, and Gen Ys. In Part Two ("Where Are We?"), I look at two issues that so many women—of all ages—brought up as critical to our upward momentum: (1) how women continue to sabotage ourselves and (2) the important role of men. Part Three ("How Achievers Become Leaders") focuses on the Seven Practices that I now believe are essential for women to become leaders. They are the result of my best thinking based on nearly four decades of helping to push the edges of opportunity for women in the workforce, years of reading and research and literally thousands of conversations about leadership with wise women. Each leader I interviewed was eager to pass along the insight and lessons learned from her own successes, setbacks, and defining moments. I wish I could quote everyone who spoke with me because each one influenced and helped sharpen my thinking. Not one is a Queen Bee, which Dr. Julianne Malveaux, president of Bennett College for women describes as, "Women who get some psychic pleasure by being the first and only. Queen Bees don't give other women a break because no one gave them one, by golly."[9] Malveaux has written about the Queen Bee style of female leadership as well as its opposite, which she calls "The Nurturer." Every leader I interviewed for this book passionately believes that, as Dr. Rosemary Brown, the first woman of color elected to a provincial parliament in Canada put it, "Until all of us make it, none of us have made it."[10]

The next phase of women's evolution is about power—collective power. We need women's voices, values, and leadership fully engaged in every sector. Years ago, I learned that I would never succeed myself, let alone help open doors for future women sports journalists, unless I threw myself into the fire of the locker room crucible. Positive social change doesn't just happen. People have to lead it. People with vision—who can imagine a better future. People with courage—to change the status quo. People with tenacity—to get the job done even when the going gets tough. Thousands of women inspired, influenced, and, in many different ways, helped me write this book and with whom I share a common purpose: We want to recruit you. Come lead with us. The world is watching—and waiting.

Part One

Who Are We?

CHAPTER 1

So Many Achievers— Where Are Our Leaders?

The torch is being passed to a new gender. There's no doubt in my mind that we women will lift that torch. We will carry it. And we will light a new way forward.

— MARIA SHRIVER, Journalist, Author, *Insider*

Something remarkable about American women and leadership unfolded during the 2008 presidential campaign. Nearly simultaneously, three very different female leaders ascended to our national political forefront. Two of them—Hillary Clinton and Sarah Palin, fiercely ambitious, iconic leaders—came closer than any other women in history to breaking the 220-year male winning streak for two of the most powerful positions in the world: president and vice president of the United States. The third, Harvard Law School graduate Michelle Obama, who had been an executive working mother prior to her husband landing a new job, became our nation's first African American First Lady.

In very different ways, Clinton, Palin, and Obama have each raised the bar of possibilities for women, by refusing to be limited by others' assessments of their capabilities. They instill a sense of wonder at their unabashed enthusiasm for *powering up*. However, despite all of their accomplishments, each stands just outside the most powerful circles of leadership influence in which they move. Clinton and Palin's campaigns were historic, but both fell short of the brass rings they sought. Michelle Obama made what *Time* magazine called "a savvy sacrifice"[1] by choosing to put her energy and drive into her husband's presidential ambitions.

Forget for a moment how you feel about Clinton, Palin, and Obama, arguably three of the most famous and influential American women on the planet—other than Oprah. Think instead about the reactions they trigger. Reactions that reveal, for the entire world to see, how conflicted we still are about powerful women.

Politicians Clinton and Palin are book-end opposites in nearly every way, from their education and experience to their politics and lifestyles.

Secretary of State and Yale-educated lawyer Clinton, whose credentials include U.S. senator and former First Lady, smashed eighteen million cracks in the American marble ceiling by coming within a whisper of beating rival Barack Obama for the 2008 Democratic presidential nomination. Clinton's assertive, no-nonsense style makes many men uncomfortable. During the campaign, a male MSNBC commentator drew laughs of recognition from his male colleagues when he quipped on the air, "When she comes on TV, I involuntarily cross my legs."[2] Yet when Clinton's eyes got a little watery during a discussion with a small group of New Hampshire women voters, those same pundits questioned whether the senator from New York was "too emotional" to handle presidential pressures.

Palin, a former TV sportscaster and governor of a vast but isolated state, touches off very different nerve endings. Barely known outside of Alaska before being chosen by John McCain as his vice-presidential running mate, Palin hit a grand slam at the Republican national convention. Her debut speech was seen by 37 million people. From the moment she uttered her line, "What's the difference between a hockey mom and a pit bull? Lipstick," Palin was embraced by her admirers as a new brand of woman leader. By the summer of 2010, she had over two million Facebook Fans and was hinting at a presidential run in 2012. Yet the mother of five children, including a Down syndrome young son and a pregnant (at the time), unmarried, teenage daughter, faced scathing criticism for putting her ambition before her family. As the *New York Times* said of her, "No one has ever tried to combine presidential politics and motherhood in quite the same way."[3]

Reactions to Michelle Obama have been equally intriguing. A full-time working mother throughout her marriage, Obama's career credentials include practicing law, commanding six-figure executive salaries, and serving on several boards. Her fierce and effective style on the campaign trail earned her the nickname "'the closer' for her ability to persuade undecided voters to back her husband.[4] But she was also caricatured, at times, as an "angry black woman[5]." Our national psyche journeyed with her as she learned to walk the tightrope that very strong, aspiring women must still navigate. Media advisers carefully crafted and softened her image. When Michelle Obama moved into the White House, she put her career in escrow, describing her primary role as "Mom-in-chief" and using her platform to support causes, particularly working mothers and ending childhood obesity. And you won't find her heading up to Capitol Hill to help shape policy as First Lady Hillary Clinton once made the mistake of attempting.[6]

Three extraordinary women—their stories and the choices, struggles, conflicts, tests, praise, and criticism they have experienced and overcome are metaphors for American women and the crossroads we now collectively face. The question is this: is individual achievement enough? If so, the path we've been on for nearly four decades is smoothly paved, brightly lit, and getting more crowded every year. The only downside is this: it's a bit like collectively treading water. We're working very hard, but too few of us are going anywhere we haven't already been.

I believe individual achievement is not enough. The human race will never reach its highest potential as long as female leaders are hampered from reaching theirs. It's time for American women to be on the move again and finally tackle our next frontier: leadership. That path is barely cleared, unmarked, lonely, and sometimes treacherous. There's plenty of uncharted territory ahead for strivers daring enough to venture forth. What I admire most about Hillary Clinton, Sarah Palin and Michelle Obama are two essential leadership qualities they each possess. They are willing to take great risks. And their fierce ambition is fueled by a sense of purpose.

Leadership Underachievers

In just a few decades, the United States has become a nation of women *Achievers.* Despite having opportunities that most of our global sisters only dream of, however, only the most daring of us are even *trying* to lead. For all of our MBA's, PhD's, medical and law degrees, Olympic medals, Purple Hearts, vice-presidential nominations, and individual striving, when it comes to positions of power and influence, American women, at the beginning of the 21st Century, are *leadership Underachievers.*

Trailblazers and pioneers are old news. I'm tired of the "glass ceiling," the "mommy track," the "good-old-boys-network," the "labyrinth of leadership," "womenomics,"[7] and all of the other explanations, excuses, and worn-out theories for why 51 percent of our nation's citizens are still so rare in leadership positions in nearly every professional sector. The reality is we've hit a plateau. Are we still up against widespread systemic barriers and deeply-ingrained cultural bias? Absolutely. However, at this point, I believe we have to begin to accept some of the blame for our glacial progress at the top. "Women want leadership served as a gift, presented on a silver platter," observes Kathleen Ligocki, Chief Executive Officer of Next Autoworks, a new American car company. "Or, they naively believe recognition comes to those who deserve it. Not always," Ligocki warns. What's her advice? "You have to fight for what you want."

Leadership Underachievers. You might bristle at that characterization. So did Lorraine Bolsinger, president of GE Aviation Systems. But even she acknowledges that something is wrong. "You say that women are a class of 'leadership underachievers.' I don't agree with that. Women want to achieve. I think they opt out (of leadership) because there are unfair practices or it's just too hard."

A Nation of Women Achievers

Bolsinger is right. The evidence of how much women *want* to achieve is now overwhelming. For over four decades, we've been breaking barriers and feasting at a banquet of unprecedented opportunity in nearly every arena you can think of. From politics to business, from medical operating rooms to judicial court rooms, accomplished, highly educated, professional women are no longer the exception. Consider a few recent developments:

- In early 2010, for the first time, there were more women in the U.S. workforce than men, due in part to significant job losses by men in the predominantly male manufacturing and construction sectors. The number of women who are the primary breadwinners for their families has increased dramatically.[8]
- Nationally, women have been dominating higher education for several decades. According to data from the U.S. Department of Education, the last time that men earned more master's degrees than women was 1984-1985. For the graduating class of 2009, here are the stunning facts: Bachelor's degrees: for every 142 earned by women, men earned 100. Master's degrees: for every 159 earned by women, 100 were conferred on men. Doctoral degrees: 107 PhDs were earned by women scholars for every 100 by men.[9]
- The highly respected global magazine, *The Economist,* made the case nearly five years ago that ". . . women are now the most powerful engine of global growth."[10]

- In early 2010, the Pew Research Center reported that a dramatic gender role reversal is underway in marriage, as growing numbers of men are married to women whose income and education exceed their own. The Pew study calls this development "The Rise of Wives."[11]

Interlopers, Insiders, Innovators

The United States is now home to three generations of the highest educated, most professionally accomplished, and politically savvy women in the history of the world. They are half of our nation's leadership gene pool. It is from their ranks that women leaders, who are so desperately needed to bring gender balance to decision making, will come. American women are uniquely positioned to bring fresh leadership skills and solutions to the complex problems gripping Mother Earth. Furthermore, we now have three generations of high-achieving women ready for the big leagues. In the next three chapters, you'll meet three distinct waves of ascending American women. Ambitious, accomplished, educated, skilled women who are now so abundant in the United States that we have reached that magical "critical mass" tipping point where there's no going back. Our leadership pipeline is bursting at the seams. I've developed a typology so that you can easily recognize the defining characteristics and values of each cohort group, which tend to be (but aren't always) generational. I call these three very distinct groups of women *Achievers:*

- *Pioneering Interlopers*: think of Barbara Walters, Supreme Court Justice Ruth Bader Ginsburg, tennis champion Billie Jean King, former Secretary of State Madeline Albright, Oprah and Oscar-winning director Kathryn Bigelow.
- *Influential Insiders*: think of Facebook COO Sheryl Sandberg, Condoleeza Rice, Michelle Obama, astronaut Sally Ride, Sarah Palin, the first women graduates of the military academies and the first wave of post-Title IX athletes.

- *I'll-Do-It-My-Way Innovators*: think of Google Vice President Marissa Mayer, Indy race car driver Danica Patrick, Lady Gaga, PhD student Chelsea Clinton, Beyoncé Knowles and Rachel Gingell, who has already distinguished herself, at 18, as a world class auctioneer.[12]

I'm sure you'll have no trouble identifying with one of these unique cohort groups, although you might feel your experience and attitudes straddle several. Regardless of where you fit, the other groups will resonate, as well, reminding you of your mother, daughter, mentor, mentee, or even a few rivals! In the next three chapters, you'll meet the *Interlopers*, *Insiders*, and *Innovators* who represent one of our greatest underutilized natural resources. But first, let's face a few often ignored facts.

Dazzling Wallflowers Waiting to be Invited to the Leadership Dance

We *should be* on the verge of another major surge forward, a surge that could be every bit as seismic as the cultural changes of the 1970s, which swept millions of women out of narrowly confined roles and into previously all-male professions and economic independence. Treacherous trails once blazed by daring, unconventional women are becoming crowded freeways. Women are hungrier and better prepared than ever before to stretch our wings and take off for the mountaintops. Instead of soaring, however, too many of us are contentedly squatting on the gains of previous generations or wringing our hands over the same old barriers that continue to derail and discourage too many of us. American women are like dazzling wallflowers, all dressed up and tapping our toes to the music, but waiting to be invited to the leadership dance.

Regardless of whether huge numbers of educated, accomplished, professional women "opt out" or are systematically blocked out, there's something very wrong with 51 percent of our citizens only having the influence of a special interest group—in nearly every professional and public arena. You don't believe me? Consider a few myth-busting facts:

- The United States ranks 40th out of 134 countries for its percentage of women political leaders in their national legislatures. We lag behind Spain (5), Israel (7), Germany (15), Argentina (20), Uganda (29) and Canada (36), as well as such gender equality luminaries as India (23) and Cuba (24).[13]
- The presence of women in middle and upper managerial ranks has tripled; we now hold 51 percent of America's managerial and professional positions. Yet we made almost no progress at the top during the 1990s, according to Catalyst, whose research is considered the "gold standard" on women in corporate leadership. "Women still hold only 15 percent of board positions at Fortune 500 companies and 13 percent of those companies have no women on their boards. Ninety-seven percent of Fortune 500 CEOS today are men."[14]
- The gender wage gap has barely budged in nearly a decade. Even women in managerial positions are paid only 81¢ for every dollar earned by their male manager counterparts, according to a September 2010 report by the Government Accountability Office. That's compared to 79 cents ten years ago. Catalyst CEO Ilene Lang recently told Congress, "Until women achieve parity in pay and business leadership, they will be marginalized in every other arena."[15]
- Motherhood is often cited as the reason for the pay gap, but childless women still make less than men. And here's more bad news: the gender pay gap gets wider with age.[16]
- Women are nearly 60 percent of all college students, but only 21 percent of full professors. From 1986 to 2006, the percentage of women college and university presidents doubled from 10 percent to 23 percent. However, in recent years, progress has slowed.[17]

- Of the top 15 media corporations (including print, TV, radio, and online businesses), all CEOs are men, and women hold only 17 percent of the board seats. Since 1977, the majority of college journalism majors have been women; yet articles written by men outnumber those by women by a ratio of 7:1 at our most influential magazines, which help shape our national values and agenda.[18]
- Even the percentage of women coaching college sports—a leadership training ground—is declining. As coaching salaries for women's athletics have increased, more men are competing for and taking over those positions. Yet it remains unthinkable for top women coaches, such as Tennessee's Pat Summitt, the all-time winningest coach in NCAA history, to be even considered for positions coaching men.[19]

Women Hold Only 18 Percent of the Highest Leadership Positions

Are you still comfortable accepting the common misperception that American women are already leading side-by-side in equal partnership with men? Then let me alert you to one of the key findings of *Benchmarking Women's Leadership*, an October 2009 research report published by the White House Project, a New York–based nonprofit working to increase the number of women in all areas of leadership. The researchers took a deep-dive look at the current state of women's leadership in ten major work sectors—from the military and journalism to business and politics. What did they find? *American women hold an average of only 18 percent of the highest leadership positions.* And those numbers are much lower for women of color. The 120-page report confirms that, contrary to popular perception, American women have made strikingly little progress moving into leadership positions, in most professional sectors, within the last decade. Below is a chart that shows the percentage of women holding leadership positions in the ten work sectors studied.

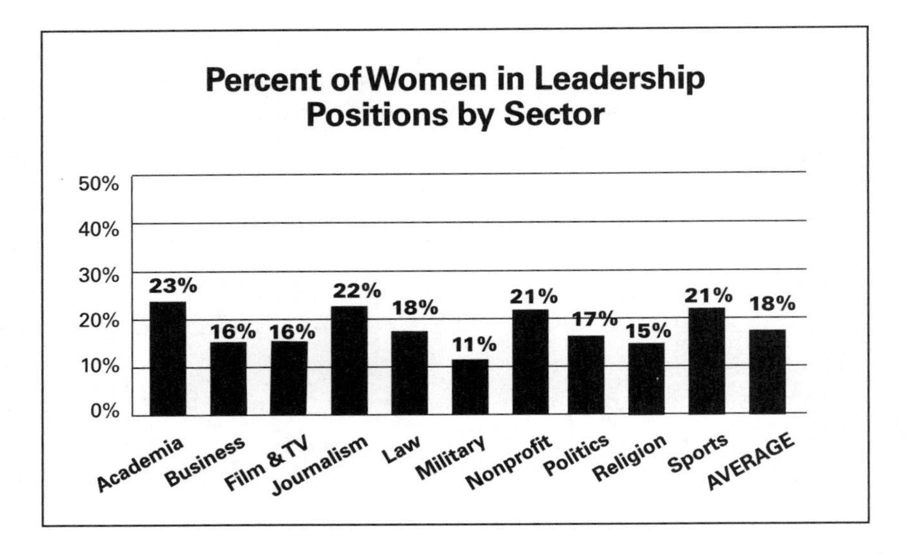

Source: Benchmarking Women's Leadership,
The White House Project Report[20]

As the *Wall Street Journal* reported in May 2008: "Surveys of powerful men feature layers of billionaires, but the most-powerful women surveys are forced to reach down into the ranks of salaried, upper-level managers to fill the lists."[21]

Of course, prominent exceptions exist. Ask any audience to name women leaders and they'll start with Secretary of State Hillary Clinton, California Congresswoman and former Speaker of the House Nancy Pelosi and Oprah Winfrey. Sandra Day O'Connor, the first women ever named to the U.S. Supreme Court, as well as Justices Ruth Bader Ginsburg, Sonia Sotomayor, and Elena Kagan also make the list. Business audiences think instantly of *Fortune* 500 power brokers Indra Nooyi, CEO of PepsiCo, and former CEOs turned politicians Carly Fiorina (Hewlett-Packard) and Meg Whitman (Ebay). And the military is quick to mention U.S. Army General Ann Dunwoody, who broke the brass ceiling in November 2008 becoming the first female four-star general in the U.S. military history. When asked by reporters whether she thought she would become such a high-ranking officer, the 33-year-military woman quipped, "There is no one more surprised than I—except of course, my husband. You know what they say, 'Behind every successful woman, there is an astonished man.'"[22]

The fact is those exceptional leaders are so well known because women at the highest levels of leadership are still so rare.

America Is Ready for Women to Lead

The rapidly increasing numbers of educated, skilled, and ambitious American women have dramatically impacted our mainstream attitudes about gender roles and women holding positions of authority. They're continuing to dilute old stereotypes while demonstrating women's growing competence in every arena. An abundance of fresh data shows that our national consciousness has come a very long way. According to research conducted by GFK/Roper Public Affairs for the White House Project report, both women and men, in large numbers, are very open to women in leadership roles, as the following chart illustrates.

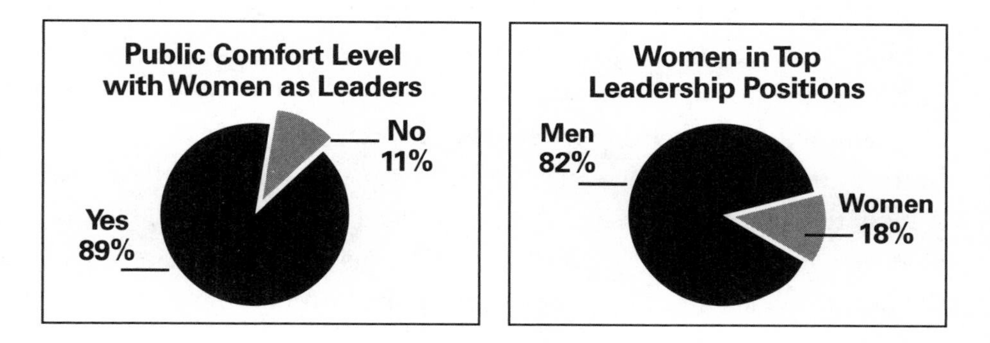

Source: *Benchmarking Women's Leadership*, The White House Project Report[23]

In addition, in a 2008 Pew Research Center study on character traits valued in leaders, respondents rated women above men in five of eight essential leadership traits: honesty, intelligence, creativity, outgoingness, compassion. Women and men were rated equally in two essential leadership traits: hardworking and ambition. Decisiveness was the only skill for which men scored significantly (10 percent) higher.[24]

The United States is clearly ready for women leaders—up to a point. But here's the problem. "This comfort level that Americans express about women in leadership," says Marie Wilson, president of the White House Project, "is accompanied by the misperception that women are already leading equally alongside their male peers."

Treading the Same, Warm Water for Over a Decade

As I was working on this book, traveling to women's leadership conferences on three continents and probing the topic with hundreds of inspiring, accomplished women, I was searching for answers to one fundamental question: Why are American women so complacent about our under-representation in leadership?

The parable about cooking frogs kept coming to mind. You can't simply drop a few frogs into a pot of boiling water because they'll leap out in a flash. The trick, as the story goes, is to start by putting the frogs into very comfortable, lukewarm water. The frogs don't mind; they relax and enjoy the soothing water. And when you gradually turn the heat up, they never know what hit them. American women have been smugly treading the same warm water for well over a decade. The "pot" of *Achievers* is about to overflow. Too few of us dare, however, to make the leap to leadership. It's time to turn up the heat on ourselves.

The Economist magazine has called women's economic evolution "the biggest social change of our times."[25] Yes, "millions of brains have been put to more productive use," as the magazine wrote approvingly, but discouragingly few are taking all of that brainpower to the top—where it's badly needed! With several generations of seasoned foot soldiers already in the workforce and fresh recruits joining the cultural revolution annually, where are all of our leaders? Perhaps we assumed that those with the credentials, vision, and passion to lead would naturally be groomed for greater responsibilities, as western, white men have always been. But that's clearly not happening, at least not in significant numbers.

And too many younger women naively believe that the world is already their oyster. New Millennial Sarah Kliff, writing about presidential candidate Clinton in *Newsweek* magazine, commented, "She doesn't inspire us to chant 'Yes we will!' because, in a sense, we already have: we have taken more Advanced Placement classes than our male counterparts . . . and graduated with better GPAs. Now, in our early 20s, most of us have not yet made any tradeoffs between family and career; we're doctors, investment bankers, and lawyers in training. That makes a female president seem hardly revolutionary or cool."[26]

A female president of the United States is "hardly revolutionary or cool"? Excuse me? The only person Ms. Kliff is kidding is herself. When Barack Obama was elected president of the United States, blacks throughout the world rejoiced, regardless of their political affiliations. They clearly "got it" that the election of the first African American president of the United States was a gigantic cultural step forward that would have long-term implications for everyone of his race. It's time for women to take off our blinders, regain our sense of urgency, and recognize that we're all in this together. Too many women still don't understand one essential fact: every woman for herself is a losing strategy. When one woman rises, we all rise.

Why Women's Leadership Matters

Why does the number of women in leadership *really* matter? It matters because when women are in positions of power:

- *Priorities are different.* Women leaders are more likely than men to address issues that impact the most vulnerable in our societies: women and children. One of the greatest examples of this occurred during the 2009 debate in Congress over health care reform. It was U.S.

Senator Barbara Mikulski of Maryland who told her colleagues—and everyone watching on C-SPAN—"For many insurance companies, simply being a woman is a preexisting condition."

- *Outcomes are different.* An abundance of research, including studies done by Goldman Sachs, Columbia University, and Catalyst, have examined the relationship between bottom line results and women in corporate leadership roles. There is a growing body of evidence that companies with multiple women officers and board directors outperform those with no women. One or two token women in a group aren't enough to significantly impact strategic conversations and decisions.
- *Institutions are different.* Women impact values and ethics and are much more likely than men to be whistleblowers. Remember *Time* magazine's "Person of the Year" in 2002? Instead of one person, it was three courageous women: Sherron Watkins, Cynthia Cooper, and Colleen Rowley—the whistleblowers (when men stayed silent) at Enron, WorldCom, and the FBI.[27] In 2010, *Time* once again featured three women on its cover, calling them "The New Sheriffs of Wall Street." Of Sheila Bair, Chair of the Federal Deposit Insurance Corporation (FDIC); Securities and Exchange Commission (SEC) Chair Mary Schapiro; and Elizabeth Warren, who chaired the Oversight Committee for the Troubled Asset Relief Program (TARP), *Time* wrote, "these women may not run Wall Street, but in this new era, they are telling Wall Street how to clean up its act."[28]
- *Work feels different.* Women's natural collaborative leadership style encourages teamwork and builds morale. Furthermore, brain research confirms that women bring skills—such as a superior ability to read nonverbal signals (emotional intelligence)—that tend to be in short supply in all-male groups.
- *Possibilities are different.* The Diversity Prediction Theorem, developed by academic experts in complex problem solving, has shown that diverse groups nearly always outperform homogenous groups by a substantial margin. "The key is diverse minds," explains University of Michigan professor Scott Page. When solving complex problems, the

diversity of a group matters as much, or even more, than the ability and brainpower of its members. "You want," Dr. Page contends, "people who categorize things in different ways."

Leadership Isn't a Job Description, It's a Risk

What do I mean by leadership? I mean putting your face into the wind, raising your voice and daring to advocate for fresh perspectives to old problems. It also requires the confidence to take responsibility for others—for those you are asking to follow you and to trust that you know the way. As a friend said to me, "What slows me down when I think about leadership is the risk; the responsibility; the weight of it."

As with most worthwhile things in life, becoming a leader isn't easy. It means exposing yourself to criticism, risking failure, challenging "the way we've always done things" and envisioning new possibilities. Leaders must be courageous, passionate and have the ability to inspire others to follow their vision. Instead of simply climbing another rung on the ladder, a leader encourages everyone around her to reach higher, and pushes the edges to find solutions, whether to the crisis in Haiti, poverty, disease, violence against women, global warming, the state of our urban schools, or achieving breakthroughs in your own company's work culture. It's a very personal journey that can often be lonely. But you don't have to be Melinda Gates or have a big title in order to lead. Mother Teresa taught us that.

Or look to Africa where Liberian women recently showed the world what's possible when mothers, sisters, daughters, aunts, and grandmothers came together and reclaimed their power. The compelling film, *Pray the Devil Back to Hell*, tells the true story of how the women of Liberia, armed only with white t-shirts and their own courage, rose up together, in 2003, to end a bloody civil war and bring peace to their shattered homeland. Just a few years later, women voters joyfully swept Ellen Johnson Sirleaf into their country's presidency. Today, Liberia is the only African nation—and one of the few in the world—with a female president.

Sometimes it takes my breath away when I think about how far women have progressed in my lifetime. At other moments, I'm discouraged and fear we're in danger of losing ground. And at times, I stagger under the weight of how far we have to go to end the oppression, brutalization and disenfranchisement of women and girls throughout the world.

Not every female Achiever was born to lead, but plenty were. Comedian Groucho Marx understood that decades ago when he quipped, "Only one in a thousand men are leaders. The other 999 are following women."

Practicing What I Preach

The fastest way for women to dramatically increase our leadership influence is for more of us—*lots* more—to run for office. The *Benchmarking Women's Leadership* report explains why. "Women leaders in politics are the most visible manifestation of women's leadership in our culture. Because they operate in the public eye, they have the potential to transform the perception of women in a far greater sphere than in any other sector."[29]

For years, through my professional speaking, workshops and leadership coaching, I've been urging women to run for office. I've also written as many checks for candidates as my budget could bear and volunteered to work on campaigns. I've had numerous people encourage me to become a candidate myself. But I never stuck my neck out and ran. The time finally came when another woman called my bluff. Mari Harvey-Edwards, the former mayor and a long-time city councilwoman in my hometown of Auburn Hills, Michigan, walked into my kitchen one afternoon and told me bluntly, "Anne, when are you going to start practicing what you preach? I think it's time for *you* to run for office." She was right.

I had been working hard on this book for nearly two years, which was a fascinating but very solitary endeavor. The truth is you're not doing much leading when you're reading, researching, interviewing, and wearing out the keys on your laptop rewriting book drafts! It was time for me to get back in the trenches. Time to test all of my theories and put to work what I'd learned from all of the global leaders I had interviewed. It was time to answer the call to leadership and give back to a community that has been my refuge for nearly 20 years. So I filed my petitions, recruited a crack campaign team, developed a web site, and tapped my family, friends, and allies to raise money. Oh, yes, and I knocked on hundreds of doors, walking nearly every street in Auburn Hills, Michigan. And in November 2009, I won my first election, coming in as high vote getter in a field of 14 candidates. I am now serving a four year term on my local City Council. You can be assured that I'm taking this journey with you.

It's Not More Leadership That's Needed, It's More Leaders

"In times of crisis, it's not more leadership that's needed. It's more leaders." Those are the words of Rosabeth Moss Kanter, the Harvard Business School professor who has been advising America's top corporations for decades on the power of diverse executive teams. I first heard Kanter's rallying cry from *Interloper* Ann Moore, recently retired long-time CEO of Time, Inc., who quoted Kanter in a speech she gave recently to women professionals.

So what's the next step? The time for resting on our laurels is long past. The game stakes are no longer simply individual empowerment. We'll make the next giant step forward when a critical mass of *Interlopers, Insiders,* and *Innovators* (whom you are about to meet) claim multiple mantles of leadership. What are American women waiting for? Within the next decade, we need women decision makers at the highest levels to be as common and expected as women are today in our law schools, medical schools, and business schools. That will be a dramatic change from where we are today. It will require collective effort, openly supporting and promoting other women leaders, actively mentoring young women and girls, and insisting on appropriate representation for 51 percent of our citizens and members of the U.S. workforce at *all* the tables of influence. And most of all, it will require taking the risk yourself to reach higher than you've ever dared before.

Even the decision to aspire to leadership takes courage. Each of us must make our own decision on which path we will choose. We need women on all paths. Not everyone is called to lead. But if you hear that voice inside calling you to dare to lead, to take the risks, to challenge old thinking, and to envision new solutions to long-festering problems, this book is for you. It's time for American women to regain our sense of urgency—to begin actively reaching across racial, cultural, economic, political, and generational lines to lift and lead one another into leadership positions—in big numbers. As the 21st Century unfolds, these are the best of times to be a female citizen of the United States. The doors of opportunity are swinging wide open. The time is at hand for women to begin ascending—in unprecedented numbers—to leadership positions and stepping up to our responsibilities as global citizens. How about you? Have you begun to hear that quiet, internal voice calling you to do more? Is there a sense of purpose or nagging injustice that's driving you to become more of a force for positive change in the world beyond your own family and career? My guess is you wouldn't have picked up this book and read this far if you weren't ready to *power up.* So, let's begin.

So Many Achievers, So Few Leaders

- ✓ A nation of women *Achievers*
- ✓ Leadership *Underachievers*
- ✓ Waiting to be invited to the leadership dance
- ✓ Why women's leadership matters
- ✓ America is ready for women to lead
- ✓ Leadership is a decision

Interlopers, Insiders, Innovators

Have you ever crossed a line when you were warned "Don't you dare."? Have you ever found yourself a solitary "other," tested at every step in arenas where the majority resented your very presence? Have you ever taken a risk because of your personal ambition, but realized that you were carrying the weight of responsibility for others? If any of those scenarios bring back memories of defining moments, I'd call you a *Pioneering Interloper*.

Have you ever uttered the words "I'm no feminist, but . . . ?" Have you worked hard to become "one of the guys," being careful not to rock the boat and keeping a strategic distance from women who were regarded as a little too outspoken? Did you discover early in your career that being a woman could actually be a competitive advantage? If your answer is "yes" to any of those questions, I'd call you an *Influential Insider*.

Or are you a woman who believes that "Girls Already Rule"? Perhaps you've earned a law degree, medical degree or an MBA. You started playing competitive sports—often against the boys—in grade school. You fully expect to have both a great career and a family, but have no intention of working 60 hours a week as your mother or boss did. If your employer doesn't understand that, you'll work somewhere else. If any of that resonates, I'd call you an *I'll-Do-It-My-Way Innovator*.

Interlopers, Insiders, and *Innovators* are the names I use to describe three very distinct types of women who have been spreading their wings and reinventing work culture for more than 40 years. There are millions of them in the United States today. You know who they are. The very fact that you're reading a book about women's leadership tells me you're probably one of them (unless, of course, you are an enlightened and curious male).

They are professionally-accomplished, highly-motivated and self-sufficient women who seem to have been born with an inner drive to achieve. They tend to be well educated, engaged in the world, and unwilling to be defined or limited by gender. They are subsets of the four major generational groups presently in the workforce. *Interlopers,* such as Maya Angelou and Barbara Walters, are primarily Baby Boomers (born 1946-1964) and some Traditionalists (born before World War II). The cultural message they faced was "No, you can't!" *Insiders* tend to be Gen Xs (born 1965-1980). Sarah Palin and First Lady Michelle Obama are two of our most visible icons of this group. As they came of age, American culture began telling women "Maybe you can." *Innovators* are part of the huge Millennial or Gen Y wave (born 1981-1995) just beginning to make its mark. The I'll-do-it-my-way independence of Angelina Jolie is characteristic of this group. Jolie and her generational peers of women grew up with the message, "Yes, you can!"

It's easy to assume that *Interlopers, Insiders,* and *Innovators* are only generational cohorts. That's often true, but it's only part of the picture. The lines of distinction can be fuzzy, because each of us tends to see the world through the eyes of the experiences that shaped us as much as by the times in which we grew up. For example, Supreme Court Justice and septuagenarian Ruth Bader Ginsburg, who favors long black robes, and 20-something race car driver Danica Patrick, the first woman to win an Indy car race and whose publicity photos are just as racy, have more in common than first meets the eye. They both share the *Interloper* experience of helping to carve out new paths where women were not always welcome. Different fields become accessible to women at different times.

Today, *Interlopers, Insiders,* and *Innovators* form a rich and deep pool of leadership talent that has barely been tapped. Yet rather than feeling connected by our similarities as aspiring women, too often we are fractionalized by mistrust and stereotypes. You know what I'm talking about.

The savvy executive who wants nothing to do with those "feminists still carrying chips on their shoulders," or the fast-track whiz kid who has no patience for working mothers trying to juggle office and family deadlines. Women may bond outside of the office in professional organizations or with parents of their children's friends, but all too often, we shy away from strong, overt alliances with one another in the workplace. That's a mistake that men don't make.

It's time for women *Achievers* to set aside our differences and embrace the shared priorities and unique life rhythms that connect us. Imagine the possibilities if we ever collectively flexed our muscles of influence. That will only happen when we get to know one another a little better. Let me introduce you.

CHAPTER 2

The Pioneering Interlopers

When Detroit Tiger GM Jim Campbell told me, "Over my dead body you'll go into our Tiger Clubhouse," I knew I had to open those locker rooms—not just for my own credibility, but for every woman sports reporter who would come after me.

— ANNE DOYLE, TV Sports Broadcaster, *Interloper*

The dictionary defines *interloper* as "one who intrudes into some region or field without a proper license." When I say *Interloper*, I think of Sandra Day O'Connor. Although she graduated at the top of her Stanford Law class in 1952, the only job she was offered was as a legal secretary. But she overcame gender bias to become the first woman justice on the U.S. Supreme Court.

I think of Billie Jean King, one of the greatest athletes of our time, who became the wind beneath women's wings in the 1970s after she beat former Wimbledon champion and self-proclaimed "male chauvinist" Bobby Riggs in a nationally televised match dubbed "The Battle of the Sexes."

I think of C. Vivian Stringer. A talented athlete, she had to fight to become the first African American on her school's all-white cheerleading team, which was the only "sport" offered to girls in 1964 at her Pennsylvania high school. She is now one of the all-time winningest coaches in college basketball. You may know of Stringer and her Scarlet Knights women's basketball team for the way they stood up to shock radio's Don Imus for describing them as "nappy headed hos."

I think of Carolyn King, who was only 12 years old in 1973 when she made headlines around the country by trying out for and *making* her local Little League baseball team.[1] She just wanted to play ball, but national Little League officials demanded that she be kicked off the team because "no girls were allowed." With the support of her teammates and coach, King played anyway, facing boos and some fans screaming "go home and play with your dolls!" Within a year, Little League backed down, and girls all over the United States were trying out for local baseball teams, thanks to a very young *Interloper.*

I also think of Shannon Faulkner, who was an *Interloper* in 1995 when she became the first female cadet to be admitted to The Citadel Military College of South Carolina.[2] She suffered legal, academic, and social humiliation as well as brutal treatment from her fellow cadets and didn't last very long. But she unlocked the doors and pointed the way for the more than 200 women cadets who have now graduated from the prestigious school.

Each of those remarkable leaders epitomizes the courage, ambition, and sheer mental toughness that characterize this unique breed of American women. Today, most *Interlopers* are in their 50s and beyond, their resumes heavily sprinkled with the word *first.* Who are these unconventional and once-considered "uppity" women who chose to follow roads least taken? First of all, they were lucky—lucky enough to come of age at a point in history when a cultural window was opening. Not all women dared or wanted to break out of the gender comfort zones of the 1960s and 1970s, but hundreds of thousands, perhaps millions, did. Today, their achievements seem mainstream. For their times, they were extraordinary.

Shaped by Seismic Cultural Shifts

To understand *Interlopers,* you first need to look at the environment that formed them, where their roots still run deep. Most grew up in the late 1940s, 50s and 60s. Their career role models were basically teacher, secretary, nurse, or, if they were pretty, airline stewardess. Few dared even dream that they would ride a tsunami of cultural change to historic heights. Every *Interloper* I interviewed mentioned the stunning cultural upheavals of her early defining years as major influences on her life choices. In addition to the Vietnam War and three devastating assassinations in five years (President John F. Kennedy, 1963; Martin Luther King, Jr. and presidential candidate Robert F. Kennedy, 1968), three other developments were key springboards to the *Interlopers'* pioneering professional breakthroughs.

- *The Civil Rights Movement.* Title VII of the Civil Rights Act of 1964, which outlawed employment discrimination on the basis of race, color, or gender, unlocked the doors of economic opportunity for women as well as racial minorities. The landmark legislation gave ambitious *Interlopers* the legal momentum they needed to pursue careers in every professional arena, from journalism, law, and medicine to business, police work, and even the unionized trades. Women began knocking—hard—at the doors of nearly every previously all-male profession.

- *The Women's Movement.* Unless you lived through those times, it's hard to imagine how intoxicating feminism once was. Betty Friedan's *The Feminine Mystique,* published in 1963, awakened a sleeping giant of women's activism. Gloria Steinem, Coretta Scott King, Bella Abzug, Shirley Chisholm, and many other women leaders inspired grassroots political pressure against a multitude of discriminatory laws and practices of the times. Singer Helen Reddy's "I Am Woman, Hear Me Roar" topped the pop charts as a joyful rallying cry for women's growing sense of power and possibility. "It was the women's movement that put the movement in me," recalls former Maryland Congresswoman Connie Morella. "I was on the Montgomery County Commission for Women, lobbying for equality in housing, employment and education. It was the 1970s, and women couldn't even get a mortgage in their own name, or credit. Women today do not realize how their so-called foremothers had to work to open the roads of opportunities they now have. They think, 'Oh feminists, radical women. Against men and all that.' Baloney." Although few wear it on their sleeves today, rare is the *Interloper* who isn't a feminist deep in her soul.

- *The Pill and Roe v. Wade.* If it hadn't been for unsung heroine Katharine McCormick,[3] women might have remained at the mercy of their reproductive organs for several more decades. McCormick, a wealthy American philanthropist, provided most of the research funding throughout the 1950s for development of the birth control pill. Considered one of the greatest scientific advances of the twentieth century, it was approved by the FDA in 1960. Thirteen years later, the U.S. Supreme Court gave women the right to safe, legal abortions. The Pill, as well as *Roe v. Wade*, triggered the sexual revolution and decades of cultural furor that still simmers and often boils. But there was no turning back. For the first time in history, women felt the exhilarating freedom of having control over their reproductive rhythms and their lives. In addition, new laws made it illegal for employers to fire women who chose to become pregnant. As a result, millions of women of reproductive age began to remain in the workforce.

Take the seismic social shifts I just described, add the largest group of women in American history graduating from college, and the seeds had been sown for the growth and rise of a new breed of American leaders.

Marines Taking the Beach

I understand *Interlopers* because I was one of them. We were like marines landing on a strange beach. Most of us encountered heavy fire as soon as we ventured into waters that had long been the sole domain of men. Unlike women today, who can build their skills and confidence for years before running into serious gender barriers, *Interlopers* were tested before we had a chance to get our professional sea legs. Right out of the gates, we had to routinely fight for every inch of professional ground we gained. In 1972, when I was fresh out of Northwestern University's Medill School of Journalism and trying to get my first broadcasting job, the news director at WWJ Radio in Detroit told me, "No one will ever listen to a woman on the radio. Your voices are too high." He was one of many who advised me that I was "pursuing the wrong career." All of the naysayers—who believed that I was trying to insert myself where I didn't belong—just increased my determination.

A few years later, when I was hired by WJBK-TV in Detroit to be one of the first women TV sportscasters in the nation, I had to steel myself to enter press boxes and locker rooms where team management, athletes, many sports fans, and even male sportswriters thought I had no business intruding into their male inner sanctums. Once again, the resistance I encountered just strengthened my resolve to prove the skeptics wrong, not only because of my own ambition but also because I knew that any woman who followed in my path would be judged on whether or not I passed the tests.

Barbara Whittaker, who rose to become one of the highest ranked African American executives at General Motors, explains the mindset shared by the early trailblazers. "I think many of us understood we were behind. We understood that there was a challenge before us. We didn't see it, know it, or understand it, but we had a hope and a belief. The younger women today believe they can be anything, because they have *seen* others do it. For us, it was possible only because we made it possible."

The Work Environments They Faced

Interlopers were rarely welcomed with open arms. The running joke in those days was that a woman had to be twice as good as a man to even be considered for a position, but luckily it wasn't that hard. Only it wasn't a joke. Susan Davis, chairman of Susan Davis International, a Washington, D.C.-based global consulting firm, tells this story of cracking the "good-old-boys club" of presidential advance work.

"I was working in Washington, D.C., in 1972 and told my boss, Donald Rumsfeld [later Secretary of Defense], that I wanted to do advance work. But the call I got was from guys at the White House saying, 'We'd like to talk to you about being Mrs. Nixon's scheduler.' I didn't want to do that. I wanted to be what they called an 'advance man.' But girls had never had that job before. So I went to the interview, which I will never forget. There were five guys sitting around the room. They seemed really old to me because I was 21, but they were probably about 28. They were smoking cigars and drinking scotch. It was after hours, a totally different White House than today. They said to me, 'Would you like to be Mrs. Nixon's scheduler?' Mostly they were looking at my short skirt and my long red hair. I was very conscious of what was going on and I said, 'No, I want to be an advance man.' They literally spit out their scotch and cigars. And one of the guys said, 'My dear child, girls cannot be advance men.'"

But Susan Davis proved them wrong. "I got the job over Haldeman's dead body, Ehrlichman's dead body, and all the dead bodies of every person in that room. I got it because Don Rumsfeld went to bat for me and told them they couldn't discriminate. They had to give me a shot at it. And then they said, 'If you want this job, you have to quit your job and be in Manchester, New Hampshire, by ten o'clock tonight. If you are one minute late, you're fired.' And that's how it started."

Unapologetic discrimination, sexual advances, hostility, and open mockery were all part of the work environment *Interlopers* customarily faced. "I'll never forget my first day of class at Georgetown Law School," remembers global tax attorney Marjorie O'Connell, of Washington, D.C.

"The professor made the few women in his class stand up, introduce themselves, and indicate whether they wanted to be referred to as 'Miss, Mrs., or Manuscript.' His little joke was intended as an insult for those of us who wanted to use Ms."

Others took their jokes a few steps further. The late and widely admired Judge Hilda Gage, the first woman to chair the American Bar Association's National Conference of State Trial Judges, told me about an incident with a torts professor on her first day of law school. "I was one of only a handful of women among nearly 200 men," she recalled. "In front of the entire class he asked me, 'Miss Gage, would you fornicate with me?' That's how the law professor chose to make a point to the entire class that it's not assault if you ask first." It would be years before sexual harassment in the workplace was taken seriously, let alone made illegal.

The Only Woman in the Room

Being an *Interloper* is lonely business. It's not just that these early career trailblazers were nearly always the lone woman in the room. Unfortunately, that's still not unusual today, particularly at senior levels. It's that *Interlopers* were usually the first professional-level women most of their male colleagues and supervisors had ever worked with. "You had as many different attitudes toward you as people around the table, some curious, some resentful," recalls Anne Stevens, recently retired CEO of Carpenter Technology Inc., who was one of *Fortune* magazine's "50 Most Powerful Women in Business" while COO of the Americas for Ford Motor Company. "You never went into a room as just another person or with anything close to 50 percent support," she recalls. "We had to protect ourselves because there were plenty of men trying to sabotage or discredit us. And there were lots of environments where women were pitted against each other because there was only room for one of us."

As difficult as it was to be constantly under the microscope, *Interlopers* were driven to excel by a powerful sense that they were part of something bigger than themselves. Bankruptcy lawyer Barbara Rom, a former managing partner with law firm Pepper Hamilton, put it this way: "I was ambitious enough to want to do well for myself. But I also felt I was representative of women, and would be the first experience that many men I was encountering would ever have with a woman lawyer. So I felt the burden of responsibility to make a good impression so that the women behind me, whose names I would never know, whose faces I would never see, wouldn't pay the price if I didn't succeed."

Interlopers: Differences that Divide

Ironically, the very skills that helped *Interlopers* succeed are frequently the source of misunderstanding with younger women. *Interlopers* are often seen as:

- *Individualists, not team players.* In order to break out of the confining gender roles of their times, *Interlopers* needed to be strong individualists who nearly always had to go it alone. In addition, as pre–Title IX girls, few had the opportunity to develop team skills by playing organized sports. Plus female role models were rare, which is why *Interlopers* are often criticized for not mentoring younger women. As Carol Hollenshead, director emeritus of the University of Michigan's Center for the Education of Women put it, "We muddled and fought our way the best we could, with few allies, no mentors and even fewer road maps on how to get where we wanted to go."
- *Men in skirts.* First Wave professional women were measured by male standards of dress, professional demeanor, language, and personal style. Adapting the navy blue power suit as their uniform, swearing, and telling off-color jokes with the guys were some of the ways many *Interlopers* tried to fit in. Femininity was a card they rarely played, because misplaying it, even in a light way, could too easily be misinterpreted. "*Neutralize* is a good word for what we did back then," says Joan LeMahieu, general manager of Mountain Winery in California's Napa Valley. "I think women of our generation were, initially, very uncomfortable with our femininity because it was so

associated with the softness we were struggling so hard to overcome. Today I am much more lighthearted with men. I think we are finally beginning to integrate the pieces of our lives."

- *Too tough.* Tested over and over, *Interlopers* learned to develop a thick skin. That protective layer is often interpreted as rough edges or "having a chip on their shoulders." Beth DunCombe one of the first African American attorneys to pass the bar in Michigan, tells the story of standing before a judge for a rape trial. "The judge looked at me and asked, 'Are you the victim, Miss?' I simply replied, 'No, Your Honor, I'm the lawyer.' You came to expect that kind of thing and got used to it," she told me. Duncombe and many other *Interlopers* I interviewed confided they have spent years trying to shed what *Insiders* and *Innovators* often regard as the inexplicable toughness of their older professional sisters.

- *Not supportive of work/life balance concerns.* The concept of achieving a magical "balance" between ambitious career goals and the traditional responsibilities of motherhood and homemaking didn't occur to *Interlopers*. Most felt they had to make an either/or choice. They were fighting to prove they could do "a man's job," which meant picking up and traveling on a moment's notice and working long hours and weekends as easily as men who had stay-at-home wives. Many delayed marriage until very late or chose not to have children at all. Others found the pool of men who were comfortable dating a "career woman" or, even worse, a "feminist," was pretty small. I didn't marry until age thirty-six and chose a man eleven years my junior. I was in my early forties before I became a mother, thanks to the privilege of adoption. It was common for *Interlopers* who became mothers to be advised not to display pictures of their children in their offices lest they create the impression of not being "serious" about their careers. Many still carry some personal sadness and regret about the choices they felt they had to make between career and family. Is it any wonder that *Interlopers* often have little empathy for the work/life balance expectations of the huge waves of high-potential younger women who are now hot on their heels on professional fast tracks?

What We Can Learn from *Interlopers*

- *How to dress to impress.* Thanks to John Molloy's 1975 best seller, *Dress for Success, Interlopers* learned early to dress for the job they wanted, not merely the one they had. Whether it's on a football field or a golf course, in the military, or in a conference room, men use clothing to signal their membership in a group and to telegraph their level of power and influence. If even a hint of cleavage and form-fitting clothing are your idea of leadership attire, you might ask an *Interloper* for a few tips.
- *A sense of sisterhood.* The last few decades have seen unprecedented individual achievement by American women. Yet too many still regard other women as their primary competition. Systemic change is never achieved by isolated individuals. It requires collective effort. *Interlopers* rode the waves of change together. True, they had to be strong individualists to break away from expected female roles of the times. But they also felt a strong sense of sisterhood as they worked to open doors for younger women who they knew hoped to follow them. It's been decades since significant numbers of women joined together, with a sense of being part of a shared cultural tribe, to achieve mutually beneficial goals. *Interlopers* remember what's possible when women fully engage our collective power.
- *The responsibility to give back.* All the major milestones for women's equality were achieved in the 20th Century. The Suffragettes fought for nearly 75 years, chaining themselves to the White House fence and enduring hunger strikes, forced feedings and beatings to win the right to vote. (If you haven't seen the movie *Iron Jawed Angels*, starring Hillary Swank as Suffragette Alice Paul, rent it. And invite friends and family—including sons—to watch it with you.) Other women fought for decades to open higher education to female students, which only began to occur in the late 19th Century in the western world. *Interlopers* paid their debt to the women upon whose shoulders they stood by fighting for the economic and legal breakthroughs of the 1960s and 1970s. It's time for each of us, regardless of our generational cohort group, to ask ourselves: What am I doing to help other women?

How am I supporting my sisters who are today's leadership *Interlopers*? Will your daughter, niece or granddaughter look back one day and thank you for the contributions you are making to accelerate women's forward momentum?

A Few Words to *Interlopers*

There may be two generations of ambitious younger women snapping at your high heels and wishing you'd turn off your Blackberry or iPhone and get out of their way, but don't even think about it. The world needs you. I predict your full legacy is yet to be written. Why? Because you've passed the tests. You don't have to prove yourself anymore. If 50 is the new 30 you're in your prime, with perhaps two decades (or more!) of productive work ahead. Chances are you will outlive most men of your generation, and with your child-rearing days behind you, it's likely you now have more time than many younger women to take on significant leadership roles.

My challenge to you is twofold: First, take pride in the paths you forged and the foundation you laid for women who followed you. Now, take it up a notch. Run for office. Write a book. Produce a film. Mentor in ways you wish you'd been mentored. Donate money for a new building at your alma mater—and name it after yourself, as men routinely do! Share the wisdom and wealth you've earned, the lessons you've learned. Stick your neck out, once again. Whatever you do, don't rest on your laurels. No one knows better than you that positive social change doesn't just happen. People with vision, courage, skill, and tenacity must make it happen. You led once. It's time to lead again.

Finally, if you are still carrying around resentment about the opportunities that younger women take for granted but you never had, let them go. My mother frequently reminded me that the only way humanity evolves is by each generation reaching and rising higher than the one whose shoulders they stand on. Of course younger woman went further and faster than we did by climbing up our backs. Remember, we had some pretty broad shoulders that helped lift us, as well.

Interlopers cut a wide swath across the American work landscape. Their defining moments are scattered like fertile seeds that have sprouted from Maine to New Mexico and are taking root throughout the world. They hacked their way through jungles of gender barriers and shattered stereotypes about women's capabilities. Along the way, they reinvented the world of work. The *Interlopers* are the women who, as *Miami Herald* columnist Leonard Pitts, Jr. so eloquently put it, "prepared the banquet of opportunity that women today are dining upon."[4] No one has been feasting longer at that banquet than the generation of women who surfed the *Interlopers*' wake: a group I call the *Influential Insiders*. They are a very different breed.

CHAPTER 3

The Influential Insiders

We all worked very hard to fit in. We don't like to highlight our differences as females or focus on being women.
— MAGGIE WOODWARD, Commander General, U.S. Air Force, *Insider*

If the *Interlopers* were the Marines establishing the first beachheads of professional opportunity, then the *Influential Insiders* were the diplomats who followed on their heels. Rather than aligning themselves with the *Interlopers,* whom they often considered too radical, *Insiders* tended to be more interested in fitting in than rocking the boat. They were savvy enough to realize that different skills were needed to get seats at the tables of influence than were required to crowbar open locked doors. How many times have you heard a woman utter the words, "I'm no feminist but . . ."? That's a tip-off you're talking to a woman with the mindset of what I call an *Influential Insider.*

Major General Maggie Woodward, Commander of the 17th Air Force articulated this group's perspective. Woodward, who entered Reserve Officers' Training Corps (ROTC) in 1978 as a college freshman and started her active duty pilot training in January, 1983, told me how differently she presented herself compared to a slightly older female officer. "There were very distinct differences between Jackie and me," Woodward recalled. "She was what you might consider your typical 'women's libber type.' She was always trying to hold the line, saying, 'You can't say that to me.' I was the complete opposite. I was just trying to be one of the guys as desperately as I could. The only kind of splash I wanted to make was through my flying. You'll see a similar theme with other women of the same period. We had to fit in very carefully."

Kathleen Ligocki, who became one of the first women CEOs of a Fortune 500 automotive supplier when she led Tower Automotive through bankruptcy several years ago, echoed that sentiment. "When I joined the car business nearly thirty years ago, I wasn't thinking about the fact that women had begun a multi-generational struggle to rebalance the male-dominated world to a better, more equal place. I just wanted a level playing field, not a gladiatorial battle."

When I think of *Insiders* in business, I think of Charlene Begley, president and CEO of General Electric Home and Business Solutions. Named one of *Fortune* magazine's "Top 50 Most Powerful Women" when she was thirty-nine years old, Begley is the youngest senior vice president at a company renowned as a fiercely competitive breeding ground for leaders. And I think of Facebook Chief Operating Officer Sheryl Sandberg, mother of two, who earned her MBA from Harvard with "highest distinction."

In sports, I think of Dara Torres, who smashed the paradigm of what a 41-year-old mother is capable of when she not only made the U.S. Olympic swim team—for the fifth time—but won three silver medals in Beijing during the 2008 Olympic Games. Displaying her toned and lean physique on the cover of *Sports Illustrated* magazine, Torres epitomizes the physical fitness and athleticism that is also a defining characteristic of this breed of American women.

In the world of entertainment, I think of comedian, actress, writer and one-woman social catalyst Tina Fey. She was chosen "Entertainer of the Year" in 2008 by the *Associated Press* as the performer who had the greatest impact that year on American culture and entertainment. And she's just getting warmed up!

And of course, I think of Michelle Obama and Sarah Palin. They are as different as their politics. But they are each very comfortable with their feminine, even glamorous, sides. And neither felt the need to choose, as *Interlopers* often did, between career and family. They both married young and combined hands-on mothering with high-powered careers.

The Soil They Grew In

When the *Insiders* began entering the workforce in the early 1980s, professional environments were much more welcoming than those most *Interlopers* faced. By 1985, half of all college graduates were women, the number of two-income families had increased dramatically, and women were expanding their presence in nearly every imaginable occupation. *Insiders* weren't nearly as alone in the workplace as *Interlopers* had been. They were much more likely to have career role models and were supported with growing social acceptance for their professional ambitions. Rather than fighting to prove their capabilities, *Insiders* were able to build confidence during their early career years. As a result of all of these factors, they often achieved higher levels of success, and at much younger ages, than *Interlopers.*

As the number of dual-income families gradually became the norm in the U.S., even women with preschool children began entering the labor market in record numbers. While *Interlopers* were considered radical for choosing to use Ms. rather than Miss or Mrs. and keeping their maiden name after marriage, *Insiders* made both choices mainstream. Never one to miss a fresh trend, Hollywood stretched America's imagination with several hit series, including *Police Woman*, *Cagney & Lacey*, and *Murphy*

Brown, about women working in once male-only environments. During the decade of the 1980s, being an assertive woman with career ambitions became cool rather than contrary.

The second wave of professional American women also had more graduate degrees, including law, medical, and business degrees, than any previous generation of females. According to the U.S. Department of Education, undergraduate and graduate school enrollment by women began increasing dramatically in the late 1970s and has continued to soar.[1] With both academic credentials and ambition, *Insiders* pushed against glass ceilings with such force that they began to inch upward. Many achieved positions of influence and authority that *Interlopers* only dreamed about. Today, *Insiders* are beginning to dominate the innumerable lists of influential women, from the *Wall Street Journal's* prestigious "Women to Watch" to *Forbes*' "Most Powerful Women in the World." *Influential Insiders* are in their prime career years, just hitting their stride.

Not Quite One of the Guys

Something else was different by the time the *Insiders* began arriving on the professional fast track. Rather than a barrier to opportunity, being a woman was actually becoming a competitive advantage. "You had to be top-notch and know your stuff," *Insider* Sandy Pierce, CEO of Charter One Financial in Michigan and leader of the Michigan Turnaround Plan, a coalition of 75 CEOs, recalls. "But because there were so few of us, the spotlight was always on us. A woman who was good could stand out and get noticed quickly. Any woman of my generation who doesn't admit that isn't telling the truth."

Insiders didn't feel the need to neutralize themselves as *Interlopers* often did, leading to the demise of the navy blue power suit as the uniform of an ambitious woman. Of course, they also had the help of the fashion industry, which had discovered that there was big money to be made in stylish clothing for working women. *Interlopers,* particularly lawyers and women who worked in conservative, corporate environments, told me story after story of having to buy men's suits and have them tailored to fit because there were so few appropriate alternatives early in their careers. But by the late 1980s, *Insiders* found entire floors of department stores filled with stylish women's suits, from entry level to designer label.

Not One of the Girls Either

The cohort group of professional American women I call *Influential Insiders* has often been criticized for reaping the benefits of the heavy lifting done by the generation before them, while not being particularly supportive of other women. Perhaps that is because they were often pitted against one another. By the time *Insiders* were entering the workforce, U.S. corporations and employers in all sectors were beginning to feel the heat from federal government Affirmative Action policies that required them to demonstrate their hiring and employment practices didn't discriminate against women and minorities. That opened up new opportunities, but only a few. Rather than being considered equally with men for *all* positions, by the 1980s and early 1990s women often found themselves competing against one another for what was commonly known as "the token woman spot." Regardless of their shared gender, *Insiders* were more likely to view other women as rivals for limited opportunities rather than potential allies for mutual advancement.

Insiders also tend to shy away from publicly aligning themselves with other women and women's issues. Brigadier General Barbara Faulkenberry, who was part of the third class of women to graduate from the Air Force Academy, recalls behavior she says was typical of "second-wave" military women. "When I walked into a room for a class, I never sat next to a woman. We didn't gather as women. The interesting thing is the difference today, when you fast forward 25 years. Recently, the brass wanted a number of senior women to put together a conference honoring the 60th anniversary of women in the Air Force. We sat around the table and said, 'We don't want this conference. We don't want to separate ourselves and have just a women's conference,'" Faulkenberry told me. "That's our hang-up from the era when we were first making our mark. The younger women see no issues with getting together as women. And the conference turned out to be a great thing."

Superwoman, Opting Out, the Mommy Track

Another distinguishing characteristic of *Insiders* was their determination to prove they could "have it all," which usually meant *doing* it all. According to the Families and Work Institute, Generation X has always been more family-focused than Baby Boomers.[2] It was *Insiders* who inspired the TV ads that mythologized the American superwoman. She was often shown as a beautiful (of course), stylishly-dressed businesswoman greeting her children after school, then picking up a frying pan to whip-up a gourmet dinner, and finally slipping into something sexy for a romantic evening with her husband.

The truth was more complicated. *Insiders* may have been ascending to levels of higher responsibility, but nearly all carried a heavier share of the parenting and household workload than their male peers (and still do!). This led to two work culture trends that began to take root in the late 1980s and early 1990s: *The Mommy Track* and *Opting Out.*

Catalyst founder Felice Schwartz (now deceased), who was a business executive when she took time off to raise her three children, first proposed the concept of two career tracks for women in a 1989 *Harvard Business Review* article.[3] She suggested that corporations should offer women a choice: the opportunity to compete on the traditional *Fast Track* with male peers whose wives were nearly always full-time homemakers and a separate track for women who wanted to slow their pace while their children were young. It was the media that came up with the catchy but derisive "Mommy Track" name. And of course, there was no *Daddy Track* for men, nor guarantees that women would ever get back on the *Fast Track* once they stepped off. The *Mommy Track* was a controversial idea that the most ambitious *Insiders* were quick to resist. Those I interviewed who managed to successfully juggle both demanding careers and family life nearly always credited supportive husbands, who encouraged their careers and pitched in on the home front, as essential to their success.

Significant numbers of *Insiders* did "opt out," choosing full-time motherhood over their once high-flying careers. The trend had been building for years by the time the *New York Times Magazine* published "The Opt-Out Revolution" in April 2003.[4] The article featured photos and interviews with former executives with Harvard MBAs and law degrees who had chosen to return home to full-time motherhood. It triggered a backlash for its elitist focus on women whose finances allowed them the luxury of choosing whether or not to work. It also put its finger directly on the pulse of the growing divide between career women with young children who continued to work full time and those who chose to return home to become so-called "full-time mothers." The tension between professional-level women who make different family choices is still in the air today.

It was the determination of *Insiders* to find a way to balance the push and pull of career and family that led to work culture innovations such as on-site daycare, job sharing, flexible work schedules, and telecommuting. They also are the group most responsible for the dramatic increase we've seen in the number of fathers more actively involved with day-to-day parenting and the continued softening of the once rigid gender roles for both men and women.

Springboards to Their Success

Influential Insiders were rarely the women featured in magazine articles as "the first" in any unconventional career, but they played a major role in expanding and reinforcing women's presence and achievements in public arenas. From raising the glass ceiling and changing work cultures to encouraging men to step out of their gender-defined narrow comfort zones, the impact of *Insiders* over the past few decades has been dramatic. There were five key factors essential to their tremendous success.

- *Role models. Influential Insiders* grew up watching Geraldine Ferraro run for vice president of the United States, astronaut Sally Ride go into space, and tennis champion Billie Jean King defeat Bobby Riggs, the man who had declared to the world that no female athlete could ever defeat a male athlete. *Insiders* were the first generation of American women to come of age *suspecting* that they truly could do anything. Their defining roots are planted in soil fertilized with plenty of evidence to support their dreams. They couldn't help but be influenced by pervasive media coverage on interloping female judges, surgeons, police officers, construction workers, and even TV sportscasters.

  I will never forget the day I stood in front of the TV in my kitchen and watched a *CBS Evening News* story on the first women to graduate from the U.S. Air Force Academy. When I saw female pilots dressed in flight suits climbing into jets and taking off into the sky, my eyes filled with tears. It was the first time in my life that I ever truly believed—regardless of all my public bravado as a young feminist—that I could have flown a plane. The power of role models, at any age, cannot be overestimated. *Insiders* grew up with an abundance.

- *Title IX.* Another huge differentiator between *Insiders* and generations of women before them was Title IX of the Education Act. Passed in 1972, this federal law outlawed gender discrimination in education, including sports.[5] In the stroke of a presidential pen, female students had the legal right to participate in sports at every level, from grade school through college.

  Of course, nothing that dramatic changes overnight. It took courageous girls and young women to insist on those rights. Those who did frequently experienced the kind of hostility I witnessed as a TV news reporter in Grand Rapids, Michigan, covering the implementation of Title IX in the mid-1970s. I'll never forget the look in the eyes and the set of the chins of a handful of middle school girls as they walked to their school track for their first meet. They had to walk directly past jeering, angry parents who were upset that the girls were insisting on their right to run on the school's previously all-boys track team. Several outraged fathers and mothers, who apparently thought females should stick to cheerleading, told me they were afraid their sons could be emotionally damaged if they happened to be beaten by a girl.

As tough as it was in the 70s for young girls who were some of the first females to play on school sports teams, the benefits they received prepared them well for competing with men in the workforce. "I was nine or ten when I started playing baseball with the boys," recalls Karen John, one of the coaches of the 2008 U.S. Women's Olympic softball team. "It was right after Title IX, but girls' sports weren't really organized yet. So we had the option of playing baseball with the boys. I learned to manage heckling and how to lead, because we weren't really wanted. And I learned that I could be a peer with them."

In 1979, I interviewed Betty Harragan, author of *Games Mother Never Taught You,* the 1977 best seller on corporate gamesmanship for women. Her groundbreaking book sold over one million copies. Harragan was a strong advocate of sports opportunities for girls. I interviewed her for a TV documentary, *Playing to Win*, that I produced for WJBK-TV in Detroit on the impact of Title IX. Looking at the video over three decades later, it sounds very dated. But Harragan's words were prophetic. "Sports are very mental activities," she told the young sports reporter. "It takes a lot of planning and decision making. It takes a lot of risk taking and guts. Those are the very words that employers then say, 'Oh, women don't have what it takes to get ahead. They don't take risks. They aren't competitive. They don't try hard enough.' All the very skills that men have been taught through sports. It isn't that women *aren't that way*. It's that a part of their education has been almost universally cut out."

Insiders were the first beneficiaries of the sports opportunities triggered by Title IX. Betty Harragan would smile today if she could see the growing numbers of female athletes who are powering up to leadership positions.

- *Landmark lawsuits.* During the 1970s and 1980s, shudders went through corporate boardrooms after women prevailed in multiple landmark, class action lawsuits against major employers, including AT&T, United Air Lines, and even *The New York Times.*[6] Companies facing millions of dollars in damages for back pay and penalties discovered that gender discrimination and sexual harassment could have expensive consequences. It was primarily *Interlopers* who stood up and publicly challenged discriminatory practices. Those who did, such as journalist and *Interloper* Mary Lou Butcher Casey, whose lawsuit against the *Detroit News* opened up opportunities for female reporters at newspapers across the country,[7] paid a high price. The lawsuits dragged on for years and the courageous women who were involved nearly always lost their jobs and often found themselves labeled "problem employees" for the rest of their careers. The *Detroit News* made life so miserable for Butcher that she eventually left journalism for a very successful public relations career. *Insiders*, who began moving into the workforce just as professional playing fields were leveling out just a bit were the beneficiaries of the heavy lifting done by their older professional sisters.
- *Military service.* The military has long been considered an excellent training ground for the development of leaders. For men, that is. It took an Act of Congress in 1975 to open the U.S. service academies, including West Point and Annapolis to women.[8] The first female cadets, who entered in 1976, were true *Interlopers*. Several have written fascinating personal memoirs that describe the sometimes harrowing environments they overcame to graduate in 1980 as members of the first dual-gender classes of officers. One of my favorite such memoirs is *In the Men's House* by Carol Barkalow.

  As women proved they were up to the physical, psychological, academic and even hazing tests the military threw at them, attitudes began to change quickly. By 1990, over 229,000 women were serving on active duty as officers and enlisted personnel in the Army, Navy, Marie Corps and Air Force.[9] It was primarily *Insiders* who led the way into the military. Their numbers continue to grow, as women today are serving courageously and risking injury and death alongside their male comrades, including in Iraq and Afghanistan.

Insiders, such as Air Force Colonel Dawn Dunlop, the first (and only at this writing) female pilot flying the *F-22 Raptor* combat jet, is a big believer in actions speaking louder than words. "When you first show up (as the only woman), there are all kinds of questions from the men like, 'Why are you here? Why would you want to be a fighter pilot? Can we tell jokes around you?' The best approach is to just do your job. Not to start telling them why this is right for you, and right for them and right for the nation. But just *showing* them. That takes time."

- *Professional development resources.* Finally, it would be hard to overestimate the value of the wealth of books, workshops, training and individual mentoring specifically tailored for professional women that were becoming widely available as *Insiders* were coming of age. Bookstores opened entire new sections as a proliferation of "self-help" books for professional women were published. Some of the classics, such as *He Said, She Said* (Deborah Tannen), *Hardball for Women* (Pat Heim), and *Play Like a Man, Win Like a Woman* (Gail Evans), are still relevant today. Personal coaches, mentoring programs, women's professional organizations, and training on everything from assertiveness and presentation skills to business travel etiquette all gave *Insiders* an edge over *Interlopers,* who had to figure it all out the hard way—on their own.

Influential Insiders: Differences that Divide

Insiders and *Interlopers* share all of the fundamental qualities essential for professional achievement: ambition, drive, perseverance, versatility.

But the dramatically different work environments and social attitudes they encountered early in their careers created differences that run deep. Here are the two most common criticisms I hear about *Insiders:*

- *They separate themselves from Interlopers.* Many trailblazing professional women are still a little bitter about *Insiders* who tended to distance themselves from and criticize the very women who had paved the way for them. GE Senior Vice President Charlene Begley recalls her impressions, early in her career, after she attended a meeting of a very prestigious women's network: "I spent two days at an exclusive forum for high-achieving women. When I left, I told our HR executive, 'I'm never going back.' It was all senior, very successful women that had huge chips on their shoulders and seemed angry at men. They had worked their way up the hard way and it was a very bitter group. I just couldn't relate and I wanted no part of it." Begley's perspective of *Interlopers* is one I hear often from this cohort group, primarily because few *Insiders* can relate to the very difficult road that most *Interlopers* walked. As a result, *Insiders*, as a group, have shown little interest in learning from or supporting the advancement of *Interlopers.* Few admit it, but many believe they're just a little savvier, smarter, and, yes, sexier, than their trailblazing older sisters.
- *They are reluctant to lead change.* One of the harshest and most common complaints I hear from women of all ages about *Insiders* is that few of them are willing to be catalysts for change. "I felt I needed to be accepted by the old boys club," *Insider* Judith Mühlberg, who rose to executive levels in two very male industries: autos and aerospace, explained. "I remember one former CEO asking me to help him break the glass ceiling. My response to him was, 'That would be career suicide for me! I can't be seen as the person who's going to lead in that frontier.'" You could argue that trailblazers had nothing to lose when they openly challenged the status quo, while *Insiders,* who achieved greater financial benefits and positions of influence, had—and still have—plenty to lose. "It's a risk, and many women don't want to jeopardize their positions," says *Insider* and The 85% Niche CEO Miriam Muley, who held executive positions

at several Fortune 100 companies, including Avon and GM, before starting her own marketing firm. She acknowledges it's time her generation of women *Achievers* put their hard-earned influence to work to make a difference beyond their own resumes. "I think the real distinction of a leader is someone who's willing to right the wrong in an organization," says Muley. "Not to do it blindly, of course, but to leverage your business savvy and understanding of the politics of the organization to step out and do what's really needed today—to get the pipelines in place, salaries aligned, and leadership tracks expanded."

What We Can Learn from *Influential Insiders*

- *Diplomacy.* One of the keys to *Insiders'* success has been their ability to fit in to male-dominated work cultures and work effectively with men as peers. Yes, many were also constantly under the microscope. But because they didn't face nearly as much rejection, hostility, or open sexism as *Interlopers,* they weren't nearly as defensive. They also had an edge on *Interlopers* in the art of being assertive without seeming too aggressive. And they're more likely to have a sense of humor about gender differences. Mastering those skills early in their careers served them well in work cultures just beginning to get used to the idea of a woman being the boss.
- *Confidence. Interlopers* needed courage to tackle the mountains they did, but it was often backed up with more bravado than rock solid confidence. Many *Insiders* developed true confidence in their own abilities at a much younger age. The opportunity to compete in sports, an abundance of female role models, and growing up in a culture that was beginning to celebrate women spreading their wings all built *Insiders'* self-esteem. Believing you can do absolutely anything is essential. For some, it comes with the DNA; others develop it over time. Either way, confidence is key.
- *Womaninity.* This is a word I coined for this book to describe a powerful feminine quality that women are just beginning to fully

utilize. Think of it this way: Womaninity is to masculinity as Ms. is to Mr. It has nothing to do with sexuality and everything to do with being relaxed in your own skin as a female human being. *Insiders* have an edge on both *Interlopers*, who downplayed their femininity, and *Innovators*, who, too often, seem to be leading with it. Later, in chapter 13, you'll learn more about *Womaninity*, which is one of the seven leadership Practices we'll explore in Part Three. We can all learn a thing or two from savvy *Insiders* about finding the right balance of yin and yang for business hours.

A Few Words to *Influential Insiders*

If you recognize yourself in this section, I encourage you to think about what a pivotal role you and your peers are positioned to play in continuing women's upward momentum. One of the biggest challenges on the horizon is the talent war. Companies that figure out how to develop and retain women leaders will have an advantage. If you are in a position of influence, what are you doing to help other women achievers break through to leadership opportunities? Are you a catalyst for work culture changes that reflect the different rhythms of women's lives? Or are you satisfied to go along with old school attitudes, policies, and practices that continue to waste women's capabilities? If you are an *Insider* who dialed down your ambitions because of family obligations, have you given up ever getting back on the fast track, or are your eyes open to the growing possibilities for women who aren't afraid to go after them? Finally, I hope you'll think about your attitude toward *Interlopers.* Do you find yourself judging them as a little too tough or not quite as professionally savvy as you because they rarely achieved the heights your generation has? If you do, consider asking a few *Interlopers* to share some stories about the defining moments they faced early in their careers. It might give you a deeper understanding of who they are today.

Now let's meet the third wave of high-achieving American women: the *I'll-Do-It-My-Way Innovators.* Their impact on women's influence in the 21st Century could be as great as both the *Interlopers* and *Insiders* combined.

CHAPTER 4

The I'll-Do-It-My-Way Innovators

My sex has nothing to do with it. I believe in myself as a driver.
— DANICA PATRICK, Race Car Driver, *Innovator*

The most openly ambitious generation of American women ever to pick up an iPhone or slip into the driver's seat of a high-performance race car, the *Innovators* are a very different breed from *Interlopers* and *Insiders*. The daughters of Baby Boomers and Gen-Xs, *Innovators* are high-achieving female Millennials—the 80-million strong, Gen-Y generation, born approximately between 1981 and 1995. The oldest *Innovators* are in their mid 30s; the youngest are still in high school, as I write. Universities, corporations, politics, mainstream culture, and workplaces from Maine to Hawaii are just beginning to feel the rumblings of what, inevitably, will be their seismic impact. These technically savvy, multicultural, global-thinking future leaders have very different ideas on how, where, when, and why they will put their talents to work.

When I think of *Innovators,* I think of Danica Patrick, the first professional woman driver ever to win an Indy car race. She doesn't give an inch on the track to the big boys. She doesn't lose any sleep, either, about not being taken seriously because of all those photos on her website of her draped across a race car in tight-tight, short shorts.

I think of Marissa Mayer, the 35-year-old engineer and vice president of Search Products and User Experience for Google. She's the youngest leader ever named to *Fortune* magazine's list of the "50 Most Powerful Women."

I think of Jessica Mendoza, a standout athlete on the silver-medal 2008 U.S. Olympic softball team, the 2009-2010 president of the Women's Sports Foundation, and an inductee into the International Latin Sports Hall of Fame. At age 28, this bilingual California native has already traveled all over the world, visiting troops in Afghanistan, creating awareness about genocide in Darfur, and conducting sports clinics for girls in Harlem, Guatemala, and South Africa.

I think of Jennifer Sharpe, the fifteen-year-old Michigan Girl Scout who, in 2008, sold an astonishing 17,328 boxes of America's favorite cookies—using the Internet, of course.

And I think of Angelina Jolie. Yes, she's a gorgeous movie star, flies her own plane, and is a hands-on mother of a multiracial family. More importantly, she has strategically used her fame and wealth to become an influential force for causes she believes in. *Forbes* recently named her the most powerful celebrity in the world.

Never before has there been a cohort of women so well prepared and perfectly positioned to ascend to leadership in record numbers. I call them the *I'll-Do-It-My-Way Innovators* because they have no intention of playing by anyone's rules but their own. If you are an *Interloper* or *Insider,* don't expect *Innovators* to wait patiently for promotions, to accept being paid less than their male peers, or to stick around long in work cultures that offer little flexibility for their lives beyond the office. "Their requirements are ones that the rest of the generations in the workforce will welcome," says Susan Peters, vice president of executive development for GE. "They (Gen Ys of both sexes) want more flexibility, less relocation and more opportunities to 'do it my way and on my time, as long as I do a great job.' That's going to help us all in a broader way."

If you are an *Innovator,* I'm counting on you to help write the newest edition of the leadership playbook—for both genders.

Masters of technology and social networking, these forward-looking American women practically grew up with computers in their cribs. Brimming with confidence and high expectations, they are more likely to have multicultural friendships and progressive values about homosexual rights and gender roles. They have little knowledge, however, of how far women have progressed in very recent history. I was astonished when a young lawyer and member of the 2007 class of White House Fellows, a prestigious year-long leadership program, told me she had never heard of Betty Friedan, author of the searing 1963 manifesto *The Feminine Mystique.* The *New York Times* credits the brilliant and tenacious New York crusader with "permanently transforming the social fabric of the United States." In the most diplomatic way I could manage, I told the young lawyer, "Betty Friedan is to the Women's Movement what Martin Luther King and Rosa Parks are to the Civil Rights Movement. You are a White House Fellow today because of Betty Friedan." She responded, "No one ever told me about her."

It's true that U.S. history classes include little more than passing mention of the key leaders and events responsible for women's ascent toward legal and social equality throughout the 20th Century. Perhaps that's one reason why *Innovators* feel little personal connection to the struggles of their more seasoned, professional sisters, be they *Interlopers* who marched in the streets for the Equal Rights Amendment in the 1970s or *Insiders* who still faced widespread bias throughout the 1980s. For example, in 1982, legendary Indiana University basketball Coach Bobby Knight ordered college basketball player Carol Hutchins and her Michigan State Lady Spartan teammates, practicing in their home gym, to "Get off the court! The men's team practice is more important than yours."

Even the historic significance of a woman running for president in 2008 warranted little sisterhood support from *Innovators,* who heavily supported Barack Obama. Is it any wonder that trailblazers such as Jane Kay Nugent, who was the lone woman executive for several decades at a Midwest utility company, keeps her hard-earned wisdom to herself? "I don't give speeches anymore," Nugent told me. "Young women today don't believe my stories. They just think I'm some out-of-touch old lady who wasn't as smart or savvy as they are."

Forces that Shaped Them

Just as *Interlopers* and *Insiders* were shaped by the cultural forces and attitudes at work during their coming of age years, *Innovators* are reflections of the cultural forces shaping their generation. Their attitudes, values, and behavior have been heavily influenced by:

- *Technology, technology, technology.* High-speed Internet, iPods, Kindles, hundreds of channels on cable TV, YouTube, Facebook, MySpace and texting are all part of the diet that this generation has grown up on. Practically born with a mouse in one hand and a cell phone in the other, they seem to have an extra gene that gives them an intuitive, technological edge over more experienced workers. *Innovators* barely remember a time when they didn't have information instantly at their fingertips, from local job opportunities and movie times to global news and entertainment trends. This has given them a window on the world that has no geographical or cultural boundaries. Theirs is the generation that has led the explosion of social networking on the Internet—and, more importantly, understands how to use this powerful tool better than their more seasoned professional sisters.
- *Ethnic and multicultural America.* Whether they were growing up in New Orleans, New York City, the Southwest (where Spanish is the second language), or Detroit (where African Americans are the

majority and nearby Dearborn is home to the largest Arab population outside of the Middle East), *Innovators* are coming of age in a United States that looks and thinks very differently. As a result, their cultural comfort zones are fluid. They're more likely to judge people and choose friends based on common interests than previous generations. And they're less burdened with old social patterns that categorized people first by gender, race, religion, or social class. Case in point: 66 percent of voters aged 18-29 years old voted for Barack Obama for president. That's 14 percentage points higher than any other age group.[1]

- *Oversexualization of women.* Perhaps it was the influence of Britney Spears, hip-hop lyrics, and America's obsession with sex. Or maybe it was just the cultural pendulum swinging in the opposite direction after several decades of women struggling to be measured by their mental abilities rather than their physical attributes. *Innovators* have grown up steeped in a culture so sexually charged that even the clothing available for them, since the time they were young girls, reflects it. Low-cut jeans, bared midriffs, tattoos, and plenty of cleavage are practically their trademarks. When the fashion industry is pushing high heels for pre-schoolers and breast implants are a growth market among 19 to 34-year-old women, you can be sure that we've moved 180 degrees away from the days of *Interlopers* protesting the sexism of the Miss America pageant.

The Millennial Edge

For the past six decades, Baby Boomers have been shaping America's work and social cultures. And Millennials are taking their time about taking over, with many delaying adult responsibilities and living with their parents longer than recent generations. But as older generations begin to retire, the economy surges, and the talent wars start heating up again, it is *Innovators* who will be holding a winning hand. All the early research indicates that this generation of women Achievers will play their cards very differently than *Interlopers* and *Insiders*. Here are a few early clues into their mindset.

Innovators:

- *Truly believe that girls rule.* During the 2008 presidential campaign, *Newsweek* magazine reported that large numbers of young American women never jumped on the Hillary Clinton bandwagon. *Innovators* are used to being equally influential with their male peers in shaping the arenas they've competed in. This gives them a strong sense of entitlement to an equal share of the spoils of professional competition. Only an *Innovator* would write, as the young author of the *Newsweek* article did, "A female president does not seem like change."[2]
- *Are both androgynous and overtly sexual. Innovators* feel little conflict between their ambitions and their gender, as evidenced by the cleavage they so often display during business hours. Because they don't carry the weight of limiting stereotypes of the past, they tend to be much more comfortable with fluid gender roles. They fully expect their husbands to be full partners on the home front. Yet they also routinely dress in a sexually provocative manner. What's going on? "There is a huge sexualization of women of my generation," acknowledges Olympic medalist and long-time member of the U.S. Women's National Softball team Jessica Mendoza. She's concerned about young girls feeling "as if they need to show more skin and be sexual all the time," but also understands the other side of the coin. "Among my friends, there is almost this sense of 'no sex,' meaning it doesn't matter if you are a man or a woman," she explains. "We're not stereotyped by sex anymore. It's more about being who you are and doing what you want to do."
- *Will flee work cultures that don't work for them. Innovators* grew up watching their working mothers struggle to do it all, which was nearly always *too much*. As a result, they have very different expectations of the companies they will choose to work for. Part of a generation accustomed to instant gratification, their expectations are high for money, opportunity, and work environments with social values that match their own. At the same time, they are much less likely than any previous generation to stick around and "pay their dues" in unfulfilling jobs with inflexible career tracks. "Despite the recent

flurry of media speculation that Gen Y women are planning to 'opt out' of the business world, our research shows a much more complicated picture," reported Kellyanne Conway on the findings of a year-long study of educated Gen Y that was commissioned by Lifetime Television.[3] "They are a highly ambitious group of young women with great expectations," said Conway, president and CEO of the Polling Company, Inc., which conducted the research. Flexibility is one of *Innovators* top career goals.

***Innovators:* Differences that Divide**

Ask any manager of Millennials about the work ethic of this new breed and you'll get an earful. The headline on a 2007 *Fortune* magazine cover story on the widespread disconnect between *Innovators* and older professionals said it all: *"Manage us? Puh-leeze . . . Today's 20-somethings have their own rules. You just don't understand them."*[4] Here are the not-too-complimentary themes I heard over and over from *Interlopers* and *Insiders* about *Innovators:*

- *Big ambition, no perseverance.* The jury is still out on how hard *Innovators* will be willing to work to achieve their high career expectations. Many accomplished women leaders I spoke with have their doubts. "We have a lot of young women in our health leadership tracks," Nancy Schlichting, president and CEO of Henry Ford Health Systems, told me. "They have it in their heads that they're just going to continue to move right up. I think they underestimate what is required, the depth and breadth of learning that needs to take place before you are really prepared to move into senior leadership roles."
- *Unable to handle criticism.* Often raised by so-called "helicopter parents" who hovered, coddled and built up their self-esteem with oodles of positive reinforcement, few *Innovators* have grown the Teflon skin that *Interlopers* and *Insiders* needed to arm themselves with. "There's no thick skin. Theirs is about as thin a veneer as it can be. And I think their answer to everything is, 'I'll just quit,'" observes

Lorraine Bolsinger, president and CEO of GE Aviation Systems. But she also believes that making the effort to retain talented *Innovators* is critical. "We have to find ways to communicate what's required in a way that's compelling so that they don't simply say, 'I don't have to listen. I'm going elsewhere.'"

- *Naive about gender barriers ahead.* Because they are still at the very beginnings of their career paths, where so many women have already smoothed the way, *Innovators* have rarely encountered gender barriers or experienced the "good old boys club" in action. Not until they reach higher levels, where the financial stakes are so much greater, will *Innovators* discover that plenty of gender land mines still await. In addition, most have barely begun to face the complexities of family "speed bumps" that slow many a promising woman's ascent to leadership opportunities. Dr. Judy Rosener, a University of California/Irvine business professor and nationally recognized expert on gender and leadership, has observed, "My female MBA students think the gender barriers are behind us. Then they come back to me in five years and say, 'What happened?'" Few *Innovators* realize it yet, but they'll discover soon enough that Congresswoman Carolyn Maloney had it right when she titled her 2008 book, *Rumors of our Progress Have Been Greatly Exaggerated.*
- *Don't dress for success.* If I've heard that complaint once, I've heard it at least 100 times from mystified professional women who are astonished at the inappropriate ways legions of young women are dressing for work. *Innovators* with leadership ambitions are underestimating the confusing signals they are sending, particularly to men, when they wear sexy clothing at work. *Interlopers* in particular, who struggled so mightily to emerge from the confining box that measured women first on their "physical assets," are watching in stunned amazement at the way young women are boldly playing—some would say misplaying—the sex card. Regardless of how seductively lawyers, FBI agents and surgeons are dressing for work on America's top-rated TV series, real-life women who aspire to leadership must be highly conscious about not sending mixed signals with their clothing. Even those who are not dressing provocatively are frequently dressing too

casually for their ambitions and underestimating the significance of professional attire.

While I was working on this book, I was asked to serve as a judge for a high school speech competition sponsored by one of our local Optimists clubs. I was dismayed by the dramatic difference in the way the competitors were dressed. Every one of the young men was wearing a long-sleeved shirt and a tie: the male professional uniform. One boy, an Asian American, was even wearing a suit jacket. The young women, on the other hand, seemed to be clueless about how to dress to impress an audience, despite the fact that "Appearance" was one of the elements we were asked to judge. Not a single female competitor was wearing anything that signaled professionalism or "Take me seriously." You think I'm being overly critical? One of the high school *Innovators* was wearing her school hoodie. Why, I wondered afterward, did those top female students have no sense of how to dress for success in a competitive situation while their male peers had it down pat? What are parents teaching their sons about dressing to impress that their daughters aren't learning?

For all their thin (and exposed) skin, naïve bravado and rough edges, *Innovators,* however, have enormous potential to transform our culture's definition of professional achievement and leadership. "Unlike previous generations focused on climbing the proverbial corporate ladder," says The Polling Company CEO Kellyanne Conway, "these young women are redefining the terms of success across a broad spectrum of personal and professional goals."[5] Women of any age can learn plenty from this fascinating group of newcomers to the professional fast track.

What We Can Learn from *Innovators*

- *Technology skills.* Growing up with technology has given *Innovators* an invaluable competitive edge. The quicker *Interlopers* and *Insiders* admit we have some catching up to do, the better off we'll all be. I was frustrated for months about my difficulty getting in touch with my teenage son, Kevin, who rarely answers his cell phone and never checks voice mail. When I looked at my phone bill and realized he was sending or receiving over 1,000 text messages a month, I asked him to show me how to text. I've never had trouble reaching him since. We're not going to lick 'em, so we might as well learn from them. Are you LinkedIn? Have you learned to use Facebook to expand your social and professional networks? Do you have a presence on Wikipedia? When was the last time you checked out the "most popular" video on YouTube? Or have you tried tweeting, just to know what all the buzz is about? If not, ask one of your favorite Gen Ys to get you started.

- *Mentoring and connecting with other women.* This generation doesn't have the hang-ups that *Insiders* did about aligning closely with other professional women. They recognize and welcome the benefits of coming together as women, without any concern about jeopardizing their ability to bond effectively with men. They also embrace mentoring opportunities, which are in greater demand than ever. Progressive companies are figuring out that this powerful developmental tool shouldn't be reserved only for highflyers already on the leadership track. The savviest of *Innovators* have caught on quickly to the value of finding mentors and advocates early in their careers who will open doors as well as help them avoid damaging mistakes. You can never have too many allies.
- *Global world view. Innovators* didn't have to read author Tom Friedman's best-selling book to discover that the world is flat. They already knew it. These future leaders have traveled overseas in record numbers and will accept international assignments as readily as *Interlopers* and *Insiders* relocated within the United States. From a very young age, the Internet has been their membership card to a world without borders. They are much more likely to think globally and are comfortable engaging with diverse people of different genders, cultures, and life experiences. We can learn plenty from *Innovators* about getting out of our comfort zones and becoming engaged citizens of our complex planet.

A Few Words for *Innovators*

Perhaps the glass ceiling will be a forgotten metaphor by the time you reach leadership levels. I hope so. Recent trends indicate that it is highly likely that the men you marry will be more involved with parenting and partnering at home than their fathers, uncles, and grandfathers ever were. Insist on it! "Research has shown that women with families who work full-time experience far higher levels of stress than their male counterparts, and that their excessive stress is due not to the demands of their employment but to the weight of their responsibilities at home," report authors Linda Babcock and Sara Laschever in *Women Don't Ask: Negotiation and the Gender Divide:* "Make sure the men you choose to share your life live up to all the promises they make. Those negotiations must be worked out between each couple."[6] Or, as Facebook COO Sheryl Sandberg advises when she speaks to audiences of career-focused women, "Make your partner a real partner."[7]

There is every reason to believe you will be change agents, helping to lay the foundation for greater flexibility in how, where, and when you and millions of your generational peers will work. I'm counting on you to lead the way. But it won't be easy. Don't believe all that talk about your ability to write your own ticket because of pending talent shortages. The recent global recession and Wall Street meltdown that wiped out billions of dollars of retirement savings and financial security means Baby Boomers will be working longer than anybody expected. Until you are in charge, I encourage you to remember that you are being evaluated by colleagues and superiors who will measure you by their standards, not yours. Individuality is great. However, don't underestimate the importance of matching your work ethic, demeanor, and attire to the highest standards of your workplace.

Finally, think about the concept of 360-degree mentoring, which is all about two-way learning—from those above, below, and at your side. You have plenty to learn and plenty to give, especially to colleagues who seem to be missing your "technology gene." Make sure you are truly open to the wisdom and advice that more seasoned professionals can offer. And remember, the more you give, the more you will receive.

Interlopers, Insiders, Innovators

I hope you recognize yourself in one of these fascinating cohort groups of high-achieving women. Don't typecast or limit yourself though. You may identify with qualities and defining experiences of each. If we continue to stretch, challenge ourselves, and empower one another, we can all learn valuable lessons from each of these distinctly American waves of ascending women. Now that we have a sense of who we are, let's take a closer look at where we are.

Part Two

Where Are We?

CHAPTER 5

Why Girls Don't Rule

There is a special place in hell for women who don't support other women.

— MADELINE ALBRIGHT,
Former Secretary of State, *Interloper*

When Xerox CEO Anne Mulcahy stepped to the podium to open her corporation's May 2009 Annual Stockholder meeting, everyone in the world headquarters auditorium knew they were about to witness history—or, more accurately, *herstory*. Topping the agenda was confirmation of what Wall Street had known for months: 50-year-old Ursula Burns, Mulcahy's hand-picked successor, would be named the next CEO. Not only is Burns the first African American female chief executive officer of a global corporation the size of Xerox, her ascent marked the first woman-to-woman CEO handoff in *Fortune* 500 history.

Savvy executives Mulcahy and Burns would say Xerox's leadership selection was simply good business: the best person won. No doubt. But look a little deeper and ask yourself this: What did it take for two, high-powered women executives—of different races and different generations—to become trusted business partners, mutual mentors, and unusual allies working toward common goals? It took Mulcahy and Burns to realize they could be more influential and effective as a partnership than operating alone. At some point, these two ambitious leaders became a team. Their example was a headline-worthy exception to the norm.

The more widespread reality, however, is that most women view one another as their primary competition—for everything: men, jobs, the spotlight, you name it. As a gender, we have little concept of a fundamental principal that men figured out centuries ago: teams can accomplish much more than even the most talented individual.

"Most women have all other women as adversaries; most men have all other men as their allies," quipped American humorist Frank Gelett Burgess in the early 1900s. Unfortunately, his observation is as true today as it was then. American women are like individual superstars on a team that has never won big. We have an abundance of *Achievers—Interlopers, Insiders,* and *Innovators*—carving out impressive careers and making their marks in nearly every walk of life. But here's the problem: in leadership, as in sports, it takes more than exceptional individual performance for a group to excel. I'm convinced that one—but not the only—of the primary reasons that *girls don't rule* and women still do not have appropriate influence and power in shaping our nation and culture comes down to one simple fact: *Women haven't learned that leadership is a team sport.*

Every Woman for Herself Is a Losing Strategy

The first way I assess a woman is by a very simple litmus test. Is she a female who supports and feels a natural allegiance with others of her cultural tribe? Or does she separate herself from and undermine other women? If she's in the first category, I consider her a potential ally. A cultural sister. Perhaps a leader whose vision I would consider following, a peer with whom I'd share my network, or even a potential mentee. I'm interested in learning more about her. If she's in the second category, however, I keep my distance. I don't trust her. We will never be more than acquaintances. I'd be unlikely to follow her lead or go out of my way to help advance her goals. Why do I give this question so much weight? Because I've learned that *every woman for herself is a losing strategy.*

Think about it. Gender is the first way that human beings categorize one another. All the other clues we use to identify with or differentiate ourselves from one another, be they race, heritage, religion, age, economic class, sororities, or even favorite sports teams, pale in comparison to our instant categorization of one another by gender: male and female—nature's primary differentiator. Have you ever noticed how uncomfortable people are when they can't immediately tell a person's gender? That's because we've been socialized to treat people in different ways based on gender identity. If we don't know a person's sex, we're not sure how to appropriately interact with her or him.

As females, we are born into the same cultural tribe. Regardless of the titles on our office doors, our golf handicaps, or even our military records, we are never, *ever* going to be one of the guys. Every woman is still viewed through a gender lens of broadly held conscious and unconscious attitudes and archetypes. That lens is so distorted and clouded with outdated images of what leaders look like that even women have a hard time thinking of ourselves and other females as having the *right stuff* to lead. In addition, non-Caucasian women of every shade, who are earning college and graduate degrees in record numbers, face the double jeopardy of being viewed through both a gender *and* a color lens.

Stand If You Ever

The biggest mistake women continue to make is to distance ourselves from our own natural allies: other women. Yet I see it happening every day. What am I talking about? There's a fantastic exercise called "Stand If You Ever"[1] that confronts women with common examples of how we undermine one another and, in the process, ourselves. Developed by organizational development practicioners Anne Litwin, Rita Andrews and Mary Lou Michael, the exercise asks participants to stand if they have ever done any of 25 items on the list. For example, if you tried the exercise, you would be asked to stand if you ever:

- Laughed at a joke told by a man at the expense of women,
- Assumed a woman got a job because of a quota,
- Made a commitment to a woman and then broke it to be with a man,
- Said or thought "You can't trust women,"
- Were more critical of women in leadership than of men.

The only place *that* behavior gets us is where most of us are right now: individually trying to break through glass ceilings while men keep getting a hand up from their tribal "big brothers." "How often have you heard a woman say, 'I'd never work for a woman' or 'I'd never vote for a woman,'" asks former Maryland Congresswoman Connie Morella, now a board member for Vital Voices Global Partnership, which works "to identify, invest in and bring visibility to extraordinary women around the world." "I think it is lack of respect and confidence in oneself that makes women pull other women down. I think anytime a woman is elevated all women are elevated."

When the day finally comes that large numbers of women recognize that we're all in this together, there will be no stopping us. But right now, three of the biggest reasons that girls still don't *make the rules*, let alone *rule,* are staring right back at us in the mirror. We don't believe in ourselves. We don't believe in each other. And we've barely begun to pull together to raise our collective game. Leadership is a team sport because it requires both strong individual performance as well as groups of people pulling together in the same direction. Women will continue to be *leadership underachievers* until we stop making the following three critical mistakes:

- We eliminate ourselves;
- We fail to join team women; and
- We play the other guy's game.

Each of these behaviors is like a pick in basketball. If you don't know what a pick is, you never see them. But once you recognize these blocking moves that players make to create scoring opportunities for teammates, you'll realize they are happening constantly in games. The same is true for culturally bred habits, which Dr. Ruth Yopp-Edwards, an African American scholar and *Interloper*, says ". . . develop over generations through both institutionalized and internalized oppression."[2] In order to escape their debilitating effects, it's important to realize how pervasive and destructive they are. By the end of this chapter, you'll not only recognize these behaviors when they raise their sabotaging heads, you'll also have new tools for stopping them in their tracks.

Mistake #1: We Eliminate Ourselves

My father, who was a naval officer, an athlete who played minor league baseball, and a sports broadcaster for nearly 40 years, knew a thing or two about leadership and winning. He gave every one of his seven children the same advice: "Never eliminate yourself." I don't know if my Dad coined that phrase or picked it up from someone else. But his three simple words are the most powerful mantra I've ever found for countering that little internal voice that never tires of warning "No you can't!" or "What if you fail?"

Here's how Vince Doyle explained to us what he meant by his advice. "If you're not good enough to make the team, get hired for a job you want, or earn the promotion you're going after, the world will eliminate you. There is plenty of competition out there. But if you never go for it because you think you're not ready or you're afraid of being embarrassed if you fail, then you've eliminated yourself."

That is the biggest mistake I see women still making today. We continuously eliminate ourselves from leadership opportunities. "Women hold themselves back. We don't have the bravado of men" is the way Leslie Desjardins, CFO of Amcor Limited, the world's largest packaging company, put it. "You have to fake it till you make it." Here's the pattern I've seen over and over: a man can be 30 percent qualified for a job and he thinks he's the perfect choice. A woman can be 90 percent qualified and the only thing she's worried about is the 10 percent of the experience she doesn't have. We still don't believe in ourselves. Too few of us have the confidence to see ourselves as authority figures. And because we don't believe we can do it (whatever *it* may be), it's comforting to believe that *no woman* can do it. So we default to the status quo: passively going along with 49 percent of the population—men—continuing their firm grip on well over 80 percent of leadership positions.

Speaking of a firm grip, don't underestimate the power of a weak handshake to eliminate you from consideration for leadership opportunities. Deedee Corradini, the former mayor of Salt Lake City (1992-2000) and current president of the Women's Ski Jumping Association, makes a point of teaching young women how to shake hands. "I am so sick of women with wimpy handshakes," she told me. "I do a lot of speaking on leadership. High school girls are always surprised when I talk about the importance of learning how to shake hands well. They tell me, 'No one ever talks to us about that.' So when I finish my remarks, I tell them, 'Come on up and let's shake hands.' Every girl who takes me up on my offer gets a firm handshake before I will let go of her hand."

When we eliminate ourselves in small ways—wimpy handshakes, holding back as men step up first to chair committees and claim small leadership roles, convincing ourselves it doesn't matter who gets credit for work as long as it gets done or carrying more than our share of the family load—it becomes that much harder to step forward and openly compete for leadership and power when bigger opportunities arise. It's similar to lifting weights. The more reps you do, even with small weights, the stronger you get. Yet too many of us are still reluctant to present ourselves as experts for speeches, professional panels and media interviews. We are dramatically less likely than men to negotiate our salaries and ask for promotions. And our widespread tendency to hold back, to wait to be asked, and to allow others (and men are happy to comply) to go first is the primary reason we have so few women in elected office today.

"Men wake up in the morning and say to themselves, 'I think I'll run for office,'" says Marie Wilson, founder and president of the White House Project, which is working to increase the numbers of women in political office and leadership. "Even highly qualified women have to be asked, even urged by others to run for office before they are likely to present themselves as candidates." Despite how deeply I believe that our country will be stronger when a critical mass of women is elected to political office at all levels and how many times I have urged other women to run, it took me years to throw my own hat in the ring. I had eliminated myself from opportunities for political leadership.

And no discussion of how women eliminate themselves would be complete without tackling another one of the elephants in the room. Droves of *Interlopers* and *Insiders* are howling in disbelief at the way so many young women (are you listening, *Innovators*?) are pairing their lofty ambitions with provocative clothing. "I find it amazing how many women are volunteering these days as sex objects," says Dr. Sonya Friedman, a psychologist in private practice, author, and host of the long-running CNN interview show, *Sonya Live*! "We used to talk about women who slept their way to the top. It seems today an awful lot of women want to expose their way to the top."

Why are growing numbers of girls and young women buying into today's pop culture drumbeat that an empowered female is both sex kitten and career driven? "Young women today have never experienced a media environment that didn't over exaggerate the centrality of sex and 'hotness' to everyday life," writes author Susan Douglas in *Enlightened Sexism: The Seductive Message that Feminism's Work Is Done.*[3] Douglas' analysis of the sexist stew that American movies, TV, magazines, and music videos have been force feeding us since the 1990s is wickedly funny and right on the money.

My college-age niece, Chicagoan Lucy Doyle, pushed back hard against my criticism of young women of her generation over-playing their sexuality card. "Women my age like dressing that way because we love our bodies," she told me. "Society is just going to have to get used to it. In ten years it won't seem so provocative." We'll see. Dressing for the workplace in ways that draw attention to her sexual attributes is guaranteed to get a woman plenty of attention. However, it is also sending a powerful mixed message—that immediately undermines any leadership aspirations she may have. Dr. Friedman also believes the trend is dangerously narcissistic. "My advice is for a woman who aspires to leadership to reflect on how busy you are with yourself versus how busy you are with what you're doing."

The issue of the oversexualization of girls and women that permeates American pop culture also has implications far beyond individual fashion choices. Kah Walla, a young political leader from Cameroon, Africa, asked me to share this message. "America makes the movies and music videos that are being sent out to the rest of the world. The images of how women are portrayed by western culture are horrible and have a very strong affect on how young women believe they should dress and act," Walla said. "There is a huge battle to be fought and won around the ways that women are portrayed in mass media. And American women are the only ones who can lead it."

Buying into pop culture's prevailing theme—that women's greatest attribute is our sexual impact on men—is one of the most insidious ways that we continue to eliminate ourselves and allow other women to be eliminated from becoming truly empowered.

American culture, still very macho yet infused with a fantasy that women have already achieved full equality in the United States, is the cultural dye that we all soak in. To move forward into the leadership frontier, a critical mass of women, not just a few exceptional leaders, must consciously emerge from this enfeebling brew and lift other women with us. When we allow our internal voice to keep us in the passenger seat, we eliminate ourselves. When we dress for work in a sexually provocative way, we eliminate ourselves. And when we ignore the impact movies, TV, and music that degrade women have on every one of us, we accept our cultural gender chains and eliminate ourselves from greater possibilities.

I've been a professional woman for four decades. I've been tested in some pretty tough leadership laboratories. I'm no rookie when it comes to taking risks. And I've never been shy about speaking up. Yet even today I often find myself turning to my father's advice to quiet that little voice in my head that never tires of insisting "What if you fail? Why rock the boat?" or "Maybe you shouldn't." *Never eliminate yourself*—three simple but powerful words. Make them your mantra. Share them with everyone you know. Put them in your purse or your briefcase, so you'll always have them with you when you need them. They are three Aces. Play them.

Mistake #2: We Fail to Join Team Women

Have you ever heard the phrase "It's bros before hos"? It's a vulgar expression that demeans all women. But it's also common enough in U.S. culture today to be OK to say on mainstream radio. That's where I heard it used (all in good fun, of course) by two male announcers. I was irritated to hear those values expressed so casually by male DJs. But I nearly drove off the road when the men's 20-something, female "sidekick" laughed and agreed with them. Did she not realize how demeaning their "lad humor" was to her and all women listeners? Or perhaps she felt her job would be at risk if she were so uncool as to object. Can you imagine how men would react if two women broadcasters were to vulgarly proclaim to their listening audience, "Sorry guys, but it's chicks before dicks"? As competitive as men are with one another, they all understand the unwritten rules of male bonding: guys stick together. Why don't gals?

How many times have you heard or thought: "We are our own worst enemies." I've lost track of the women I interviewed who used those exact words when they shared stories of how other women had been some of their fiercest critics and toughest adversaries. One of the most perplexing ways that women continue to sabotage our collective progress is by what I call "failing to join *team women.*" Every time I bring this topic up, I get moans and sighs of agreement from women. "Oh boy, that's huge" is a common response.

There is a book with a catchy title, *Tripping the Prom Queen*, which is all about this dysfunctional female behavior.[4] I'm not recommending you read it, because it's a sad book, filled with examples of "mean girls" of all ages, displaying their talons and clawing one another. But I am advocating that it's time we understand what this woman-to-woman sabotage is all about—and cut it out!

The most disturbing example I've heard of women being our own worst enemies was told to me by Wayne County Prosecutor Kym Worthy. A graduate of Notre Dame Law School, she is the daughter of one of the first African Americans to graduate from West Point. Worthy earned national respect for her unflinching prosecution of former Detroit Mayor Kwame Kilpatrick for a sex scandal and felony perjury charges that sent him to prison. When I asked her if she felt that women tend not to support other women, I was stunned by the response of this formidable leader. "I know that's true and I'll tell you why," Worthy immediately responded. "Rape cases are some of the hardest to prove. Whenever you've been a prosecutor for a period of time you learn to kick women off your jury because that's the only way you have a chance of getting a conviction. Women are very judgmental of other women. For a rape trial, I'll pick a jury of all men if I can get it."

I would never suggest that women should support other women without question. But the cultural myth that we are more likely to get in cat fights than be the wind beneath each others wings isn't all stereotype. Scratch a stereotype and you'll usually find the seeds from which it originally grew. Yes, American TV and movies perpetuate (and make plenty of money from) images of women as catty, competitive Queen Bees and Mean Girls who can't work together. It's up to women who are leadership material—*Interlopers, Insiders,* and *Innovators*—to start playing like a team. To do that, we need to face up to three major divides that separate us and dilute our collective power:

- The Tribe Divide,
- The Color Divide, and
- The Mother Divide.

Let's take a look at each.

The Tribe Divide

G23 is a first-of-its kind, all-women strategic consulting group within Omnicom Group, Inc., the largest advertising agency in the world. It was the brainchild of Janet Riccio, a senior vice president, who brought together an all-women team of communications executives from disciplines and divisions throughout the agency's giant empire. That was revolutionary enough and actually made many of the Omnicom men a little wary. But what I found most fascinating was Riccio's vision of women as members of cultural tribes who share characteristics across the globe. Under her leadership, G23 funded and published "The 8 Female Tribes that Power the Global Economy," an unprecedented study of women's economic lives in 16 countries.[5] For Omnicom's clients, the tribe theory is all about tapping women's exploding global buying power. For women interested in powering up to leadership, it's more evidence that our fastest way to the top is through our own tribe. "Imagine the possibilities for amplifying and activating female power," Riccio urged me, "once we as women begin to look at ourselves as a shared cultural group across the globe." Yet we remain a tribe divided.

Think about the Queen Bees, who are all too happy to be the only woman in the room. They have no interest in mentoring or giving another woman a hand up because they love being the exception in the room. They don't want to share the spotlight. Shirley Stancato, CEO of New Detroit and an African American *Interloper* who rose to senior leadership in the banking industry, told me, "I could write a book about all the obstacles that have been put in my way by women, much more than men." Stancato recalled an incident at a very large, lavish banking industry dinner. "I commented to another female banker, 'Wow, there aren't very many women here.' She looked at me and said, 'That's fine with me.' I think women are socialized not to like each other," Stancato says, "Not to hold each other up, not to help each other." There is no room on a winning team for Queen Bees.

And how about the women who are so fearful of killing the goose that lays their golden eggs that they won't risk ruffling any feathers? They've been so successful at mastering the men's game, they've secured their corner office or department chairmanship and aren't willing to risk their piece of the pie by even slightly rocking the boat to help other women rise. You rarely find them standing up as advocates within their companies to make sure that women (other than themselves) are paid equally with men or that female-focused nonprofits such as the Girl Scouts receive the same level of corporate support as the Boy Scouts. Nor will you see them leading the way to tackle practices and policies that make it more difficult for women to crack executive tracks.

I ran into this attitude recently in a state-wide political leader who had just thrown her hat in the ring for higher office. Her party affiliation was one I don't usually align with. But I told her, "We women need to stick together," to signal my openness to possibly publicly and financially supporting her. But instead of welcoming the tribal bond I offered, she looked away from me uncomfortably and said, "Oh, I take a different view of all that." In an instant, she told me a lot about herself. She had clearly signaled that she was unwilling to align herself too closely with women, even privately. To me, her reaction signaled that I could not count on her to stand up and fight for public policy that would help empower women.

Here's another example of the tribe divide. Have you noticed that male leaders think nothing of surrounding themselves with lieutenants of all white men? They think they are being inclusive if they have *a* woman on their team. And if they have more than one woman, plus a person of color, they feel they deserve a diversity award. Yet women leaders rarely openly promote or surround themselves with multiple other women for fear of being considered biased or anti-men.

Finally, young women often unwittingly abandon their cultural tribe by assuming that the professional playing fields were leveled years ago. Because they've faced few gender barriers during their academic years and at entry levels of most professions, many *Innovators* don't realize how many gender land mines are lurking ahead and how much they're going to need the support of their older sisters.

"You know what I think is the biggest problem hurting women right now?" the father of a 20-something daughter told me. "Women are so critical of one another and don't help each other in the workplace. Men compete with one another. But we also network all the time and know that we have to pass along opportunities and business to each other. I just don't see women doing that enough."

A lawyer friend recounted a disturbing example of exactly the behavior that father had observed. "One of the ways that men frequently bring new business into our law firm is by helping their friends land positions with companies that will need legal support," she told me. "Once the friend (often a fraternity brother or golfing buddy) lands the job, he returns the favor with legal business. But women don't reciprocate in the same way. When one of my clients asked if I could recommend anyone for an executive position they were about to fill, I opened the door for a woman I knew. I was glad to help her, but I was also anticipating my billings would increase. Not only did she not return the favor, one of the first things she did after getting the job was drop me as their corporate counsel and hire another firm! I was flabbergasted. She told me she appreciated how I had helped her, but she felt others would see our relationship as a conflict of interest."

That's the difference. When it comes to business, too few women have learned the fundamental rule: you scratch my back, I'll scratch yours. There's nothing unethical about this. Yet as long as men routinely do business with other men and women are reluctant to be seen as aligning too closely with other women, the status quo will prevail: males will have a major leg up in the rainmaking department and will continue their vice-like grip on the lion's share of power and influence.

The Color Divide

One evening during the 2008 presidential campaign, I was part of a political discussion with a group of about 40 women leaders. It was a professionally and racially diverse group, full of lawyers, doctors, judges, journalists, and business executives. We were discussing the Democratic nomination, which was still up for grabs with Senators Obama and Clinton running neck and neck. At one point, I suggested that a Clinton/Obama ticket would be unbeatable. I can still see the angry look that instantly flashed across the face of an African American woman with whom I have been friendly for years. She was sitting just a few feet away when she glared at me and snapped, "No, an Obama/Clinton ticket." I was stunned by the harshness of her unexpected psychic slap and merely responded, "Sure, or an Obama/Clinton ticket." She had made it abundantly clear to me that for her, race trumps gender.

I wallowed in my wound from that incident for awhile. It took me several months of thinking, reading, interviewing academic experts on racial divisions, as well as multiple courageous conversations, to begin to comprehend the other woman's feelings and my own naïveté. I've come to better understand that her split-second reaction sprang from decades of experience living in a world of assumed "white entitlement." I was oblivious to the depth and price of that experience, just as most men have little understanding of the psychic wounds many women suffer regularly from the patriarchal values that saturate our culture. I've always felt a sense of kinship with other minority groups, be they African Americans, Hispanics, Asians, or Native Americans, who, like me, were not born with the "white male table stakes" required to compete equally in most professional circles. But it rarely occurred to me that my "whiteness" stands as an invisible, sometimes impermeable, barrier between myself and women of color.

It was Barbara Whittaker, who rose to become one of the highest-ranked African American executives at GM, who offered me stunning insight into the depth of the color divide among American women today. Whittaker told me how dismayed she felt while listening to a report on trust levels among women during a Women of Color conference sponsored by *Working Mother* magazine. Using InstaPolling at Town Hall conferences throughout the country, researchers sampled the views of over 5,000 women; most were multiracial. Whittaker was among the attendees who squirmed uncomfortably in their seats as responses flashed instantly on the screen. Fifty-nine percent of the respondees reported that they trusted women of their own ethnic and racial groups. However, the responses changed dramatically when women were asked about trust levels with coworkers of different ethnic groups. Here's how the magazine reported the research results to its readers:

> *No single question sparked more gasps of surprise than when Town Hall attendees were asked whom they did not trust at work. Thanks to the Instant Polling technology, seconds after attendees voted on their handsets, the results flashed up on a 12-foot screen: 7% said they distrusted African-American women in their workplace, 7% distrusted Asian-American women and 8% distrusted Latinas—but a whopping 32% of those polled said they didn't trust Caucasian women. (The only group less trusted than white women was men, with 47% of respondents saying they did not trust this group.) An audible gasp filled the room, followed by an awkward silence. Many Caucasian women looked around the room in disbelief wondering: Could I be part of the problem?*[6]

When I began to probe why the circle of trust that women of color often share so rarely includes white women, three themes came up repeatedly:

- *White women are more closely aligned with white men than with women of color.* Anne Litwin, a PhD expert in diversity and organizational development at the American University, says that white women are often mistrusted by people of color because—among other things—"We're sleeping with the enemy." This is pretty tough stuff.

But Anglo women can't ignore how intimately entwined we are with the cultural group still holding most of the power. As long as our organizations and social mores continue to minimize opportunities for people of color, white women will remain in a limbo zone. Because of our gender, we'll never truly be one of the guys. Yet our "whiteness" excludes us from acceptance in the sisterhood shared by women of color.

- *Class differences impact how women view their opportunities in society and their relationships with other women.* "Women of color who are products of middle class upbringings have a sense of possibility and personal power that women who grew up in poverty or extremely modest circumstances don't have," says Dr. Glenda Price, president emeritus of Marygrove College. "Women who were poor when they were children fought very hard to be successful. That has a real impact on the whole question of trust. Do you look to other women for friendship and support or do you feel you have to go it alone and do it on your own? That's a critical differentiator."
- *White men are most likely to hire, promote, and mentor women of their own race.* We all know the mantra "Women have to work twice as hard as a man to be considered half as good." Most women of color believe their "work harder" quotient is a multiple of three or four, not just two. "It's rare for white women to even notice that women of color aren't represented. They don't see that we're not there and are rarely advocates for the value that we might bring to the table beyond gender," is how one highly-accomplished African American health care executive put it.

"White women generally don't understand the level of mistrust and the ways that we keep feeding it. One of the ways that we feed it is by being oblivious to it," said Dr. Litwin, who has spent three decades working to help women, in particular, bridge diversity differences. "We have enough to deal with, trying to be successful in patriarchal cultures, without having women to worry about. Yet we do worry about each other because we don't trust each other."

The deeper I delved into the complexities of the color divide, the more I had to ask myself "Have I been so focused on the barriers and inequities that came with my gender that I have ignored the advantages of being born white in America?" Black and white women in this country have a very long and painful history whose roots go back to slavery. In addition, we were—and still are—socialized very differently. "Generally speaking, we [white women] are conflict avoidant. Sugar and spice and everything nice is our socialization," says Dr. Litwin. "African American women are still socialized to be strong, independent, and direct. Many black women feel they can't trust us because we don't stand up for ourselves and we don't stand up for them."

Furthermore, we rarely talk about these differences across the color divide. "African-American women talk about these issues all the time," said Dr. Price. "My white women friends tell me they rarely or never talk about it." It's time we do. While I was working on this chapter, I had a phone conversation with a New York friend, an African American communications executive, on the usually unacknowledged dissonance that race differences create. Later, she sent me an email saying, "Anne, this question is Oprah-esque. It's huge. Women have so much work to do around this issue."

You may be a woman who has achieved deep friendships with females whose racial background is different than yours. If so, your life is certainly richer for it. Strong friendships and professional relationships that reach across color and cultural differences are all too rare. It takes years of conscious effort to achieve deep trust. How do you begin to foster those relationships? I put that question to three academics—an African-American, a Latina, and a Caucasian—whose life work and consulting practices revolve around understanding and overcoming the color divides. Here's a taste of their answers, which were rich and complex.

- "The norm in this society is that we don't discuss differences because it will only lead us to unproductive pathways. We have to acknowledge and then start talking about the positive and negative aspects of race. That requires skill and intercultural competence that I believe anyone who wants to be a leader of people in today's global world must develop." (Dr. Placida Gallegos, professor, School of Human and Organization Development, Fielding Graduate University)

- "From my study of the literature, my experience and looking at history, black women have done all that we can. We've done a lot of reaching over the years and every time we've been burned. I think it is time you (Anne) and your Caucasian sisters figure out what we need to do to heal this." (Dr. Ruth Yopp-Edwards, expert on the socialization and development of black women, principal, *Step Into Yourself, LLC*)
- "As part of the dominant group, white women must raise our consciousness about the impact that race differences and racism have on the daily lives of black women, in particular. But we shouldn't expect to get our education on these issues from women of color. We need to take responsibility for our own racial education." (Rianna Moore, PhD candidate researching close relationships between black and white women in the United States)

A great way to start peeling away the layers of this pungent onion is through an abundance of excellent books and movies. I've included my favorites in the bibliography and movie list in the appendix. Keep searching for women from other ethnic backgrounds who are interested in reaching across the color divide. You never know when the next Anne Mulcahy/Ursula Burns alliance will begin.

The Mother Divide

The once heated debate between working mothers and "stay-at-home" mothers has cooled a bit. But the guilt, resentment, and even pain associated with what I call the "mother divide" are still swirling just beneath the surface. All it takes is a scratch, perhaps a double-edged comment, to draw blood. I've followed this long-simmering drama for years. As a single parent, I have personally felt the inner conflict and guilt that working mothers often experience. But it was a story about two sisters that recently clarified for me how deeply the pain resonates on both sides of this emotional divide.

I know the sisters well. They are very close. Both are highly educated, with impressive resumes that reflect their early career success. Yet their lives took very different paths once they married and had children. One of the sisters chose to become a so-called "full-time" mother. She gave up her career to raise her sons and provide the family haven for her high-achieving husband. The family-focused sister became a gourmet cook and poured her creativity and drive into her children's schools and community leadership. She is the epitome of a Super Mom.

The other sister is a classic Career Woman. She was financially successful, independent, and didn't marry until her biological clock had just about stopped ticking. She and her husband adopted a child. When her son was very young, she went through a difficult divorce and, just a few years later, the death of her former husband. She raised her son alone, while balancing the demands of a challenging position with a global company. She managed with the help of live-in, European au pairs. Different choices, different paths. Years went by.

Then a comment during a family gathering triggered an unexpected explosion and exposed resentment, judgment, and pain that had been simmering between the sisters for years. On one side of the mother divide stood a woman who had invested decades in her passionate belief that "It *does* matter who changes every diaper, who washes every dish, who picks up your child after school every day." She insisted that her career sister admit that her son did not receive the same quality of mothering that a full-time parent gives her children. The inevitable reaction from the sister who had raised her son alone with no financial or emotional support from a father was outrage. "How dare you judge my mothering as less than yours," she told her sister. "I did a damn good job, with no one else paying the bills or helping with the parenting." The full-time mother held her ground arguing, "You can't have it both ways. I gave up my career to dedicate myself to my children. You can't have your career and still insist that you have been just as good a mother as I have and that your son didn't miss something valuable that I gave to mine."

And there you have it. The bitter truth that runs like a hot, toxic stream beneath this divide. The women who feel themselves sucked into this no-win debate feel guilt and loss on each side. Women who left careers they enjoyed and chose to stay home in order to give their children high levels of mothering often pay a high price, feeling the loss of self-esteem, facing dismissive ("Oh, so you're just a housewife?") comments, and struggling to re-enter the workforce after their nests have emptied. On the other side, mothers who continued to work, out of necessity or choice, carry the guilt imposed by society's judgment. There are many ways to mother, nurture, and guide children to adulthood. Our middle-class expectations of how much time *good* mothers should spend parenting and caretaking are many-time multiples of what we expect of good fathers.

Rather than judging one another, turning our backs and aligning only with those who have made similar choices to ours, we need to put down our weapons, find common ground, and give each other a break. That's what those two sisters did, who are now as close as ever and gave me permission to share their story.

Contrary to the extensive media coverage it has received in the last few decades, the mother divide is actually quite narrow. It's primarily between women who are affluent enough to have choices whether or not to work after they have children, as well as women who have chosen not to become mothers.

Most African American women say this long-time squabble has little relevance to them because few grew up in families that embraced the post-World War II middle-class model of a father as the sole breadwinner and a mother whose domain was the family. In African American culture, mothers, grandmothers, and aunties nearly always worked outside the home. During slavery in this country, females were forced into hard labor side-by-side with men, often while pregnant or carrying children on their backs. Today, 64 percent of African-American women work outside the home and 45 percent are household heads. Women of other ethnic and class groups, be they Jewish descendents of World War II survivors, Hispanic immigrants, or the working poor, were also much more likely to have family role models of mothers with jobs outside of the home than their Caucasian, middle-class sisters.

For decades, *Interlopers* and *Insiders* have staked out positions on various sides of the mother divide. Now *Innovators,* looking ahead, are searching for models of how to blend (forget balance!) their ambitions for fulfilling and financially rewarding careers with their dreams of a happy marriage and perfect children. "It's something my generation talks about a lot. I guess I was a little naïve coming out of business school about what reality is in the business world," said 31-year-old Chanel retail strategist Maloni Goss. "I was really surprised at the low numbers of women at the top. It just makes you think: 'What is it going to take to have a successful career and a successful family at the same time?'"

Banking CEO Sandy Pierce, the mother of three children, swears by a system she calls "slicing your personal pie." Every Sunday night, she allocates her time for the coming week, based on her *whole* life, not simply her work life. "Be very disciplined about allocating your time—for your husband, kids, work, community, friends, and for yourself," she advises. "People, particularly women, make a big mistake of trying to do more than there is actually time for. I see it constantly. You can only work and stay awake so many hours in a day. If you are trying to please everyone and stretching too thin, I guarantee you will have emotional meltdowns. Keep asking yourself, 'What's important to me.'"

More men are taking on bigger parenting responsibilities. But even younger men rarely give any thought to how they will balance parenting with their careers. And regardless of how an individual woman chooses to navigate the caretaking waters, there is no perfect solution. If you are a woman who finds yourself on either side of the mother divide, here are a few ways you can start helping to resolve our differences:

- *Look at the big picture.* Rather than judging and criticizing one another, let's recognize the divide for what it is: individuals coping in different ways with the cultural pressure surrounding gendered division of parenting and household labor that kicks into high gear when women become mothers.
- *Respect one another's choices.* Stay-at-home mothers have often told me of the subtle, psychic insults they experience from career women who treat them as less accomplished. Working mothers have their own stories of being criticized by other women for not doing their share as room mothers and chaperones or judged as "choosing their career" over their children.
- *Listen to men.* Have you ever heard a man criticize other fathers for "choosing their career over their children"? Probably not, although many often feel regret later in life for missing too much of their offsprings' childhoods. Ironically, the only way men feel the heat in this debate is when they take the role of flex parent on the home front, supporting their wives' higher-paying careers. They often experience the same psychic insults of "being just a Dad." However, that stigma is changing rapidly, driven in large part by our recent Great Recession. Six out of ten of the eight million jobs lost during the 2007-2009 economic meltdown were held by men, primarily in construction and manufacturing, which led to a major spike in the number of women who became their family's primary breadwinner.

America's work environments are notoriously anti-family. This critical arena is ripe for restructuring by visionary, courageous, and influential leaders, which is why a high representation of women in political and senior management positions is so essential. We are one of the few developed economies in the world that does not provide federally required paid leave for parents. Key reasons that Nordic countries score so high on the Global Gender Equity Index are their work policies related to parenting. In Sweden, for example, paternal leave—as well as maternal leave—is mandatory for fathers of new babies. This equalizes the economic liability between male and female employees for companies that absorb the costs of parental leave.[7] Inflexible work hours, lack of on-site child care, and leadership fast track expectations that are designed for individuals with little or no home responsibilities are other ways that our culture continues to restrain women with children from wielding greater influence in our society.

Michael S. Kimmel, a professor of sociology and highly regarded expert on gender roles in the United States, writes in *The Gendered Society*: "Without a concerted national policy to assist working women and men to balance work and family obligations, we continue to put such enormous strains on two sets of bonds—between husbands and wives and between parents and children, and virtually guarantee that the 'crisis' of the family will continue."[8]

Interlopers and *Insiders,* if you are in positions to influence policies and attitudes in your organizations, it's time to step forward. We need you to lead the necessary work culture changes that have been talked about for at least 20 years. *Innovators,* most of you have yet to hit the mothering crossroads. Before you get there, think very hard about two critical choices: the life partner you plan to start a family with and the work culture of a company where you hope to build a career. Unless you choose a partner who is truly interested in stepping up to fully sharing responsibilities at home, you will find yourself facing the same mother divide that *Interlopers* and *Insiders* have struggled with for decades. When jobs are scarce, choices are few. But when you do have a choice of where to work, make sure you critically assess a potential employer's willingness to consider flexible solutions to work/life priorities and demands. And look for examples of both women and men in senior leadership who model and support new ways of working. Sheryl Sandberg, the 41-year-old Chief Operating Officer of Facebook, who is the mother of two young children and married to Dave Goldberg, the CEO of SurveyMoneky, is known for mentoring young women. According to a *New York Times* profile, Sandberg encourages them "not to shy away from important roles simply because they were planning to start families."[9]

Just like the tribe and color divides, it's time to put the mother divide behind us. Let's give our *Team Women* sisters a break. Every good mother is a full-time mother. Every good mother is a working mother. The possibilities for being effective mothers who guide healthy human beings to productive adulthoods are as unlimited and unique as each individual woman who chooses to become a parent. Don't let patriarchal culture make you feel guilty for the way you choose to nurture your children and piece together your life puzzle.

If there are people in your life who can't seem to keep their opinions to themselves on the quality of your parenting, keep your distance. And as for that voice inside you, whether she is laying a guilt trip on you for not spending more time with your children or berating you for the career opportunities you sacrificed, turn her off. She's not the truth. She's a warped record from another time, playing the same tune over and over and over. And she rarely plays it for men. She only torments and divides women with it. Is it easy to juggle career and family? Absolutely not? Is it possible to do it well? Yes we can. Millions of us are finding creative, new ways to do it every day. Start with your mindset. I like the way Carol Bartz, president and CEO of Yahoo! and the mother of three children, responds to questions about how she manages to "do it all." "I have a belief that life isn't about balance, because balance is perfection . . . Rather, it's about catching the ball before it hits the floor."[10]

One Last Thought on Team Women

I learned about what it takes to leverage the power of a team from covering professional athletes as a sports reporter. First, you have to bring highly developed individual skills to the game. You need those to win a spot on the team and earn credibility with other players. The better you are at your position, the more your stock goes up. Then, you have to learn that the game isn't just about your stats. Wins and losses are measured by what the group accomplishes together. Players who are selfish, who won't pass the ball so another can score, and who don't celebrate their teammates' accomplishments or encourage them during slumps are resented for not being *team* players. The athletes who are respected and listened to as *leaders* are the ones who value being part of something bigger than themselves and lift their teammates to higher levels of performance.

The same goes for any woman who aspires to lead others. You must first be very clear about what team you're on. But don't get me wrong. My sister, Irene, never fails to remind me that women are not a monolithic group. She's right. We don't have to agree on everything in order to be teammates. And we need plenty of friends and allies on *Team Men,* as well. How many times have you watched professional athletes warmly greeting and even hugging friends on the opposite team before a big game? Once the game is on, however, the highest compliment athletes pay one another is to compete intensely, even against their best friends. Women, as a group, have much to learn about loyalty to a team and the power of teamwork. Rather than competing with one another for limited numbers of *women's positions*, it's time we set our sights on leadership and begin to work collectively to compete at our highest levels for *all* positions. Have you joined *Team Women?* If not, why not? If not now, when?

Mistake #3: We Play the Other Guy's Game

Learning to trust the strengths that come most naturally to us as women may be the biggest leadership leap we need to make because it requires shedding socialized behavior. American women spent the 20th Century earning full rights as citizens (although we still haven't achieved an Equal Rights Amendment to the Constitution) and proving ourselves in competitive, previously all-male arenas. That required playing and mastering the other guys' games. Considering where we started, we've made tremendous progress. But as long as women keep trying to emulate male leadership styles and squeeze our lives into work schedules and career paths designed for men (particularly those with you know who at home), we're always going to come up short. Breakthroughs in the number of women powering up into leadership positions will require significant numbers of *Interlopers, Insiders,* and

Innovators to do what every championship team does: play to our own strengths. Let's start by:

- *Recognizing the leadership skills developed through mothering.* Men have long regarded war and athletic competition as excellent training grounds for leadership. It's easy to understand why. For centuries, those were primary arenas for men to test themselves against one another. Women need to stake a claim to the skills we polish in an equally challenging training ground where our experience far surpasses that of men: the parenting and family COO hot seat. The skills required to protect, guide, and bring out the best in a maturing human being are directly transferable to leading adults. That is particularly true today as a whole new breed of ambitious, yet restless, Gen Y *Achievers* are forcing companies to rethink and retool how they manage, reward, and retain high potential talent.

But let's not hold our breath waiting for men to recognize that women who spent years running households and managing often conflicting teams of people (sibling rivalry anyone?) will bring fresh insight and skills to leadership. Once again, major American corporations (whose senior executives and board members are nearly all men) are turning to the military for fast track leadership talent. The March 2010 issue of *Fortune* magazine features a combat ready army officer on the cover and the headline: "Meet the New Face of Business Leadership . . . Why Companies Like Wal-Mart, Pepsico and GE Are Recruiting the Military's Elite."[11] I'd submit that Iraq and Afghanistan aren't the only places where life and death judgment calls come with the job description. It only takes a few moments for a young child to wander into a backyard with a swimming pool, for a teenager to become the emotional victim of bullies, for an elderly parent to take a serious fall, or for a family home to burn to the ground. If the stock of parenting and managing a household experience is going to go up (and they couldn't go much lower when it comes to equity on a resume), then women, in big numbers, are going to have to make the business case that mothering, running a busy household and caretaking elderly parents can all be leadership training grounds.

California Congresswoman Nancy Pelosi, often described as the "most powerful woman in United States history," frequently mentions her parenting experience and "mother-of-five" voice as significant reasons for her effectiveness on Capitol Hill. She made a point of surrounding herself with children, including some of her own eight grandchildren, when she took the oath in January 2007 as the first female Speaker of the House of Representatives in U.S. history. "I don't think anything prepares you for dealing with people and being successful at it better than raising a family," she told *More* magazine for an article in its October 2010 issue. "The discipline, the focus, the interpersonal skills, the diplomacy, the sense of organization, the joy. I regard my life in politics as an extension of my life as a mother." Lynn Sherr, author of the *More* profile, wrote that Pelosi is "unconcerned that playing the mommy card strikes some as a step backward." Sherr's article also included the following fascinating quote from a male described as a longtime Pelosi observer: "I really believe it helped that she raised five kids. Congress is a bunch of rowdy children. Kids, brats, egos—that's what she has to deal with now. Lots of men are just impatient."[12]

Now that women are 51 percent of the U.S. workforce, it's time to take a fresh look at the value of *all* of our work experience. *Interlopers, Insiders,* and *Innovators* who are in positions to assess and promote job candidates can be powerful catalysts for change. The next time you interview a woman who took a few years off to take the lead on the home front, don't simply write off those years as irrelevant. If you probe a little deeper, you might discover that the parental firing line can be more effective than business school book learning for fine-tuning management skills.

And if you are one of the unprecedented numbers of women who fear you may never be able to power back up to your previous professional levels once you've eased off on the fast track, I have two pieces of advice. First, immediately eliminate these crippling words from your vocabulary: "I'm just a housewife." Talk about eliminating yourself! There is no "just" about it. Women don't take or give other women enough credit for the unpaid work we do running the business of a well-functioning family. Second, don't buy into the other guy's game of dismissing your years in the "child-raising industry" as irrelevant. When you start dusting off your resume, reframe your parenting years in the language of human development. Here's my list of skills that I'd argue are as essential to well-run work environments as they are to highly-functioning families:

- Treating people as individuals and taking a personal interest in their lives
- Recognizing talent, encouraging natural strengths, working around weaknesses
- Holding individuals accountable for work assignments (homework and chores anyone?)
- Multitasking; managing multiple projects simultaneously
- Meeting deadlines
- Managing conflict
- Intergenerational teamwork (guess who raised Gen Ys)

New York Times columnist and top-selling author Tom Friedman writes in his classic book, *The World Is Flat,* that success in the New Economy will require talented people who can pair deep expertise with the ability to leverage their skills across multiple sectors. Parenting and caretaking is human development. Since when is that irrelevant to the workplace?

- *Quieting our over-developed guilt gene.* Several years ago, a photographer was sent to my office to take my picture for an article on home offices. As he was arranging the lights and setting up the shot, we started talking about our children and different ways that men and women parent. At one point, he stopped, looked at me, and said, "I just don't get all this guilt that women feel. I'm a great father, but I spend a lot less time with our kids than my wife does. Yet she feels guilty all the time."

Does that sound familiar? I'll bet you know exactly what he's talking about. No matter how much we do, women can't seem to quiet our guilt gland, which kicks into high gear when we become mothers. Women who balance paying jobs with motherhood know that feeling of never being totally at peace, regardless of where you are or what you are doing. If we are home with our children, we're stressing about the work responsibilities piling up at the office. If we are at work and on top of things with our jobs, we are feeling guilty about not spending more time with our children. It's common knowledge that women are natural multi-taskers. Thinking about and managing multiple things at the same time is practically second nature. Men, on the other hand, tend to prefer focusing on one thing at a time. When they are working, they are not worrying about everything that has to be done at home. When they are with their family, they are rarely feeling guilty about work. And when they are golfing on a Sunday morning, few are dragging around a lot of angst about not spending that time with their families. "Women make a terrible mistake by putting so much guilt on themselves about family stuff," says banking executive Sandy Pierce. "And men let them. I think that men at work and even many husbands like women to feel guilty because the weight of it slows them down. Men don't carry that weight."

One of the biggest barriers preventing women from competing equally with men for positions of leadership is "the second shift" that women of all social classes carry at home. Research studies repeatedly confirm that American women spend many more hours working in a day than men. The biggest difference is that a higher percentage of women's work is unpaid. The majority of married men in the United States still expect that their wives will do most of their domestic and child-rearing work for them. That frees men to focus more of their time on getting ahead at their jobs. It also relieves them from guilt about work related to the home and children. Even men who are more involved than average in parenting and household chores often describe what they do as "pitching in." In other words, they are "helping" their wives with *their* jobs, rather than taking responsibility for a fair share of the *family* work. Some might say, "'Well, that guilt that women carry is a positive thing—it is a strong sense of responsibility." But as long as we allow ourselves to accept all or primary responsibility for caring for children and running our homes, men will continue to be free to hold the positions that allow them to remain free to be the primary *deciders* for issues and policies that affect the entire human family.

There's an African proverb that says "If you wish to go quickly, go alone. If you wish to go far, go together." There is no question that American women have gone quickly. But we haven't gone nearly far enough. Going far in the 21st Century means pushing into our next frontier: the team sport of leadership. That will require us to go together. Why don't girls rule? Because too few of us have learned that *every woman for herself is a losing strategy*.

Why Girls Don't Rule

- ✓ We eliminate ourselves
- ✓ We fail to join *Team Women*
- ✓ The tribe divide
- ✓ The color divide
- ✓ The mother divide
- ✓ We play the other guy's game
- ✓ Every woman for herself is a losing strategy

CHAPTER 6

What Do Men Have to Do with It?

Men are more wary of the penalties for failure when competing with women, and women are more wary of the penalties for success when competing with men.

— KATHLEEN DEBOER, Executive Director, American Volleyball Coaches Association, *Insider*

Michelle Campbell was a seasoned basketball referee and former police officer who had officiated over 2,000 high school games. Dressed in the traditional striped shirt and black pants of a game official, she was just about to blow her whistle and start the competition at St. Mary's Academy in Topeka, Kansas, when she and her fellow ref got some stunning news. Campbell was told she couldn't officiate the boys' high school basketball game that night because the school didn't allow women to have authority over men. If you're assuming that incident happened a few decades ago, you're wrong. It occurred in 2008. ABC News thought the incident was unusual enough to report about on *Good Morning America.*[1] But the reality is that examples that reveal and reinforce our culture's discomfort with women having authority over men are all around us.

How many men do you see coaching girls and women's teams? Now ask yourself how many women you've seen coaching boys and men's teams. As college athletic budgets for women's sports have grown, thanks to Title IX, so have coaching salaries. As a result, increasing numbers of men are competing with women for those positions. "I don't think only men should coach men and only women should coach women. But I don't recall too many women who have the opportunity to coach men," says Carol Hutchins, an *Insider* who played Big 10 basketball at Michigan State and has built a softball dynasty during her 27 years as head coach at the University of Michigan. "If all things were equal, we could all coach each others sports. It's about opportunity. Right now, we don't have 'em." Hutchins cites an example from a few years ago when the University of Michigan was searching for a new head coach for its men's basketball team. "During an athletic department meeting, our boss told us, 'We're going to look at all of the best coaches in the country.' I said, 'So you're going to interview Pat Summitt [legendary coach of the University of Tennessee women's basketball team]?' All of the men in the room laughed," Hutchins recalled. "Summitt wouldn't even be *considered* for any of the top men's jobs, yet she's recognized as one of the best basketball coaches in the country. And it goes on and on."

The big picture evidence backs up Hutchins' personal experience. According to "Women in Intercollegiate Sport," a longitudinal national study (1977-2010) done by Linda Jean Carpenter and J.D.R. Vivian Acosta, both professors emerita of Brooklyn College, men now hold 75 percent of all intercollegiate coaching positions.[2] Consider these facts:

- There are now 9,087 women's intercollegiate sports teams in the United States, approximately 8.64 per school.
- 42.6% of the women's teams are coached by a female head coach.
- 57.4% of the women's teams are coached by a male head coach.
- Less than 3% of men's teams are coached by a female head coach.

"Men are hired to coach women all the time," Hutchins points out. "They can coach us but we can't coach them? Why?"

There is still plenty of deeply ingrained sexism in every culture, including here in the United States. What do men have to do with women moving into positions of leadership and authority? A lot. Men's attitudes about women's capabilities and appropriate roles—as well as their willingness to include, mentor, promote, align with and become sponsors and advocates for women's advancement to positions of authority—make all the difference in the world for female leaders.

Equally important is how effectively we interact with men. For women in positions of power, that requires the ability to skillfully change "gender gears," as needed. Be they our fathers, brothers, lovers, employers, co-workers, friends, partners, or rivals, men are such an important part of any discussion about women and leadership that they merit their own chapter.

Every woman interviewed for this book told me stories about the ways that the men in their lives helped them along their path to leadership. My favorites are about fathers who encouraged dreams, often becoming, as my Dad did, their daughters' most important mentors. They are also about bosses who opened doors of opportunity; male friends and allies who had our backs; brothers who helped toughen us up; and, of course, husbands who supported their wives' ambitions with actions as well as words. All play key roles in whether or not the leadership equation works for women. The importance of developing strong professional alliances with men, as well as valuing their insight, friendship, feedback, and even competitive tests of our leadership readiness cannot be overstated. And don't underestimate the contributions of men who, for one reason or another, choose to throw obstacles in our way. Every woman who has achieved positions of power and authority has been tested along the way by men who made the mistake of trying to stand in her way. It's always a mistake, because, inadvertently, those men only help to strengthen the resolve of *Achievers* who have the drive, courage, and capability to ignore the naysayers and pick up the leadership mantel.

No Place in a Newsroom for a Woman

When I was a senior at the University of Michigan in 1972, I dared to dream that I could follow in my father's footsteps and become a radio and TV broadcaster, even though I had never heard a female voice reporting the news. But there was reason to hope. Barbara Walters was appearing regularly on NBC's *Today Show*; WWJ-TV in Detroit had hired its first newswoman, Betty Carrier; and I had seen occasional TV news reports by Nancy Dickerson, the first woman to break into a high-profile position in the Washington, D.C. national press corps. I didn't know it at the time, but Susan Stamberg, who rose to become the highly regarded cohost of *All Things Considered,* had just gotten her foot in the door at National Public Radio (NPR).

I started doing newscasts at WCBN, the University of Michigan's student radio station, and was looking forward to a summer graduate program in TV News at Northwestern University's Medill School of Journalism. A few months before graduation, I managed to get an internship at WUOM, our university's NPR station. During my first few days on the job, I read and recorded books on tape for the blind, helped select music for programs, and learned what a traffic department was in a radio station. But my real interest was in the news department. So I was thrilled when the news director saw me in the hall and signaled for me to come over and talk to him. He met me at the newsroom door, pointed to the floor, and said, "Do you see that line? Don't you cross it. Don't come in here to answer the phone, to read the newswire, or even to drop something on my desk. There is no place in a newsroom for a woman."

I was angry and astonished that I would be treated that way at my own university. But as a student intern in the early 1970s, there was nothing I could do about it except prove him wrong. He was the first, but he wasn't the only man who told me I was pursuing the wrong career. Once I graduated, the news director at WWJ Radio in Detroit wasn't quite as harsh, but his message was the same when he said, "No one will ever listen to a woman on the radio. Your voices are too high." For every man who told me "No, you can't," there were many others who helped me believe "Yes I can" and gave me chances to prove it.

Interlopers of my generation nearly always credit men for giving them their "first professional breaks." There simply weren't women in positions to hire or promote us early in our careers. The man who unlocked broadcasting's doors for me was George Blaha, the news director back then at WJIM Radio in Lansing, Michigan. If you are a sports fan, you may recognize his name as the long-time play-by-play voice of the NBA Detroit Pistons and Michigan State football. I still remember sitting across from George after he offered me my first *real* broadcasting job and began explaining my responsibilities. "You'll be a radio street reporter. That means you'll be covering City Council, the School Board, the state Capitol and even getting up in the middle of the night to cover fires or police news," he told me. A little voice inside me was screaming, "There is no way you can do this. Just get up right now and walk out." But my father's words, "Never eliminate yourself," drowned out my fears. I took the job. Thanks to George Blaha and other men who gave me key opportunities, particularly Jack Hogan who hired me for my first TV job and Mike Von Ende who gave me the chance to cover sports, I went on to work in journalism for nearly 15 years in Grand Rapids, Detroit, Los Angeles, and Atlanta.

There were many other men who helped me in a multitude of ways. *Detroit News* sports columnist Jerry Green came up behind me as I stood outside the locker room doors of the Detroit Express soccer team searching desperately for the courage to walk in. He gave me a push and said, "Get going." The momentum of his nudge carried me through the doors. Baseball broadcasting legend Ernie Harwell was one of the first to make me feel welcome covering the Tigers. And when I was nominated for the Michigan Journalism Hall of Fame in 2007, it was selection committee member Jim Bleicher, the assistant news director at Channel 2 during my sports reporting years, who convinced his peers that I had helped to change the industry and open doors for other journalists. On the night I was inducted, it was Jim, now the News Director at WJRT-TV in Flint, who introduced me. As I listened to his words, I couldn't help but smile as I remembered the many newsroom battles "Bleicher" and I had fought.

The people who try to block your path to leadership will fade away—provided you stay the course and get away from them as fast as you can. I've forgotten the name of the WUOM news director who refused to make room in his world for the other half of the human race. You never forget, however, the ones who opened a door, pushed you to do more, supported you at critical moments, or believed in you—even before you fully believed in yourself.

Male Allies: Can't Lead without 'Em

Because men (white males, in particular) are born into the cultural tribe that has held power throughout all of recorded western history, they intuitively understand the rules of the game in professional arenas. Why wouldn't they? After all, the rules were written by men—and for men. Women who aspire to lead in male-dominated environments are like foreign nationals living and working in another culture. We are the ones who have had to adapt, to master their "language," and to learn the nuances of male culture.

As we enter the second decade of the 21st Century, it's not glass ceilings that women leaders must push their way through; it's "a thick layer of men," quipped Laura Liswood, co-founder and Secretary General of the Council of Women World Leaders. So far, men have had little need to adapt to women's work styles. But now that women are 50 percent of the U.S. workforce, and three women are graduating from college for every two men who earn degrees, the day is just around the corner when men must become gender bilingual, as well. In the meantime, male allies and champions are invaluable.

Christine Brennan, *USA Today* sports columnist, ABC/ESPN commentator, and one of the most respected sports journalists in the country, had so many male allies as a pioneering female sports reporter that she had to write a book to thank all of them. The *Best Seat in the House* is an inside-the-locker-room look at Brennan's experiences covering every major sporting event and famous athlete who stepped onto a court, field, track, or rink for the last three decades. Just imagine how many defining moments she has had! One of my favorites occurred August 23, 1983—the night Brennan went into her first men's locker room. She was working as a summer intern at the *Miami Herald* in between her undergraduate and master's years at Northwestern University. The Miami Dolphins were playing the Minnesota Vikings in a pre-season game, and the paper assigned their female sports intern to write a sidebar on the visiting team. Here's how Brennan tells the story of that night and what the unexpected male ally did who stepped up just when she needed him.

> *It was worse than I thought. Not the naked men. Actually, there were very few naked bodies. The players were in various stages of undress, many still wearing their football pants.*
>
> *No, I could never have anticipated the problem I was about to confront. It was a preseason game, so there were many extra players on the roster, but no names above the lockers. And even though I was carrying a flip card, the sheet given out in the press box containing all the players' names and numbers, most of the players had taken off their jerseys, so I couldn't tell who anyone was.*
>
> *To further complicate matters, I also couldn't look around. If I did that, the players could accuse me of being in the locker room for the wrong reason. And that was one thing I had to avoid.*
>
> *As it was, as soon as I walked into the steamy, overcrowded room, I heard whoops and hollers from distant corners, from players I couldn't see.*

"We don't go in the women's bathroom!" someone yelled. "What are you doing in here?"

"Here for some cheap thrills?" screamed another.

I took a few tentative steps into the room, then stopped, not knowing what to do. I was stuck. It seemed like a lifetime standing there, but really was only twenty to thirty seconds when, out of the noise and confusion, a player in uniform walked up to me. It was Tom Hannon, the Vikings' fourth-year safety out of Michigan State.

"Who do you need?"

I smiled.

"Tommy Kramer," I said.

Hannon pointed. "He's right there, putting on his necktie." I looked, and immediately recognized Kramer, the quarterback.

"Mark Mullaney," I said.

Hannon pointed out the defensive lineman.

I mentioned another lineman; Hannon helped identify him as well.

"That's all you need?" he asked.

"And, well, you."

"You bet."[4]

Brennan told me she never ran into Hannon again but hasn't given up looking for him. She'd like to thank him and let him know what a difference he made for a sports intern in a steamy locker room a few decades ago. She also wanted to make it clear that the once highly controversial issue of whether women journalists should be allowed in locker rooms has long been settled. "Talking about women going into locker rooms is like talking about whether women should vote," Brennan told me. "It's resolved and was resolved generations ago."

However, just a few months after my interview with Brennan, the long dormant issue flared up. A voluptuous TV Azteca female sports reporter covering the 2010 pre-season training camp for the New York Jets football team was the target of boorish, juvenile behavior—some would say sexual harassment—by a number of the players. The incident triggered a national media debate on whether certain women, depending on how they are dressed, are "asking for" inappropriate attention. It resulted in a National Football League training program for all 32 NFL teams on proper workplace conduct for players and coaches. It was also a red flag reminder of one of my mantras: women working in testosterone-rich environments must still walk a very careful line—regarding how they dress and conduct themselves—to be respected for their competence, let alone be considered leadership material.

Besides having your back at critical moments, male allies are an essential source of frank feedback on how to make your mark and hold your own with men. They've been invaluable for helping to sharpen my squishy edges. Two of my earliest male allies were my cameramen. TV street reporters often spend a lot of time with their photographers, driving to breaking news events and working together under pressure to meet deadlines.

I was a rookie reporter with barely a year of radio news experience under my belt when Rick Kamel and I were paired up at TV13, the ABC affiliate in Grand Rapids, Michigan. Rick was a couple of years younger than I and a high school graduate who used to joke that he couldn't read his diploma. But he was already a seasoned TV newsman, street-wise, smart, and never one to kowtow to power. He toughened me up, urged me to be more aggressive, bolder, and to ask tougher questions. Together, we took on slum landlords, discriminatory practices by local businesses and harassment of vulnerable senior citizens by teenagers. We covered accidents, murders, major fires, political elections, and the rise of our local congressman, Gerald R. Ford, to president of the United States. Rick knew just when and how to throw gasoline on my competitive streak and wasn't reluctant to tell me when my work stunk. Now the president and CEO of RK Public Relations, Rick is still a valued sounding board.

Chuck Davidson, an outstanding TV news photographer for WJBK-TV in Detroit and WBBM-TV in Chicago, taught me how to cover sports for TV. We worked together at Channel 2, the CBS affiliate in Detroit, where all the reporters jockeyed to get Chuck assigned to their stories. But his first love was shooting sports. Lucky me. In the early 1980s, TV stations had to shoot their own game footage. If your cameraman missed a great catch or was out of focus on the big play of the game, your story was in trouble. Chuck always had a perfect shot of every critical moment in any event we ever worked together. But most importantly, Chuck knew his sports. On the way to games, we'd talk about players, the opposing team, the strengths and weaknesses of both. And if he thought I had asked a stupid question, missed asking an important one, or saw a story differently than he saw it, he'd tell me, "Doyle, you're wrong on this one. Here's why." We didn't always agree. And the longer I covered sports, the more we'd argue. But he made me a better reporter.

Chuck and I went into plenty of locker rooms together, although he didn't particularly relish those moments. I'm sure he took ribbing and maybe even criticism from other men who resented my presence—even in the press boxes. But he understood that I couldn't compete with my male peers if I didn't have the same access to players, so he supported me doing my job. And there's nothing better than having a strong male ally at your side when you're encroaching on men's turf. Unlike newspaper reporters who usually work alone, TV reporters nearly always have a photographer with them. I was very lucky to have Chuck and Rick, straight shooters who held themselves and others to high standards, at my side as I learned the ropes and pushed the edges of women's possibilities. They both brought out the best in me and raised my game.

If you don't already have trusted male allies you can count on to tell you the truth, to engage with you in healthy debate, and to back you up when you need support, make it a priority to develop them. Or if it's been awhile since you reflected on the ways that special men have impacted your personal and professional growth, think about your list. Have you told them what a difference they made and thanked them? And remember, even the ones who throw up obstacles and challenges are doing you a favor. We don't usually figure that out until long after we've passed their tests.

Male Mentors Make All the Difference

A mentor, in my book, is someone whose impact on a leader's development is even more significant than that of allies. They are more seasoned, wiser, take personal interest in your development and offer invaluable counsel and guidance at critical moments. I had been covering Detroit's sports scene for over a year when I experienced one of the toughest moments of my career. It began as a public humiliation, but ended with a standing ovation—thanks to my father, who was the perfect mentor for an interloping female sportscaster in 1980.

Our TV-2, *Five Star Sports* team (four men: Ray Lane, Charlie Neal, Jim Price, and Bob Hillman, and me) was invited to speak at the prestigious and male-members-only (at the time) Detroit Athletic Club. Our hosts were the Beavers, the jocks of the DAC. They were successful businessmen, many former athletes, who began their luncheon meetings with a rousing game of a variation of water polo, which they called "basketbrawl." Lunch was served at white linen-covered tables arranged around the pool, with many Beavers clad only in their speedos and yellow, terry cloth bathrobes. It was a macho-soaked, locker room environment. When the program began, I discovered to my dismay that the Beavers were going to have me for dessert.

My first clue of the danger I was in came right after my colleague Charlie Neal answered a question about the Pistons' upcoming season. Someone yelled, "What do you think about that, Anne?" Before I could answer, the entire roomful of over 100 businessmen enjoyed a hearty laugh. The next question was about University of Michigan football. My father had been broadcasting Wolverine football games for years. I'm a U of M graduate. I'd covered every Michigan game that season, as well as quite a few of Coach Bo Schembechler's legendary practices. I answered the question with ease. But when I finished, a Beaver called out, "Oh, your father told you all that!" More laughter. Things went downhill from there, with even a few Beavers suggesting (good naturedly, of course) that we "throw her in the pool."

Not one of my sports department "teammates" came to my defense nor said one word to suggest that the Beavers' open mockery of their TV-2 colleague was rude, let alone downright hostile. Perhaps they didn't want to appear "soft" in front of all the other guys. The humiliation of that afternoon has long since faded. What I will never forget is my father's advice and the lesson he taught me about earning your stripes with men.

The following year, the Beavers invited us back. My station General Manager, Bob McBride, suggested that maybe I shouldn't go. I knew I had to. Staying away would be conceding defeat. That was when my Dad came up with a plan, telling me, "Annie, I've got an idea. It's going to take a lot of guts, but if you'll go through with it, I guarantee you'll win those Beavers over." His plan was outrageous. I thought he was kidding. But I also knew my father, who had been a professional athlete himself, understood the male, jock mentality much better than I. Without a better idea, I decided to trust him and hoped he was right.

What was Vince Doyle's plan for my second date with the jocks of the Detroit Athletic Club? Right after the Beavers finished their water polo game and the program was about to begin, two of my TV-2 colleagues, Ray Lane and Charlie Neal, suddenly grabbed me and threw me into the pool—just as I'd asked them, the night before, to do. A roomful of stunned Beavers, most still in their terry cloth robes, literally jumped out of their chairs. One dove into the pool to "rescue" me, cheered on by his fellow Beavers. Dripping wet, I climbed out but was pushed into the pool two more times—this time by various Beavers—before I escaped to the nearest locker room. That was where my Dad's plan ended. My options at that point were to catch a cab back to the TV station or strip off most of my dripping clothes and return to lunch. That was exactly what I did. Wet hair, mascara smudges and all. When I walked back in, dressed in one of the Beavers' own yellow robes (I kept on my underwear) and a grin, I was greeted with a standing ovation. This time, when the sports questions began, the Beavers were ready to listen.

How did a dunk in the pool win over a roomful of mocking, skeptical men? My father intuitively understood that I was being tested as an outsider who had dared to venture into men's territory. The brilliance of his plan was that he figured out a way for me to initiate myself into the Beavers' circle of trust. He knew that the club always threw their newly elected presidents into the pool, clothes and all. Once I'd been dunked, I was no longer an outsider. Women rarely do this kind of thing to one another, but men seem to love it. How many times have you watched football players eagerly dump a huge container of Gatorade over their coach's head near the end of a big victory? Never in a million years would I have guessed that a sense of humor and the willingness to look ridiculous in front of one hundred affluent businessmen would earn me more respect than all the sports knowledge in the world. I'm not suggesting that I didn't need to know my stuff. That was expected. But it took a wise male mentor to guide me safely through the Beavers' gender boot camp.

During my five years on the front lines of women in sports broadcasting, there were hundreds of other tests and skirmishes, some big, some very small. And I certainly didn't win them all, but my father always had my back. I didn't realize how closely he watched over me until one spring morning when my Dad arrived at my house early, asking if I had time for a cup of coffee. He sat down in my kitchen, placed the morning paper face down on the table, and took both of my hands in his. I looked at him and saw there were tears in his eyes as he began telling me about a story in the morning paper. *Detroit News* columnist Jay Mariotti was reporting that I was the "Worst Sports Reporter in Detroit," based on an informal readers' poll that he had conducted. According to Mariotti, I'd also earned second place in the categories "Least Smart" and "Least Prepared." Channel 4's Al Ackerman, the dean and highest paid TV sportscaster in Detroit at that time, beat me out for first place in both of those categories. I'm sure Al laughed about the column over his morning coffee. But to a lone woman working to earn her stripes in a high-profile and often hostile environment,

Marriotti's column cut deep. At the end of our morning visit, my father looked me in the eye and said, "Don't let this silly poll beat you, Annie. You know it's not true. Walk into the newsroom today and hold your head high. Let this be your motivation to continue to prove them wrong."

Women are still so rare at the top that they are often, essentially, on their own. Never "one of the guys." No female peers around to provide powerful allies and strategic confidants when the going gets rough, which it always does. That's why strong, trusted male allies, who can provide both professional and personal support, are so essential. How do you find them and cultivate those relationships? I'd suggest starting with men whom you've discovered have strong wives, sisters, or mothers—and great relationships with them. When you're slogging your way through that "thick layer of men," make sure you have at least one trusted and wise male mentor—who has your best interests at heart.

Credibility Is Transferable

Regardless of where you choose to make your mark, every woman leader must earn male credibility and support. The more powerful and dominant men are in an organization the more essential it is for high-performing females to have strong male allies and supporters. It's even better if some become mentors. And better yet, if you are lucky enough to have a powerful *sponsor* who will open doors and become your advocate for developmental and leadership opportunities. Allies, mentors and sponsors are all important—but don't confuse the three. They are very different. But each is critical, particularly for women on a path to leadership.

I learned these lessons during my thirteen years working at Ford Motor Company. At the time, it was one of the largest and most respected companies in the world. Even today, the auto industry is a predominantly male environment where women in senior management are few and far between. My years on the trailblazing edges of women's push into TV news and sports broadcasting were excellent preparation for Ford. As was true for so many women of my generation, I was used to being the lone woman in the room and having to hold my own and elbow my way through thick layers of men. That's not unusual for women leaders, even today, at the highest levels of most organizations.

At Ford, I worked with CEOs, the UAW, mega-dealers, and members of Congress. I held leadership positions in sales and marketing, parts and service, global product development, governmental affairs, and corporate staff. My work took me all over the world from executive suites and company jets to factory floors and congressional hearings. It was a privilege to work for one of the largest and most admired companies in the world, during good times and bad. I could never have risen to Ford Director of North America Communications without many male allies and mentors over the years, particularly David Scott, Jim O'Connor, Al Chambers, Red Poling, Pete Pestillo, Jerry Sloan and Martin Ingles.

One of the most important lessons I learned about earning professional respect with men and gaining their support is this: credibility is transferable. In the world of men, two fields, in particular—the military and sports—are highly valued as leadership training grounds. Many a man has leveraged his military experience or sports career to launch his leadership ambitions in business, politics, and even the presidency.

People have often asked me "How could you go from TV sports broadcasting to leadership positions in the auto industry?" It may seem like a big leap at first, but it wasn't. As David Scott, the vice president of global public affairs who hired me told me, "Anne, we have thousands of people who know cars; we need someone who thinks like a journalist and knows TV news." I had those credentials in spades. In addition, because I had been tested very publicly by the sports world in Detroit, I was holding an unexpected ace on the day I walked in the door at Ford. My first lesson in how my sports background would prove invaluable came when I was still learning my way around Ford World Headquarters. One morning, I was informed that one of the company's senior executives wanted to see me. I'd only been at Ford a few weeks and knew nothing about him except his name and title. I was taken up the private executive elevator to the top floor of Ford's World Headquarters in Dearborn and shown into a large office with dark, mahogany furniture and a spectacular view.

"Welcome to Ford, Anne," he said, extending his hand. "Nice to meet you, Pete," I said as we sat down and he offered me a cup of coffee. As a journalist, I learned very early not to put myself in the immediate "down position" by calling people Mr. or Mrs. If someone uses my first name, I use theirs. Unless, of course, I'm talking to a high elected official, such as a governor, member of Congress, or the president. The first thing this senior executive at one of the biggest companies in the world asked me was a question about the Detroit Tigers. It turned out he was a huge sports fan. Months later, he told me he read the sports section each morning *before* reading the *Wall Street Journal*. We chatted for nearly 30 minutes, starting with baseball and working our way through the Detroit Lions, University of Michigan and Michigan State football, Pistons basketball, and Red Wings hockey. When his executive assistant opened the door and told him, "Sir, your next appointment is here," I asked him. "Is there anything you wanted to know about me or something you need me to do?" "No, that's all," he replied as he rose to shake my hand. "I just wanted to know what you knew about sports."

Apparently, I passed his test and made the team. He became one of my earliest supporters at Ford and instrumental in several key opportunities, including a major promotion. My knowledge of sports and the fact that I had been previously "vetted" by legends such as Magic Johnson, Bo Schembechler, Sparky Anderson, Reggie Jackson, Ernie Harwell and even Muhammed Ali, not to mention by sports fans and my media peers, gave me "competency credibility" that was transferable to a completely different industry. The experience and knowledge I gained by covering sports made a difference with hundreds of men I have worked with over the years. Throughout my years at Ford, I often worked closely with the executive who called me up to his office. He nearly always brought up something about sports. One day, after I'd been with Ford for nearly a decade, he said to me, "Anne, you don't know nearly as much about sports as you used to." I laughed and said to him, "That's true, but I know a heck of a lot more about the auto industry."

Men are often very willing to mentor and guide women—as long as they remain in the authority position. I am grateful to the many fantastic men I have worked with over the years—particularly those I have already mentioned—who gave me important opportunities to develop my leadership skills. However, I never had a true *sponsor* in any industry I've worked in. One of the major differentiators of women who have cracked through to executive or high-level leadership positions is having not only mentors but powerful sponsors or champions. In large organizations, high-potential men have always been groomed and positioned for bigger responsibilities, just as sports teams are constantly scouting and cultivating young talent for their pipeline. Women must be strategically developed for leadership roles in the same way. But talent, drive, ambition, passion, skill and executive coaches aren't enough for *Achievers* to break through. You need powerful advocates willing and able to use some of their "political chits" and influence on your behalf.

As I was writing this chapter, I had a very frank and enlightening conversation about the distinction between allies, mentors and sponsors with a male executive with whom I worked very closely for several years. I discovered that our definitions of what it means for a male leader to be "pro women" were very different. For him, and I believe for many men in authority positions, being "pro women" means appreciating, respecting, and sometimes even mentoring high-potential subordinates and colleagues. But my definition goes further. When it comes to fully developing humanity's leadership talent, men who are "pro women" are those who actively champion break-through opportunities for high-achieving females as ardently as they do for high-potential males. And the most evolved men are those who understand why the continued exclusion of anyone of the female gender from prestigious good-old-boy business networks – Augusta National Golf Club comes to mind – is not unrelated to why more than 10 percent of Fortune 500 companies still have not a single woman serving on their boards.

Xerox CEO Ursula Burns speaks openly about the senior executives who recognized her leadership potential and began to groom her early in her career.[6] She traveled with several high-powered male leaders, sat in on their important meetings, and was coached by them on her leadership strengths and missteps. Such relationships are not easy for women to find. Start with men with whom you've already earned some stripes. Then ask for their help. Be very clear about your goals, and when the time comes, *ask* them to step forward and speak up on your behalf.

Competing with Men

A woman who grows up with brothers—the more the better—has a jump start on another essential skill for women leaders: the ability to be very comfortable with men as platonic peers. If you've had the "privilege" of being tested, poked, harassed, teased, insulted, embarrassed, and challenged by brothers from a young age, chances are pretty good you've developed a comfortable template for working and competing with men.

I have my three brothers, Dan, Tom, and Vince, to thank for years of schooling in male thinking and behavior. I learned early that complaining about things not being "fair" and playing the guilt card is useless. Brothers see no need to help with your chores just because you helped with theirs. They don't think twice about grabbing the last brownie even though they've out-eaten you five to one. And they love nothing better than winning—at anything and at any cost. Have you ever noticed how men seem to bet on everything—football games, rounds of golf, the March Madness office pool? My son and his friends don't even play miniature golf without betting. It's not about the money. It's the fun of trying to beat one another. They also expect you to pay off on your bets, whether it's one dollar or fifty. Perhaps that's the hunter in them. I can't remember the last time a woman friend challenged me to a bet.

The ability to compete head-to-head with men for positions of influence and power is essential for women leaders. As women, we've been programmed to become masters at building relationships and getting along. Perhaps that was one of our foremothers' earliest survival skills. Men, however, approach life as one big competition. It's every man (or woman if she chooses) for him or her self. "We're all in this together," one of women's favorite mindsets, even when leading, doesn't come naturally to males. Men seem to be most comfortable in hierarchies, which is why the military, business and most professional environments are organized that way. Women, on the other hand, naturally tend to relate with others in what has been described as interconnnecting, web-like relationships. It all works great when men interact with men and women with other women. The complications kick in when we begin competing with the other group—and don't understand we each have very different rules.

One of the best books I've ever read on this topic was written by *Insider* Kathleen DeBoer, the executive director of the American Volleyball Coaches Association and a former All-American athlete and coach. In *Gender and Competition: How Men and Women Approach Work and Play Differently*, DeBoer delves into the psychological differences in male and female behavior in competitive environments, which she believes make leadership development (for women) a real challenge.

> *"When entering hierarchical work environments, realize that struggle is part of the rite of passage," DeBoer wrote. "Plunge ahead, observe the behavior of your superiors and those of your own rank, fake it until you figure it out, make decisions, take risks. Do not expect feedback, instructions, encouragement, or help. To be accepted and rewarded, you must succeed, initially, on your own."*[7]

I couldn't have said it better. As long as women are the minority in professional environments dominated by men, it's up to us to adjust our game to theirs.

There's a wonderful line in the movie *The Young Victoria* that is great advice for all aspiring leaders. It is whispered to the future queen of England by her first cousin, Prince Albert, who would later become her husband and trusted adviser. The two are playing chess, but their conversation is all about the multiple individuals and political forces trying to control the young and inexperienced woman. "Then you had better master the rules of the game," he advised, as he moved one of his chess pieces in position for checkmate, "till you can play it better than they can." Queen Victoria did exactly that. In an era when women in power were rare indeed, she ascended to the throne at age 18 and reigned over the massive British empire for 64 years (1837-1901), longer than any other monarch in Great Britain's history.

The insight that women with leadership aspirations need to understand is this: competing with males for positions of power and authority requires a skill set that is intuitive to most men, but women must learn, almost like a second language. "Whether we like it or not, our current reality, even today, is you have to be able to play ball with the guys," advises Susan Peters, GE's vice president for executive development. "I don't believe the future enables women to just be pure women [in the public world]. Women have to be able to cross the cultural [gender] divide. But I also believe it's becoming true both ways. In other words, the best male leaders are also capable of interfacing with and understanding women in a broader way."

What about male rivals? Sooner or later, every ambitious woman finds herself going up against men who want the same spot she does. If you've never competed one-on-one with a man before, it can be unnerving. There are rivals who bring out the best in us and those who bring out our worst side. I've competed with and learned from both.

When I was hired as a TV news reporter for Channel 13, the ABC affiliate in Grand Rapids, Michigan, the news director, Jack Hogan, told me "You have some very big boots to fill." He was talking about Martha

Teichner, who had just left for a bigger job with the CBS affiliate in Miami. Teichner, who went on to become a CBS news correspondent covering every hot spot in the world while CNN's Christiane Amanpour was still in grade school, not only had big boots (which she kept handy under her desk), she had set a high bar in the TV13 newsroom. Jim Riekse, the veteran male reporter on the staff, had competed fiercely with Teichner for years to see who would come up with the "lead story" for each night's newscast. Although I never met her, I wasn't about to let down the station's first female reporter by ceding the "top dog" position to her rival without a fight. I picked up right where Martha Teichner left off. If you can take the heat, there's nothing better than a great competitor to bring out your best.

There was only one man that I competed with over several decades in journalism, the auto industry, and politics who crossed the line from rival to what I would call a professional "enemy." He brought out the worst in me. Our paths intersected late in my career at Ford Motor Company. Ironically, he was someone that I had known and had a good working relationship with before he joined Ford. The dynamics between us changed the second he walked in the door. Initially, I thought it was just peer friction, learning to work with a new person as he made the adjustment, which I had done years before, from journalist, characteristically an independent operator, to an upper management position in a complex, gigantic organization. I tapped all of the excellent training I'd been given at Ford to try to find a way to work with him. I had learned long before that you don't have to like someone to work effectively together. But try as I might our relationship only grew worse. He was your classic bully who used information as power and worked behind the scenes to undermine people who were in his way. He demanded that those who worked for him do the same. It was demoralizing and somewhat of a shock for me to realize that I had to guard my back from one of my co-workers. Eventually, our rivalry broke out into open hostility that provided entertainment for those who witnessed our clashes, but accomplished little for the company or either of us.

What did I learn from going head to head with such a rival? I'll be the first to admit, I didn't handle the test very skillfully. I let him get under my skin and found myself acting defensively and leading from weakness rather than my strengths. Do not allow a negative rival to suck you into his or her game! I was also astonished at how much damage an unethical, fiercely aggressive individual driven primarily by his own agenda can do in a short time. What did my enemy's tactics gain him? They worked, but only for a while. He was promoted several times before he was eventually given the "opportunity" to leave the company.

Most people don't like confrontation and back down from bullies. I'm convinced that you have to take them on—strategically. Pick your battles carefully, but once they begin, don't blink. And make sure you've lined up support before you make your move. Find allies who have the stomach for hardball politics. Battles with hostile rivals can get ugly.

The political culture within Ford, which deteriorated in the late 1990s, beginning with the Firestone Tire/Ford Explorer business crisis, eventually became so toxic that I lost my joy for the hunt. After profits plummeted and CEO Jac Nasser was fired in 2001, I jumped at the chance to take an early retirement package. Those were dark days at Ford. And even darker days lay ahead as the entire U.S. auto industry teetered on the verge of collapse during the 2007-2009 Great Recession.

No one was more pleased than I when I learned that one of the first things that CEO Alan Mulally tackled when he arrived at Ford in 2006 was the dysfunctional internal culture he discovered. Mulally has been credited, rightly, with leading Ford's stunning turnaround since he arrived in Dearborn. However, it was the vision of Chairman Bill Ford, who had the courage to go outside the auto industry and convince a brilliant leader to leave Boeing and take the helm of a dangerously tilting corporate ship, that set the stage for one of the great business comeback stories.

The next thing I'd like to see Ford and the other automotive companies do is to turn around the stunning talent drain of senior women, who have been leaving the auto industry during one of the worst periods in its history, for the past decade. Every five years, *Automotive News*, the industry trade paper, announces its list of the "100 Most Influential Women in the North American Auto Industry." I was on the first list, which was published in 2000. For the third list, announced in September 2010,[8] editors of the paper told me they had "fewer women nominated and had to reach down into lower levels" to compile their prestigious list. Today, however, the auto industry has a bright future just ahead. Women in the industry rejoiced when General Motors made history in January 2011 when it named 49-year-old (*Insider*) Mary Barra its Global Vice President of Product Development. With 36,000 people in her organization, Barra oversees GM's global engineering, design and quality and is the only woman on the company's 15-member executive leadership team. The global auto industry is a fascinating and exciting business that I believe will soon begin offering high-achieving, talented women tremendous opportunities to lead. Because my blood is still "Ford blue," as we say in Detroit, I hope Ford Motor Company sees the light first about the competitive edge companies gain when they tap the entire leadership talent pool.

The Sports Edge

Some women are born competitive; others develop the streak through sibling rivalry, academics, or through sports. I'm one of those pre-Title IX *Interlopers* who never played on an organized team nor had the benefit of a coach pushing me to give my best. *Insiders and Innovators* who played sports have a leadership edge. I'm a huge believer in the benefits girls and women gain from playing competitive sports. However, I agree with athlete and author Kathleen DeBoer that the value of sports for males and females is very different. "Women need sports to learn how to compete with men. To have the necessary toughness, but in an authentically female way," she told me. "It's not personal—not on the playing field and not with men in the workplace. It's OK to want to win; to be a star. That's what sport does for women, because we don't come to those things naturally. On the other hand, we don't need to teach men how to compete. They grew up doing that. But they need sports to learn how to connect, to build relationships, to give of yourself to something else."

Team sports are particularly valuable for teaching what it means to be a team player in the work world. Because I never had the opportunity to play on a team during my school years, it took me years to understand what male bosses meant when they criticized me for not being a *team player.* By my definition, I was the epitome of a team player. I shared information. I worked for the good of the overall group. I supported my peers and mentored those who worked for me. What were my bosses complaining about? "The mindsets of the hierarchy (male) and the web (female) lead to different concepts of team play in workplace settings," explains DeBoer in her book. "When men say that someone is a team player, they mean that the person is willing to accept their role in the structure, follow orders and do their part, even if, in the short run, it is not in their individual best interest. When women say that someone is a team player, they mean that the person is helpful, friendly and shares the spotlight with others. The differences are subtle but significant."

You want to lead? Play sports. Or if you're not an athlete, join any kind of competitive team. "The participation and empowering of girls in this country—just like boys—to learn about winning and losing and learning sportsmanship at a young age has been one of our great breakthroughs," says nationally syndicated sports columnist Christine Brennan. "In the next 20, 30, and 40 years, we'll have women running for president in this country. And the one common denominator for all of those women—on any ticket, Republican or Democratic—will be that they played sports."

The Men We Love

Fathers. By now, it should be very clear that I was blessed with one of the world's great fathers. The opportunity to work in the same field with my father and spend summer and winter nights sitting by his side in press boxes as we covered the same games for different stations was an unexpected gift from the gods. The importance of fathers is a theme that runs like a quiet but powerful river through the stories of so many women who have made the leap to leadership. Here are two examples:

- "As a young girl, I think I was about four, someone asked me what I wanted to be when I grew up. I knew the choices were teacher, secretary or nurse. I said nurse. My father happened to be listening and asked me, 'Why not a doctor?' I wasn't even in school yet, but my father's question changed my thinking about what was possible for me as a girl. I guess from that time, I never looked back." That memory belongs to Barbara Barrett, who became a lawyer rather than a doctor and whose long list of accomplishments includes serving as the U.S. ambassador to Finland and the former chairman of the U.S. Advisory Commission on Public Diplomacy. She lost her father when she was only 13, but his powerful, positive influence during Barrett's formative years was a gift that kept on giving long after he was gone.
- *Best Seat in the House . . . A Father, a Daughter, a Journey through Sports*, by *USA Today* sports columnist Christine Brennan is a sports-filled memoir of the remarkable role Brennan's father played in her life and trailblazing career. It's a wonderful Father's Day present for any man who has been given the gift of a daughter to parent. Or a daughter who was blessed with a great Dad.

Brothers. As merciless as most brothers are to their sisters as kids, they can be some of our greatest and most trusted male allies as adults. If you have a brother or brothers you are close to, tap into their wisdom. They can be a valuable source of unending insight into the mysteries of competing with the male tribe for authority and power. Plus, unlike parents, who are often our greatest fans, brothers can usually be counted on to tell their sisters the unvarnished, no-holds-barred truth.

Husbands. A woman who finds a life partner who supports her dreams, encourages her to pursue them, and equally shares home and family responsibilities is a lucky woman indeed. If you are married to such a man, count your blessings. If you are still searching for him, pick carefully. And be very clear about the "rules of engagement" that will shape your relationship from the moment you say "I do." Cultural programming is a powerful thing. It's all too easy to slip into traditional wife/husband roles that can feel as confining as straitjackets and be just as difficult for either one of you to escape down the road. I know; it happened to me.

"I have never forgotten the words of my mother who gave me excellent advice that has made all the difference in my marriage and my career," said Kim Casiano, president and CEO of Casiano Communications, the largest Hispanic publisher of magazines and periodicals in the United States, who earned her MBA at Harvard and serves on several corporate boards. "'Make sure that you have a very clear understanding with your husband that your careers are equally important, even if your career is unpaid,' my mother told me. 'And don't waver from that. It's hard to pull back,'" Casiano recalled her mother saying. "Somehow or another, Daddy being tired from paid work is more valid than Mommy being tired from staying home with the children and the work that goes with that. Shame on us if we allow that."

I'm the last person to give advice about building a great marriage partnership. Although I've loved and enjoyed the company of my share of interesting men, I've been single most of my life. I waited until my mid-30s to marry a charming Irishman, Mike Farrell, who was eleven years younger than I. It didn't last. Mike and I went through a painful divorce after only eight years of marriage. My son, Kevin, was less than two years old when Mike and I separated and only seven when his father died. So I understood exactly what Academy Award-winning actress Sandra Bullock meant when she publicly expressed her joy, from the podium at the Golden Globe Awards over the support she felt from her husband. "I never knew what it was before to have someone have my back," she told the world as she thanked her husband sitting in the audience. My heart ached along with millions of others when Bullock discovered what her husband was actually up to *behind her back.* Just days after Bullock's public yet very intimate thank you to a man she thought she could trust, Hollywood tabloids broke the story of his multiple sexual liaisons.[9] I can only imagine how empowering it can be for a woman to know—without question—that her life partner is also her most trusted ally. There's a great line in the movie, *Eat, Pray, Love.* After Julia Roberts complained that she was "so tired of people telling me I need a man," her male friend responded, "You don't need a man, you need a champion." Amen.

Sons. Relationships with our sons are powerful, complex, and can have a significant impact on a woman's leadership style. When he is young, a son can soften a mother's heart and influence her attitudes about the other half of the human race in a way that no other males can. As he grows into adolescence and beyond, forming his own opinions about females, a son can be a powerful source of unfiltered male feedback. A son can also toughen you up for dealing with challenges to your leadership authority. Thanks, Kevin, for all the practice!

As was true with many *Interlopers,* in my 20s and 30s I carried a good-size chip on my shoulder over the blatant gender discrimination toward girls and women that I experienced and witnessed. There is no better antidote for old scars from the gender wars or a tough divorce than falling in love with a little boy. My son, Kevin, is a young man now, just beginning college. Over the years, his influence on me has been like sandpaper, smoothing my rough edges. Kevin has never hesitated to call me out when he felt I made comments, even in jest, that were sexist toward men. His criticism can be hard to take, but I listen. And his views on our culture, through fresh male eyes, has provided invaluable insight on how men of Kevin's generation are approaching the age-old and ever-fascinating mysteries of gender differences.

Finally, sons provide a leadership opportunity for every mother to lend a hand in helping the next generation to break our cultural cycle of sexual chauvinism that limits our vision of cross-gender collaboration. "One of the leadership challenges for women is not just to develop their own skills but to do a better job of mothering the sons that will become the leaders of tomorrow," says CEO Kim Casiano, the mother of a teenage son and college-age daughter. "We should be raising the next generation of men to respect women, to respect their abilities, and to have very different attitudes than their fathers and grandfathers about women's leadership capability. We have the power—by the way we raise our sons—to break the cycle that limits women."

Sons' attitudes toward women are reflections of the females who raised them.

The Mindset of Men

The mindset of men will play a major role in how quickly humanity discovers that the world will be a better place when women—equally—help to run it. We're making progress, but we're not there yet. I never cease to be amazed at the outrageous, insulting, and sexist comments that are all too common on American radio and TV. I nearly drove off the road when I heard radio commentator Rush Limbaugh refer to comedian and TV talk show host Joy Behar as "Joy Be-ho." And during the Supreme Court confirmation hearings for Judge Sonia Sotomayor, nationally syndicated radio broadcaster G. Gordon Liddy told his listeners, "Let's hope that the key conferences aren't when she's menstruating or something, or just before she's going to menstruate. That would be really bad. Lord knows what we would get then."[10] There are uncomfortable days just around the corner for the likes of Limbaugh and Liddy who still cling to old, patriarchal notions of natural male superiority.

For centuries, women and ethnic minorities of every shade and gender have been measured by white, male metrics. Men born into the "elite norm" had little adjusting to do. Those days are nearly over. Our flat and ever smaller world is rapidly changing and the players diversifying. "The End of Men" was the unsettling but attention-grabbing headline on an *Atlantic* magazine article published in the summer of 2010. It asked the question, "What if equality isn't the end point? What if modern, postindustrial society is simply better suited to women?" The article's author, Hanna Rosin, provided compelling evidence that women throughout the world are rising rapidly, while the days of men as the dominant sex are changing "with shocking speed."[11] Men who are threatened by the ascent of women are making a critical mistake.

At every stage in our lives and evolution from *Achievers* to *Leaders* men provide multiple opportunities to encourage, influence, test, and stretch us. Every important interaction and relationship we have with males of any age is worth this question: "Does he build my strengths and bring out the best in me or does he trigger my weaknesses and bring out my worst?" It's equally important to pay attention to what impact we are having on the men within our circles of influence. Whether you are a mother, mother-in-law, grandmother, or future mother, I challenge you to raise great sons and grandsons!

At every step we take toward leadership, male influence is critical—either supporting or sabotaging our aspirations. What do men have to do with women's leadership? Plenty.

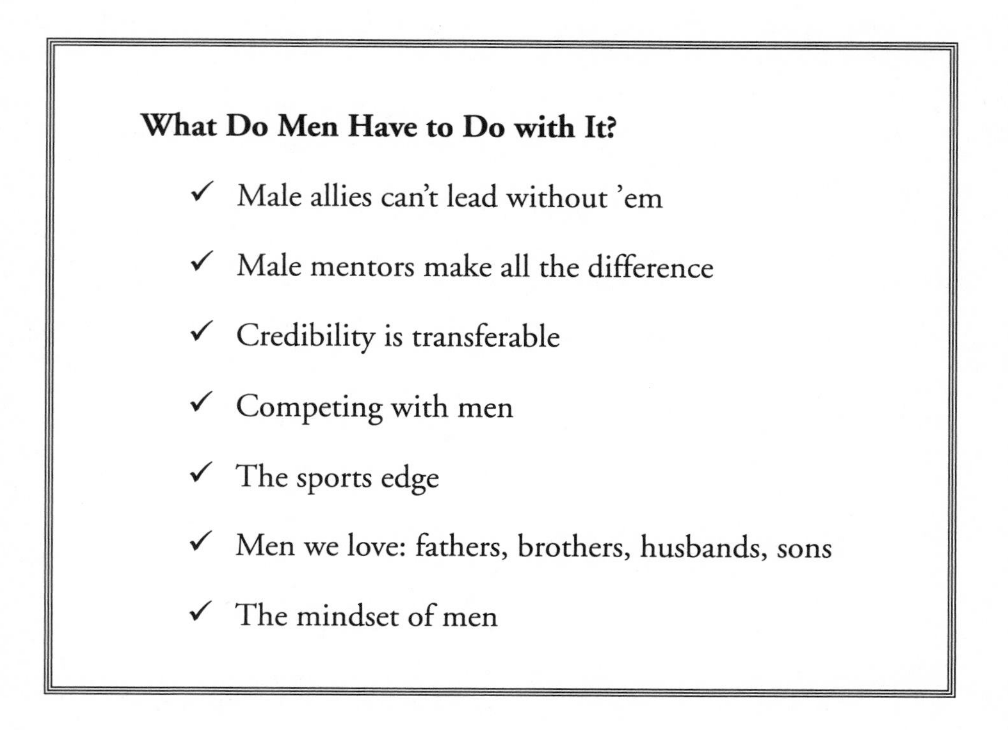

What Do Men Have to Do with It?

- ✓ Male allies can't lead without 'em
- ✓ Male mentors make all the difference
- ✓ Credibility is transferable
- ✓ Competing with men
- ✓ The sports edge
- ✓ Men we love: fathers, brothers, husbands, sons
- ✓ The mindset of men

Part Three

How Achievers Become Leaders

Seven Leadership Practices

The desire and drive to put your face into the wind, to have a hand in shaping the world around you, and to inspire others to join you in accomplishing something much bigger than your self-interests come from within. If you've heard the call, you know it, even if it has only been a whisper. Yet, just as musical, artistic or mathematical talent must be developed for a skilled musician, artist, or engineer to emerge, so it is with leadership. Becoming a highly evolved, effective leader requires the same thing it takes for musicians to get to Carnegie Hall: practice, practice, practice.

This final section of *Powering Up!* guides you through Seven Practices that I believe are essential for women *Achievers* to become *Leaders.*

How did I develop this list? I started with the classic qualities that come to mind right away: Vision, Courage, Judgment. I ended up with about 20 bullet points that I sent to several hundred female leaders to get their reactions. "What was missing?" I wanted to know. "What behaviors were more important than others?" I ended up with an even longer list—but clear winners. Certain qualities made nearly every woman's top ten. I then thought through the connections between specific qualities and leadership behaviors, asking myself, aren't "willingness to take risks" and "courage" related? That's how I arrived at the Seven Practices that are the subject of Part III.

So here's my list. Only one—*Womaninity*—is unique to women. The other six are equally important for men. What's different is how we integrate these practices into our personal leadership style, which must be authentic to our gender and our times.

At the beginning of the 21st Century, aspiring women—regardless of our generation—must still struggle to emerge from the cultural quicksand that seeps under our skin, grips us to stay in place, and resists our efforts to emerge to new and higher ground. Becoming a leader is a process that begins with a decision, but is worth the effort. Are you ready to head for deeper waters?

CHAPTER 7

Discover Your Purpose

As I thought about strong women of history, I realized that they stepped out in some way.

— MELINDA GATES, Philanthropist, *Insider*

Sometime early in the morning on Sunday, August 12, 1973, Mary Doyle, my 22-year-old sister, took her own life. She got up before the rest of the family was awake, went out to the garage, turned on her car, and laid down near the exhaust pipe, pulling a sleeping bag over her head to keep the deadly fumes close. By the time we woke up and found her, Mary was gone.

I'm the big sister and second child (my older brother, Danny, came first) in a very close family of seven children. When my first sister arrived, I took her under my protective wing from a young age, braiding Mary's golden hair, holding her hand as we walked to school, and mentoring her as my closest ally in the inevitable "girls against the boys" pillow fights, water balloon battles, and neighborhood skirmishes. As a young adult, Mary was fun, capable, crazy about Detroit Tiger All-Star catcher Bill Freehan, and a bit of a risk taker. She bought a powerful 450cc motorcycle and insisted I learn how to drive it, laughing at my terror. She was much better in math than I ever was and started programming computers when they were the size of small garages. The *Detroit News* put her in charge of running their employee payroll while she was only a college sophomore. I was 25 years old when Mary spun into a downward cycle of depression, lost all sense of her glorious value, and gave up on herself. Her death was the end of Camelot for my family; you go on, but you're never the same after such a loss.

What went so terribly wrong in the life of a young woman full of promise? It's a tragic story, triggered by a first romance with the wrong guy. So why include such painful memories in a book meant to inspire women to stretch their wings? Because, as my own path has unfolded over the decades since that terrible Sunday morning, I've come to realize that my sister's suicide has been one of the driving forces of my life.

When I was a young sports broadcaster standing alone outside the doors of team locker rooms, trying to muster the courage to walk in, Mary was with me. My willingness to face whatever was waiting for me inside every locker room I ever entered was all about the other Marys growing up, watching a woman sports broadcaster on TV. I wanted each one of them to believe in their unlimited potential—that they could be anything they wanted to be, no matter how many times culture, stereotypes, or negative people around them signaled, "No you can't." As a mid-level executive at Ford Motor Company, every time I took the professional risk of pushing, in some way, against the auto industry's entrenched "steel ceiling," my sister was with me. Whenever another woman asked me for help or mentoring, to me, it was Mary asking. My answer, whenever I could, was always "Yes." And during my darkest hours and seasons of greatest discouragement (and there have been plenty), she was with me then, too. Mary Doyle is the fire in my belly, the eternal flame burning within that gives my work purpose. Have you found yours?

Making the Leap from Me to We

Discovering your purpose is the first quantum leap an accomplished *Achiever* must make in order to become a *Leader* capable of inspiring others to action. "If a woman is just about herself, then she's not seeing clearly. We exist meaningfully in relation to others, in relation to the world," is the way internationally known spiritual leader and author Marianne Williamson put it during a "Sister Giant" conference in early 2010.[2] Over 500 women (I was one of them) traveled to Los Angeles from all over the United States and parts of Europe in response to Williamson's call to "Awaken the Sleeping Giant in American Womanhood." "The reason that so many people in American society are so lost in their weakness is because they've only been given a narcissistic model of personal growth. Me, me, me," Williamson told us. "Once you get it that we are here to serve this big WE, something rises up within you. Your power has purpose, which is much bigger than ME."

My sister's suicide, I've come to understand, has fueled nearly every step I have taken to help change attitudes, policies, and practices that limit possibilities for half of the human race. It's one thing to strive for excellence and take professional risks in pursuit of your own career ambitions. That's a great start. It's another thing entirely, and a much more enduring source of energy, to be driven by a clear sense of purpose to make a difference about something bigger than yourself—something that you care passionately about. However, you don't have to endure personal tragedy to find your purpose. Finding joy in your work can be equally inspiring and powerful.

Dr. Judy Rosener, a University of California at Irvine business professor and nationally recognized expert on women's leadership, told me, "Women start companies for very different reasons than men. Men start them if they think they can make money. Women start companies for a passion. You find very few women-owned companies that aren't started because the women really feel something." Rosener gives the example of Dr. Taryn Rose, an orthopedic surgeon and founder of Taryn Rose Shoes. "Taryn was operating on women's feet all the time and thought, 'God, their feet are terrible!' She came to the conclusion that most of women's foot problems are because of the shoes we wear. So she decided to manufacture shoes that would be stylish but wouldn't hurt women's toes. Eventually, she sold her company for a lot of money. Now she's working to develop beautiful, sheer stockings that will still give women support," says Rosener. "So here's a physician who became a very successful entrepreneur because she was also interested in helping women have clothes that work for them but are still stylish. That's passion."

Dr. Rosener, who wrote "The Ways Women Lead,"[3] a ground-breaking 1990 article published by *Harvard Business Review*, is currently working on a book about sex-based brain, hormonal, and socialization differences and their implications for decision making in the workforce. She sees the need for a sense of purpose as an essential driver for *women's* ambition, in particular. "If you look at women-owned and women-led companies, the woman tends to be very identified with the product or service. That's not the case with men. They often don't care what the service or product is, as long as it makes money," says Rosener. That explains something I've always wondered about: why are the senior executives and board members for companies that make feminine-specific products like brassieres and tampons mostly men, even today? Rosener believes that for most men, money, success, and power are the catalysts for their ambition. Most women, her research has shown, need something more to fuel their drive to lead. We need a sense of purpose.

Lead with Your Passion, Leave When You've Lost It

Years ago, when I was a newlywed, my husband Mike (now deceased) and I were talking about how unhappy he was at his job. I asked him, "What is it about your job that gives you joy?" I'll never forget the puzzled look on his face. He didn't seem to understand the reason for my question. "I like the money," he responded, with a shrug. I was astonished when I realized that Mike wasn't expecting to find personal satisfaction in his work. He sought that in other parts of his life. I can't imagine, however, staying very long in a professional position where I had lost the joy that comes from knowing you are making a difference.

People often ask me why I left successful careers in TV and the auto industry. My answer is always the same. In both cases, I left when I felt I was no longer making a difference. When I was fighting for equal access to sports locker rooms and helping to change TV viewers' attitudes about women's ability to cover sports, I had an endless supply of energy, tenacity, and passion for my job. But once my work as a change agent in Detroit was done, and I realized that it would be years before the TV networks would be ready to hire women reporters to really cover sports, not just provide sideline eye candy, I knew it was time for me to move on.

The same was true of my 13 years in corporate America. For the first 11 years working in communications and governmental affairs at Ford Motor Company, I thrived on the often grueling pace. During the 1990s, Ford was a stimulating environment. It was one of the most successful automotive companies in the world, and women were on the move. The long-entrenched auto industry "steel ceiling" was being pushed higher than it had ever been before. Highly skilled women were ascending to positions as plant managers, lawyers, engineers, designers, and even made a few inroads into the executive ranks. The higher you went, the fewer women there were. But our numbers were increasing, our opportunities were growing, and we knew we were bringing valuable, fresh perspective to critical discussions and decisions.

Even during times of intense crisis—and I went through plenty, including serving on the executive team for the deadly and devastating Ford Explorer/Firestone Tire business crisis[4]—the work was challenging and often exhilirating. The joy I felt in my work was fueled by my belief in the company's values and leadership, as well as my own ability to make a difference within the company. But my last two years at Ford, 2000 and 2001, were the most painful and discouraging of my professional career. It's often been said that we learn the most from our toughest times. I learned plenty in those two years. Following the Firestone/Explorer crisis and the firing of CEO Jac Nasser and several of his senior lieutenants, Ford was in a downward spiral, and the perfect storm was brewing in the auto industry. I'll leave it to others to write the books about how a once great company drifted dangerously close to the rocks and has now, once again, become one of the most admired automotive corporations in the world. What led me to leave was the dramatic change (at the time) in Ford's internal culture. A work environment that was once fueled by teamwork and the pursuit of excellence around a clear vision had become Machiavellian. When watching your back and worrying about internal politics are essential for survival, in my book it's time to leave. Once I realized that it would be years before I could make a difference in what had become a very dysfunctional culture, my passion, commitment, and energy dried up very quickly. That's what happens when you lose your sense of purpose in your work.

Some would argue, correctly, that we need leaders who are willing to hang in there and be the change agents in dysfunctional or outdated work cultures. I agree. Women, in particular, have been deserting large corporations and starting their own businesses in record numbers. Women-owned firms now account for 16 percent of all jobs in the U.S. workforce and are expected to create more than half of the new jobs anticipated by 2018, according to the Center for Women's Business Research.[5] Most women who leave large and medium-sized employers to follow the entrepreneurial path tell researchers they are seeking greater professional opportunity, personal satisfaction, and work/life flexibility. They also mention "being sick of worrying about office politics" as another key factor in their decision to strike out on their own. Am I concerned that long overdue work culture changes will take even longer if too many women simply throw up their hands and leave large organizations? Absolutely.

But it's also essential for a woman with the ability and desire to lead to honestly address these critical questions: Are you fulfilling your sense of purpose through your present work? Do you believe you can truly make a difference in your present position? If your answer to those questions is "Yes," hang in there. Your leadership is needed. On the other hand, do you have a nagging sense that you are wasting precious time furiously treading water while getting no closer to the sense of purpose that gives your work meaning? If so, remember: leading is not about making money or achieving impressive titles. It's about making a difference.

Know Thyself

Author and *Interloper* Dr. Sonya Friedman was one of the most recognized psychologists in the country during the eight years she hosted CNN's *Sonya Live* informational TV show. She's also a friend of mine who has a deep commitment to the issues and concerns of women, counseling thousands throughout her long career. Sitting in her home office, sharing her thoughts on what it takes for women to reach their full potential, Sonya zeroed right in on sense of purpose. "I think it's very important to figure out what you really want in your life. If you don't know who you are then you are always going to be a seeker and you are never going to find your answer," she told me. "No one can tell you or teach you this. You have to discover it for yourself."

Figuring out where True North lies for you is essential to discovering your leadership purpose. It takes time. Lots of time. Years. Leaders are rarely very young. That's why I see *powering up* to leadership as graduate work—the next step for *Achievers* who already have a strong grasp on the fundamentals needed for professional success. When I speak to university students, I always tell them that the most important thing they need to do in college is to discover their talents and begin developing them. We are all born talented. "What comes so easily to you that you often underestimate that ability and take it for granted?" I ask them. And just as importantly, "What gives you a sense of personal satisfaction and makes you come alive when you're doing it?" That's what I consider to be talent: the combination of the natural abilities we are born with that also give us joy when we use them.

Discovering our natural talents, such as the ability to draw or write well, to inspire an audience, or to figure out complex algorithms, is just the beginning of finding our purpose. It then takes years to hone raw talent into skill through experience, missteps, lessons learned, defining moments, flashes of insight, and growing expertise that we earn (often the hard way) during our 20s and 30s. Pairing our skills with the drive to excel is the work of *Achievers*. In *Outliers*, a fascinating book on what sets highly accomplished people apart from others, author Malcolm Gladwell talks about the "10,000-Hour Rule."[6] He says it takes 10,000 hours of practice—or about five years of 40-hour weeks—to become an expert in a specific task. There are no shortcuts, but some get there faster than others, Gladwell claims. (If you're curious how, read the book!)

Another great resource for learning how to develop your natural talents into powerful skills is *Now, Discover Your Strengths*, by Marcus Buckingham and Dr. Donald Clifton, chair of the Gallup International Clifton Strengths-Finder Profile. They've concluded that one of the biggest mistakes people make is wasting time working on their weaknesses. Their advice: Become very clear about what your strengths are and develop them into highly polished skills. What about our weaknesses? Buckingham and Clifton advise finessing around them by surrounding ourselves with people whose strengths complement ours. I highly recommend taking their 180-question, web-based strength-finder assessment (www.strengthsfinder.com).[7]

Leslie Murphy, an *Interloper* who was one of the first wave of management track CPAs hired right out of school by Plante & Moran in the early 1970s, got a jump start on learning her strengths. She was put through a battery of tests early in her career. "I remember the psychologist saying to me, 'You are going to really struggle for the first couple of years here because you are not a detail person and the work you will be required to do will seem mundane and repetitive to you. You really need to feel that you are making a difference, so you're going to have to figure out your own motivational system. As long as you get that satisfaction from your work you will be fine.'"

Murphy was lucky to receive such excellent insight on the psychological needs her work had to fulfill in order for her to excel. She took the psychologist's advice and disciplined herself to master the fundamentals of her profession as an essential stepping stone for her to achieve positions of greater influence. Murphy rose to a position of national leadership, becoming only the third woman in 100 years to chair the board of directors of the 360,000-member American Institute of CPAs (AICPA). She is a leader who learned early what fuels her passion for her work.

"One of the nuances of leadership is figuring out where you can make a difference. The specific aspect of where YOU bring a dimension that isn't there," advises Murphy. "Organizational leadership really comes from a whole complement of people, of things, of structures, of systems. Stepping up into a leadership role requires recognizing where your distinctiveness comes from. What's your passion? What unique dimensions can you bring to the table that aren't already there?" Once Murphy has accomplished what she has set out to do or senses she's no longer making a difference, she moves on. In other words: *Lead with your passion; leave when you've lost it.* Sometimes, that requires leaving your present employer. Other times, it simply means asking for what you need next, whether it's more responsibility, a new challenge or work that is more closely aligned with something you are passionate about.

If you've ever played cards, chances are pretty good you've learned the importance of leveraging your trump. Your natural talents and strengths are your personal trump. Learn everything you can about yours. Hone them into high-level skills. Then put your strengths to work in an environment, for a goal and with people whose values are aligned with your personal sense of purpose. Those ingredients—when combined—are a powerful mix that has spring-boarded many an *Achiever* into leadership roles.

Purpose Helps You Persevere

Another reason why "Discovering Your Purpose" is where I believe every woman's leadership evolution should begin is because leading is too hard, too lonely to do for very long without it. You must clearly understand both *where* you want to lead people and *why*. The *where* is your vision, which will change depending on what you're trying to accomplish and external influences. *Why* is all about your purpose. It's what gives you that "fire in the belly" to persevere. It's the tenacity to get back in the ring when you stumble and fail (which you must or you're not taking enough risks; we'll talk more about that in chapter 13). It's the passion that gives your work meaning during the inevitable rough spots that life throws everyone's way.

"Being connected to a higher purpose has given me a great deal of comfort, confidence and energy to keep putting one foot in front of the other, despite any challenges that I experienced along the way," says *Influential Insider* Miriam Muley, whose husband died suddenly in his sleep, leaving her to raise their two children alone. A marketing executive of Caribbean/African descent and author of *The 85% Niche . . . The Power of Women of All Colors*, Muley has persevered. She moved with her children to South Carolina to be closer to family, but continues pursuing her passion: advising Fortune 500 companies on the growing economic power and influence of African-American, Hispanic, Asian, and other women of color. "Knowing that I have a unique purpose has been a driving platform throughout my entire professional and personal life."

It's often been said, "It's lonely at the top." It's even lonelier for women who are still so rare at leadership levels everywhere that you are essentially on your own, with few female peers around to provide powerful allies and strategic confidants. Knowing you are making a difference about something personally meaningful goes a long way toward helping you handle the *aloneness* that so many women in positions of leadership grapple with.

Having a sense of purpose that's bigger than yourself or your career also protects you from needing constant affirmation from others. "If you're reliant on external validation to have a good feeling about what's the right thing to do, then you get whipsawed a lot," says Teri Takai, a nationally respected IT expert who was recently named Chief Information Officer for the U.S. Department of Defense. "Looking back, I've realized that the times my career stalled were when I lost sight of what I felt were the right things to do. I was trying to be a political animal. When you're chasing what you think someone else wants, you can become very bitter when things don't turn out as you hoped." But Takai is not implying that a leader should always go it alone or accept feeling isolated. "Earlier in my career, I felt that reaching out and asking peers for their perspective on issues I was grappling with was weakness. I've changed my thinking 180 degrees. I've learned that being able to gather a group of trusted confidants around you is actually a sign of strength."

If you are an *Interloper* or *Insider* who fears you may be losing your mojo because you no longer have the same passion and energy for your work, it may be time to re-evaluate whether the fast track you're on is taking you where you really want to go. *Innovators*, it's never too early to pair your drive and ambition with work that is personally fulfilling. Here are a few examples of the sense of purpose that fuels several amazing women, including a few you'll recognize.

- I am seeking the fullest expression of myself as a human being on earth. Keep on using me till you use me up. That's what I say to God all the time. (Oprah, media mogul, philanthropist, *Interloper*)
- Using humor, I strive to comment on and make light of our confusing world. (Megan Grano, NY comedian, *Insider*)
- To live up to Mahatma Gandhi's words, 'You must become the change you see in the world,' by creating maximum healing when people are most vulnerable and in need. (Dotty Deremo, Hospice CEO, *Interloper*)
- Be right. Be wrong. But be somebody. (Felisha Leggett-Jack, women's head basketball coach, Indiana University, *Insider*)
- My personal journey is all about turning dust into diamonds, rebuilding things that were badly broken and the effect that can have on people's lives. Once I realized I had found my calling, I've never looked back." (Lynn Tilton, CEO equity firm Patriach Partners, *Insider*)
- I am driven by action -- action to make the world better in some way. I live to do, to have impact upon the world. My fire burns brightest

when I am a part of achieving progress to help people who are broken or lost find their worth in a new global economy. (Jennifer Granholm, Governor, State of Michigan, 2003 – 2010, *Insider*)

- To save the oceans by igniting public support for a global network of marine protected areas. Every time I slip into the ocean, it's like going home." (Sylvia Earle, oceanographer; founder Mission Blue, *Interloper*)
- My purpose is helping people become healthier and living better everyday lives. The setback is it is such a hard task to get people to do that. (Florine Mark, President and CEO, The WW Group, the leading Weight Watchers franchise holder, *Interloper*)

Where Are You Going—and Why?

"I don't think it ever occurred to women that you could do what you are passionate about," *Influential Insider* Michelle Fanroy, president of Access One Consulting, told me. "In the past, we were always busy breaking down barriers and just trying to get through the door. But now that we're in the game, we can start asking ourselves, 'How and where do I want to play?'"

Do you know how, where, and why you want to lead? If not, start by searching within. Your answer lies with that very private, internal flicker that is patiently waiting to becoming your empowering flame. It will be ready whenever you are. If you haven't felt your flicker of purpose or heard its soft call, it's time to pause long enough to listen. Reflect. Search your soul. I like the way Ann Moore, long-time chairman and CEO of Time, Inc. put it to an audience of women professionals. "Forget the clock," she urged. "Get yourself a compass instead. The direction you are headed is far more important than how fast you are going."

Discover Your Purpose

- ✓ Make the leap from Me to We
- ✓ Lead with your passion
- ✓ Know thyself
- ✓ Purpose helps you persevere
- ✓ Accept and handle the *alone-ness*

CHAPTER 8

Raise Your Voice

What do you believe, how do you articulate it, and what happens if you get brushed back?

— CAROL JENKINS, Founding President, Women's Media Center, *Interloper*

The Rutgers Scarlet Knights women's basketball team had a great 2007 season, making it to the NCAA Final Four and advancing for the first time ever to the national championship. They lost in a hard-fought final against the University of Tennessee Lady Volunteers, 59-46. But the defining moment of their season came next. The following morning, Don Imus, one of the most widely listened-to talk show hosts in the United States at the time, talked about the women's basketball championship on his MSNBC show, *Don Imus in the Morning*. Imus described the Scarlet Knights, eight African-American and two white players, as "nappy-headed hos." Sportscaster Sid Rosenberg, who was on the air with Imus that morning, piled on, adding, "The more I look at Rutgers, they look exactly like the (NBA's) Toronto Raptors."[1] Imus built his career on his arrogant, salty (some would say slimy), and controversial style. The more outrageous he was, the bigger his audience and his paychecks grew. But the morning of April 4, 2007, Imus not only went too far, he met his match: a leader who wasn't afraid to raise her voice.

Rutgers Coach C. Vivian Stringer called a news conference, which was carried live on TV, to publicly hold Imus accountable for his insulting comments. Stringer and her athletes—one by one—courageously spoke up to express their outrage. The national news media took notes as the Scarlet Knights collectively refused to let a powerful talk show host's racist and sexist slurs "pass" as "all in good fun." Coach Stringer not only stood up for her athletes, she also taught her players an unforgettable lesson in what this chapter is all about: the power of *Raising Your Voice.*

Don Imus apologized. He was fired anyway. And of course, he was back on the air within eight months, broadcasting from the studios of WABC-AM radio. But anyone who was paying attention as the drama unfolded witnessed a powerful example of what can happen when individuals summon their courage, speak up, and raise their voices to make a difference. Raising your voice is much more difficult than *finding your voice*. It's also an essential skill for leading. Women, in particular, need to be strong communicators in order to have the authority and presence to command a room. Few of us have the height and deeper voices that give men who want to be heard an edge. Raise your voice; otherwise, you don't have a shot at influence.

Communications Skills: The Fundamentals

As a long-time journalist, media trainer, and communications executive, I've witnessed innumerable examples of powerful, knowledgeable leaders—both men and women—whose weak communications skills undermine their message and effectiveness. Many refuse to do live TV and radio interviews on short notice, even when news is breaking. Others ramble when asked a direct question during an employee Town Hall meeting or industry panel. Or they are unable to speak extemporaneously. I remember my astonishment when a CEO I admired simply read prepared remarks during an intimate, Washington, D.C. dinner with some of our top dealers. He knew the issues inside out and would have strengthened his own and the company's relationship with important business partners if he had thrown away the script, looked them in the eye, and simply talked to them. His discomfort as a public speaker undermined his message that night.

Leaders are expected to be able to communicate well—with all size groups and every kind of news outlet, from print reporters and bloggers to talk show hosts that now range from attack dogs to fawning allies. If you have honed your communications skills for multiple environments, they will help lift you to higher levels of credibility and influence. However, if your communications skills are not polished, your messages and voice are not strong and clear, and you haven't developed the professional *presence* to command a room, then you must master the fundamentals before you're ready for the leadership practice of *Raising Your Voice.*

Every *Achiever* worth her salt understands how essential strong communications skills are. Don't make the mistake of believing yours are "good enough." No matter how polished you think your communications skills are, you can always raise your game. Even great athletes keep practicing.

I'm a product of the 60s, so I was enthralled by Jackie Kennedy when she was First Lady. But I was dismayed when I first heard her "baby whisper voice." It's often been written that Jackie's breathy speaking style was one of the assets that made her so intriguing to men. Jacqueline Kennedy Onassis was one of the most fascinating women of her times. But there's no room today for breathy, whispery-voiced women—not even our First Ladies. Michelle Obama is a compelling speaker whose clear voice, strength, and warmth make her a strong asset on the campaign trail and an effective advocate as a First Lady. Even Laura Bush, who kept a very low profile as First Lady, has now written a book and appeared on national TV shows, including *Larry King Live*. A few decades back, Americans wanted their First Ladies to look good. Today, we expect them to use their voices—effectively and with purpose.

I still hear too many women speaking too softly and tentatively. Work on your voice. If you weren't born with a naturally strong voice or were brought up to be soft-spoken, get coaching lessons. President Theodore Roosevelt famously said, "Speak softly and carry a big stick." For women who aspire to lead, I'd fine-tune his advice to "Speak *up*, speak *clearly*, and carry a big stick."

Then, you need to back up your voice with something significant to say. What's your message? To be authentic, your message is aligned with your sense of purpose. Before you start raising your voice, you have to be very clear about your point of view. Which issues and values are important enough to you to take a stand the way Women's Basketball Hall of Fame inductee C. Vivian Stringer and her Scarlet Knights did? Next, you must articulate your positions concisely and clearly. Clarity of thought is a significant differentiator among speakers. Start listening for key messages when you hear others speak. You'll be amazed at how convoluted and rambling some speakers are. Notice which ones you understand most clearly. Whether you agree with their message or not, evaluate how effective they articulate it.

Finally, polish your ability to speak comfortably in front of groups. Whether you are addressing your local school board, testifying before Congress, or stepping to the podium as a keynote speaker or expert panelist, strong speaking skills are essential for credibility and to be able to influence and inspire others. And don't shy away from the news media. Regardless of the present meltdown in the newspaper business, the media's influence keeps growing. Today, it's all about multiple media platforms, which requires anyone who wants to be heard to be able to shift gears and tailor her messages to multiple mediums and niche audiences. These days, a leader needs to be able to have some fun with the likes of Jon Stewart on *The Daily Show* (even if it's only your local market Stewart wannabe) as well as hold her own with more traditional journalists. Remember, Americans like to take their medicine with a spoonful of sugar. Don't take yourself too seriously. If you can't have a little fun while making a serious point, work on it.

Growing up in a family of nine, with two professional speakers for parents, certainly gave me a head start. Every one of my brothers and sisters has either worked in broadcasting or has spoken publicly in their professions. As my sister Teresa says, "Communications is the Doyle family business." Here are some of the tips that I've learned through the years:

- *Listen to an audio recording of yourself speaking.* Concentrate on the sound, strength, and intonation of your voice. Is it monotone? Or does it have variety, warmth, and personality? How loud is it? How is your articulation and speed? Many people speak too fast, running their words together when they get nervous. Listeners need to be able to hear and easily understand a speaker's words. One of the best ways to evaluate your speaking voice is to use a free phone recording service, such as www.evoca.com. You can practice a speech or prepare for an important news media interview by having a friend interview you over the phone. Download the recording, play it back, and listen with a critical ear, asking yourself the questions I posed above. Then, do it again. And again. And again.
- *Never wing it.* Invest the time to prepare. I've been amazed over the years at the number of very smart, capable executives I've worked with who didn't want to take the time to practice their speeches or think through their key messages for a news media interview ahead of time. Whether you prepare or don't, it always shows. There's nothing worse than an undisciplined speaker. Even the very best extemporaneous speakers who seem to be "ad libbing" prepare their thoughts ahead of time. Developing key messages is pretty basic stuff. The challenge is holding yourself accountable for communicating them effectively. That's a little tougher to accomplish in a media interview than in a speech. Here's a trick executives and politicians use to get their messages across, regardless of a reporter's agenda. First, acknowledge and sufficiently answer (it can be short) the question. Then, pivot and transition to the key point you want to make. I've done hundreds of radio interviews and speeches. No matter how informal or short an interview or my remarks may be, I always take a few minutes ahead of time to get very clear in my head what I want listeners to

remember. Every moment you take preparing your message pays high yield dividends.

- *Visualize the results you want.* I'm a big fan of this powerful tool, which athletes use all the time. They see themselves landing the triple salchow, sinking the winning basket, or nailing their landing after their toughest vault. Picture yourself getting a standing ovation. That's not vanity or fantasy; it's programming your brain. Our brains are hypersensitive to the messages we send them. If you think "I'm going to be great," research has shown that your brain will believe it and do its best to deliver. But if you allow thoughts like "I'm nervous" or "What if they don't like me?" to creep in, your brain will believe those, too, and deliver exactly what you imagined.
- *Breathe deeply.* It's a rare speaker or professional performer whose heart doesn't speed up and adrenalin kick in before a performance. That's good. I recently heard Carol Channing, one of Broadway's greatest stars, talk about the butterflies she still gets before taking the stage. When it's show time, you need to shift into high gear. Those butterflies, however, have to be managed, or they can lead to shortness of breath. Take a few minutes before an important presentation, speech, or interview to breathe deeply and slowly.
- *Be yourself.* The biggest challenge of speaking publicly is to stay as natural as possible in unnatural circumstances. People think they have to *change* and speak differently in front of a group than when they're talking one-on-one. That's wrong. Exactly the opposite is true. Your goal should be for each person in your audience to think you are talking directly to her or him. A simple trick that professional TV broadcasters use is this: Put a face on the camera, the face of someone you know well and really like. Talk directly to that person. You'll be amazed at the difference. The same goes for a live audience. Find individual faces in the crowd who are listening intently (preferably with smiles on their faces). Look them in the eye and speak directly to them. Another effective trick that accomplished speakers use is called "one thought, one person." When you're speaking to an audience, don't scan the room. Pick a face, make a simple point (Hi, I'm Anne Doyle), and then pick

another face for your next point (I'm honored to have been asked to speak tonight). Try it; you'll be amazed at what a difference this very simple secret can make.

- *Seek constructive criticism.* In order to continue raising our skill levels, we need to see ourselves as others do. That means soliciting specific suggestions on how you can get better. Ask for it. Most people will be reluctant to tell you anything negative. You really have to make sure they understand you *want it*! Give people permission to tell you the truth. And when you get it, don't become defensive. Just say "Thank you." They've given you a valuable gift. The ability to accept criticism is a strength. Listen carefully for grains of insight that ring true and let the rest roll off your shoulders like water off a duck's back. Once you learn to seek frank feedback, you'll have an edge over those who prefer to listen only to their fans.

A strong speaking voice. Succinctly expressing your ideas, positions, and vision. The ability to connect and communicate with a large audience as effectively as you do one-on-one. Comfort and skill engaging with the news media. Those are the communications fundamentals that every ambitious *Achiever* must master and continuously polish. *Raising Your Voice* is the next step.

Overcome Fear

Too many brilliant, wise, and highly experienced women are still quietly waiting to be asked their opinions, while legions of men step up to podiums, jump at media interview opportunities, run for office, and dominate discussions. Fear is the counterweight to courage. Speak up. Seek opportunities to be heard in public forums. Dare to express a different point of view. I'm not saying it's easy. Rare is the woman who was encouraged from a young age to speak up. Mary Petrovich, CEO of Axle Tech International, a Fortune 1000 manufacturing and engineering company, witnessed this pattern even among her MBA classmates. "I went to the Harvard Business School when only 20 percent of the class was women. They were all very smart. But most were soft spoken and polite to a fault," Petrovich told me. "When it came to being articulate, being inspirational, having energy and wanting to get up in front of a group of guys and feel comfortable, they weren't that impressive."

Carol Jenkins, founding president of the Women's Media Center (WMC), a New York nonprofit working to enhance women's impact through the news media, understands as well as anyone the power of effectively using your voice. As an African-American journalist breaking into TV news in the 1970s, she faced plenty of barriers. She overcame them all, building a sterling reputation during her 30 years as a reporter and news anchor at WNBC-TV in New York. It was under Jenkins' leadership that the WMC produced "Sexism Sells But We're Not Buying It," a disturbing video of clip after clip of U.S. TV commentators mocking women candidates during the 2008 presidential campaign not for their policy positions but for their gender ("A ho is a ho, right?"[2]) "We've found too many women are quietly steaming or waiting to be asked their opinions," says Jenkins, who has trained hundreds to overcome their fear and become media thought leaders. "We need more women to take the initiative with news media and actively engage in shaping public discussions and attitudes."

What do you believe? How do you articulate it? To whom do you articulate it? And how do you handle it when you are rebuffed or publicly criticized? Those are the questions, Jenkins advises, that every woman who aspires to lead must ask herself and be able to handle with strength and poise. Don't let fear hold you back. Manage it. Grace under pressure, especially when you are the lone voice speaking up or taking an unpopular stand, is the mark of a leader.

Resist Cultural Pressure

Nearly all of us have been warned in one way or another not to become too mouthy, bossy, nagging, domineering, aggressive, ambitious, uppity, challenging, independent, and, of course, bitchy. Take your pick; they're all code words for a woman who doesn't know her place.

And then there are the more subtle messages that can be just as effective at discouraging women from raising our voices too loud or too often. I'll never forget the well-intentioned advice a Ford executive gave me when I asked him what I could do to be a more effective leader. "Anne, you have to stop always seeing things through the eyes of a woman. People are getting tired of it," he told me. I looked at him in astonishment. Then I said, "You know, I'm getting tired of it, too. But if I'm not going to speak up about things that I see through my eyes as a woman that others don't see then I might as well just be another man in the room."

At the time, there were other women in upper management positions within the company. But many were *Influential Insiders* who, as I explained in chapter 3, tend to be masters at reading "the guys" and rarely took positions that would be seen as rocking the boat. There were plenty of times, of course, that I did bite my tongue, choosing to pick my battles carefully. Some of my colleagues from those days at Ford might tell you that I would have been well served to have followed the executive's advice more closely. But I didn't. Why not? Would a leader keep quiet about the long-standing and widespread discomfort that women customers still feel in automotive showrooms? Would she resist questioning whether the *Probe* was really a good name for a car targeted for women? And would she decide not to ruffle feathers by openly advocating for more women engineers, designers, and marketers to have visible roles during media launches for new vehicles? As an *Interloper,* I believed that one of the biggest contributions I could make inside Ford was to speak up. Did I pay a price for not simply going along with majority thinking? Sure, at times. But they knew I was there. And I'd like to believe that by raising my voice, I made a positive difference.

Even young *Innovators* haven't escaped the cultural conditioning that teaches women to hold back. "I think we often don't bring our voices to the table. We frequently lack the urge to fight to make our voices heard," Nicole Navratil, a 31-year-old executive and managing director with BBMG, a New York marketing and branding agency, told me. "In big meetings, when opinions are flying all around, I often find myself thinking, 'People don't need to hear my gut reaction right now.' We often don't value our perspective enough to make sure it is factored in professionally, unless somebody turns to us and says, 'What's your womanly perspective on this?'"

As an *Achiever,* you wouldn't be where you are without self-confidence, professional savvy, and skill in your areas of expertise. To lead, you must go further. You must push the edges and seek opportunities to weigh in. Women's voices are still in short supply at leadership levels in every professional sector and policy arena. Some "tone deafness" on the part of major corporations could be avoided if more women who are already in positions of influence were bolder about raising their voices. Don't wait to be asked your opinion. Dare to bring up and advocate for alternative points of view. We need your voice.

Practice Speaking Up

How do you get comfortable speaking up more frequently and with more authority than you've done in the past? The same way you build strong muscles. You start with small weights and lots of repetition. Then you work your way up to the heavier stuff. Once you are ready to begin raising your voice, pick your opportunities carefully. Each time you speak up with courage and become an advocate for new thinking, you are strengthening your leadership vocal cords and preparing yourself for tougher moments. Every one of us has multiple, real-life opportunities to lead. Life provides innumerable moments to raise your voice. By strategically and consciously choosing when and how to raise your voice, every individual can have significant impact on how people you personally interact with perceive things. Just like water dripping on a rock, consistently raising your voice—even in little ways—can make a big difference.

Every Saturday morning, I go to a spinning class at my local fitness club. There's nothing like a room full of other people on stationary bikes sweating and pedaling furiously, great music and a high-energy instructor to make me work harder than I ever would alone. The instructors use music they program on their iPods. During a recent class, I was stunned when a song began to blare with words so demeaning to women that I nearly jumped off my bike to stop the music. It was a sensual song with a male singer rapping, "I said Shush girl. Shut your lips. Do the Helen Keller and talk with your hips."

All I could think of were the millions of ways that girls and women have been told for centuries to "Shush." And just "talk with your hips." Grrrrr. I decided not to let the song ruin my workout and went back to my riding. But I didn't let it go, either. Instead of just seething, I thought carefully about how to approach the instructor after class so that she would be open to my request that she stop using the song at the club. I started by complimenting her on what a motivating teacher she is. Then, I raised my objections to the "Shush girl" song.

"I'm sure you were just thinking about the beat," I told her. "But we are a captive audience of almost 50 people. The words that you select to play are programmed into our brains as we ride. Is that really the message about women that you want to be putting out there?" The instructor and I had a good conversation. She was very open to my concerns, telling me, "I guess I can understand why those words bothered you, but it was a woman who had requested that song." Chalk one up for another example of how women can often be our own worst enemies!

We're so surrounded by cultural sexism and degrading images, music, and messages about women that we barely notice them anymore. It's easy to become numb to the negative impact that keeps accumulating. If you think I'm making a mountain out of a musical mole hill, I highly recommend *Enlightened Sexism*,[3] by Susan Douglas, a book I mentioned in chapter 4. The insulting "Shush Your Lips, Girl" song from my spinning class is exactly what Douglas calls the "enlightened sexism" that is now embedded in American culture. When you find yourself in situations that disturb you and conflict with your values and leadership purpose, ask yourself, "If I don't speak up, who will? If I don't raise my voice to make a difference, how will things ever change."

But we can't just complain or whine. Nobody wants to hear that. It takes skill to present your message so people will be receptive. It takes even more practice to hold your own in a heated conversation where there's money, lives, jobs, and important decisions at stake. If you're going to influence decisions, people have to be willing to listen to you. And when those opportunities arrive, make sure you have something worthwhile to say.

Articulate Your Vision

In January 2009, *Harvard Business Review* carried an article entitled "Women and the Vision Thing." Researchers Herminia Ibarra and Otilia Obodaru reported that female leaders received higher ratings than males in nearly every dimension except one: vision. "In a study of thousands of 360-degree assessments collected . . . over the past five years, we looked at whether women actually received lower ratings than men. To our surprise, we found the opposite: as a group, women outshone men in most of the leadership dimensions measured. There was one exception, however, and it was a big one: Women scored lower on 'envisioning'—the ability to recognize new opportunities and trends in the environment and develop a new strategic direction for an enterprise," researchers reported.[4]

Women *Achievers* are often so focused on delivering quantifiable results or sharing credit for collaborative work that we often underestimate the importance of clearly communicating our own strategic vision. Don't make the mistake of being too busy "getting the job done" to think big and think ahead. Take the time to do the work of developing your vision. It is the foundation for putting your communications skills to work. The roots of an authentic vision spring from your sense of purpose. Entire leadership books have been written on the importance of vision and how to articulate it. If you haven't read *The 8th Habit: From Effectiveness to Greatness* by Stephen Covey, it's a great place to start. The author of the classic *Seven Habits of Highly Effective People*, describes the 8th Habit as "Find Your Voice and Inspire Others to Find Theirs."

"I have this leadership speech I give my troops," Air Force Commander General Maggie Woodward, who has commanded operations in Kosovo, Turkey, Saudi Arabia, and Iraq, told me. "'You can have all the vision in the world, but if you're not able to *inspire* people to follow you, all you are is a dreamer,' I tell them. And the only way you can inspire people is by communicating well with them."

A vision kept to yourself is no good to anyone. Articulating your vision in a way that inspires others to embrace and pursue it is a high-level leadership skill. It's also the key to getting a lot done. Dr. Terry Sullivan, president of the University of Virginia, told me: "A mistake that a lot of women make is thinking that they have to do it all themselves. You will burn out that way. A critical part of leadership is getting other people to share your vision and come aboard. You've got to be able to *sell* your vision." That goes for effective advocacy as well, such as serving as an elected official where you need others' support in order to accomplish anything. Whether you are *selling* your vision, hoping to convince others to support your position, or trying to inspire those you're leading to enthusiastically join you, the ability to clearly articulate your vision is essential.

Grow Teflon Skin

"Expect to be confronted. Expect to be opposed. Expect to have to defend yourself in the face of opposition. Whatever you do, don't turn tail and retreat to the bushes." Those are the words of PhD Nancy Badore, an organizational development expert who consults with senior executives and high-potential women being groomed for leadership. Here's the bad news: as soon as you overcome your fear, develop your vision and stick your neck out, somebody's going to take a whack at it. Leading not only requires having the guts to speak up but also means not backing off when the competition and resistance heats up. The higher you go, the tougher the resistance you will encounter. Start, right now, growing your thick hide of Teflon skin. It's your first line of defense. "My clients are often surprised when they encounter obnoxious opposition, male or female," says Badore, who has worked with leadership gurus Peter Drucker and Tom Peters. "Whatever one believes leadership consists of, it inevitably means being prepared to stand out alone in the force of the gale sometimes."

In May 2010, *Time* magazine featured three women who are now some of the most powerful figures in the world of high finance. The headline read "The New Sheriffs of Wall Street." Dressed in dark black and navy power suits, standing side-by-side and staring directly into the camera for the magazine cover photo were Sheila Bair, the chair of the U.S. Federal Deposit Insurance Corporation (FDIC); Securities and Exchange Commission (SEC) Chair Mary Schapiro; and Elizabeth Warren, who chaired the Trouble Asset Relief Program (TARP), which oversaw the mega-million federal bailout of U.S. banks during the 2007-2009 Great Recession.

The article included short profiles of the three and zeroed in on a common theme that characterized the rise of each of the women. Each faced resistance—often gender-based—along the way when they dared to stray from the common wisdom and challenge the pack. For example, Bair was the first one to warn the U.S. banking community about the brewing mortgage foreclosure crisis. Her efforts to privately sound the alarm in the spring of 2007 were ignored. So she went public. "We have a huge problem on our hands," she said during a speech at a bankers' conference in October 2007. In recounting the reaction for the *Time* magazine article, she said, "They were shocked and horrified. I thought they were going to throw tomatoes at me."[5] Each of these high-powered women told stories in the article about numerous clashes with colleagues and business moguls who not only disagreed with the women's financial views but also resented their gender. For example, when Mary Schapiro was tapped in 1994 to take over the Commodity Futures Trading Commission, she was nine months pregnant. One of her first tough decisions was to refuse a request by Chicago traders to be exempted from federal regulations. According to the *Time* article, "Tom Donovan, then the head of the Chicago Board of Trade, struck back, announcing that he would not be 'intimidated by some blonde, 5-foot 2-inch girl.' Schapiro responded by telling a reporter, 'I'm 5 feet 5.'" Now that's Teflon skin.

Build Courage

When we think about courage, our mental databases draw from the thousands of cultural images planted deep into our subconscious. Most look vaguely familiar: men on battlefields charging up hills, galloping into the face of an enemy, or rescuing women and children. We have to think a bit to pull up clear images of women and courage, such as the Suffragettes chaining themselves to the White House fence or early American pioneers giving birth on the Oregon trail in the back of a moving covered wagon. Rare is the culture anywhere in the world that celebrates and consistently models women's courage. But we have it and use it every day. And it's essential for leaders. When I think of courage in terms of women raising their voices, I think of:

- The courage to lead the way things could be, rather than silently seething over the way they are;
- The courage to speak up with conviction even when yours is a minority voice; and
- The courage to stand up to criticism and welcome it as a chance to show you know your stuff.

That last one is an area women struggle with much more than men. It's in our nature to take things more personally than most men do. That's one of our strengths and directly related to our emotional intelligence skills that are highly tuned. But, too many women also allow unfiltered, random criticism to undermine their confidence and lead them to second-guess themselves.

Teri Takai, an Asian American IT expert who was recently named U.S. Department of Defense Chief Information Officer, has thought a lot about why women are more likely to absorb criticism while men seem to instinctively deflect it. She and I talked about gender differences while sitting at her dining room table surrounded by moving boxes. "I think that as women we are very personally invested in our choices. So when we don't get positive reactions to our ideas, or when somebody pushes back, we take that very personally." Takai spent the first 20 years of her career working primarily with male engineering and information systems colleagues in the auto industry. She was leaving for California the next day to join Governor Arnold Schwarzenegger's cabinet, yet stopped everything long enough to talk with me about women's leadership. "We don't see criticism and differences of opinions as an argument over the facts. Instead, we see it as a statement about us, about our intellect. About our analytical skills. That's a big mistake."

Thanks to powerful, new brain-imaging technology that allows us to observe brains in action, we're learning why men and women often respond so differently. It turns out that our reactions have as much to do with how our brains are hard-wired as with our cultural conditioning. Hormones have plenty to do with it. Higher levels of testosterone, for example, are why men's reaction to a threat or challenge is to stand up and fight, while women's default reaction is to avoid conflict and back off. Of course, our biological hard-wiring goes back to cave man and cave woman days. We know from Darwin that Mother Nature is all about survival of the species and could care less whether you are considered senior executive material or gain the confidence of voters to elect you to political leadership. However, our lives and ambitions today far exceed the female brain wiring that hasn't changed much in millions of years. My favorite book on the topic, *The Female Brain*, was written by Dr. Louann Brizendine, a neuropsychiatrist at the University of California and founder of the Women's and Teen Girls Mood and Hormone Clinic. "We are living in the midst of a revolution in consciousness about women's biological reality that will transform human society,"[6] says Dr. Brizendine. Think about that. On our watch, we can be catalysts to positively transform society. But it will require many more women finding the courage to repeatedly speak up.

Watch Women Who Raise Their Voices Well

I was very lucky to have a powerful role model from a very young age on how to be an effective advocate. Her name was Isabel Molloy Doyle. I am not exaggerating to say that my Mother was an unusual woman—not only for her times, but right up until her final breath at age 84. Growing up in Chicago, the daughter of educated parents and the youngest of five children, she graduated from Mundelein College (now part of Loyola University) and earned her master's degree in speech and drama from Catholic University in the early 1940s. She was working as a radio actress and producing films for the Studebaker Company in South Bend, Indiana, during World War II. That's where she met my father, a New Yorker and naval officer who was sent to the campus of Notre Dame to physically condition troops for combat. After the war, they married and had seven little Doyles (four girls and three boys). By the time my younger brothers and sisters were in grade school, my mother was teaching speech and debate at Indiana University's South Bend campus.

Of all her many wonderful qualities, I would say that Isabel's courage and the way she taught her children how to use our voices from a young age were her greatest gifts. The lessons began around our dining room table. We commonly "raised our voices" every night over dinner. It was nearly always a cultural shock for our friends from smaller (and probably much quieter) families to stay for dinner. They would be astonished and usually intimidated by the cacophony of hotly debated topics we took on between passing the mashed potatoes and furtively feeding our dinner "rejects" to our dog, Cinders. I remember one friend asking me after dinner, "Wow, do you guys always fight like that?" I didn't know what she was talking about. "We weren't fighting," I told her. "We were just talking."

There's nothing like growing up in a large family to learn that you can't wait to be asked your opinion, to weigh in, or for everyone else to stop to listen to your views. And my youngest brothers and sisters will attest that the little kids had to be even more relentless than anyone to get their share of attention. But Isabel's mentoring went well beyond encouraging lively conversation and debate around the dining room table. Throughout her lifetime, she repeatedly stood up and spoke up, challenging behaviors and people she felt were wrong or demeaning to others. It wasn't something my siblings and I were always proud of. She embarrassed us multiple times. She walked out of my high school junior follies when the football players came on stage, dressed as women with gigantic breasts and ridiculous costumes, to dance like the Rockettes. My Mother also walked out during sermons at our church when she felt a priest's comments demeaned women.

Even in the final months of her life, Isabel Molloy Doyle raised her voice for issues that concerned her. After she was diagnosed with pancreatic cancer and had only a few months to live, she was very concerned about being a burden to her children. Although I hoped she would spend the last weeks and moments of her life at my home (which she did), my Mother insisted on visiting end-of-life hospice facilities. So I dutifully took her to several. I will never forget sitting in a small office and listening while she asked about the cost of care at the facility. The answers offered by the earnest young man who was showing us around were too vague for my Mother. I said nothing, simply watching his reactions, as she continued to probe for specifics on cost. He clearly thought the elderly woman asking so many questions simply needed to be reassured. "It won't cost you *anything.* Medicare will pay for it all," he finally told her. The look on his face was priceless when she responded, "I am an American taxpayer. Who do you think pays for Medicare? I want to know how much all of this will cost." Isabel was never afraid to speak up, to stand up, and to be counted.

As Isabel Molloy Doyle's daughter, I grew up watching a strong woman effectively raise her voice. She spoke up to teachers, priests, elected officials, neighbors, and, of course, my Dad. But she (usually!) did it strategically. And she was not one to defend her kids unconditionally. If we asked for her to take our side, we'd better be telling her the whole truth and nothing but the truth before she did. As a parent, she held her children accountable for our actions. It was an empowering experience to know that my Mother had our backs and wouldn't hesitate to stand up to authority for her family and also for others who couldn't speak up for themselves, especially underdogs. That's leadership.

One of my favorite examples of an *Influential Insider* who knows how to raise her voice effectively is MSNBC commentator Rachel Maddow. You don't have to agree with her politics to appreciate her verbal skills. Maddow vaulted to her own prime-time, daily TV show by going toe-to-toe with much more seasoned political commentators, all men of course. Some of the guys were stunned and outraged by the audacity of the lesbian Rhodes Scholar who refused to be intimidated, talked over, or shouted down—something they had been doing to numerous other female commentators for years. When her male colleagues raised their voices, so did Maddow. Plus, she had plenty to say, didn't get ruffled by all their bluster, and did it all with a grin.

If you're going to play hardball with the guys, that's what it takes. Be on the lookout for women who raise their voices—well. If you don't have good role models around, tune in to the nightly political talk shows and find a woman whose style you like. Watch her. Learn from her. Then raise your own voice. Early and often.

Join the Collective Chorus

Have you ever heard yourself saying, perhaps to your children, "Don't make me raise my voice"? I'd call it a soft threat. You know what I'm talking about. You really don't want to escalate things. You'd prefer that everybody just cooperate and work together to get things done. But in competitive, professional environments, just as in families, it's rarely that easy. Every now and then you have to get everybody's attention and raise your voice. The American Suffragettes raised their voices and rocked the boat for nearly 75 years, finally winning the right to vote in 1920. African-American women and their sisters who supported them raised their voices and faced snarling police dogs, fire hoses, and lynch mobs during the Civil Rights movement in the 1950s and 1960s. And millions of American women and girls raised their voices again in the 1970s, standing up to mocking, hostility, sexual harassment, and professional ostracism to fight for their rights to employment opportunities, credit, protection from rape and equal opportunity in education, including athletics. All of those giant forward steps in our society's evolution were achieved because courageous females—and the men who supported them—spoke up and worked collectively to challenge and change the status quo.

Women of achievement have been too "well-behaved" and way too quiet in this country for a couple of decades now. We have passively allowed men to remain the dominant "deciders." Yet, as one crisis after another has piled up, it is practically impossible to ignore whose handiwork has gotten us into this mess. In the wake of the 2008 meltdown and bankruptcy of Lehman Brothers, once one of Wall Street's most powerful global financial services firms, one clever commentator quipped, "What would have been different if it had been Lehman Brothers and Sisters making the decisions?" Even *Time* magazine noted in May 2010, ". . . the financial wreckage littering our world is the creation, almost exclusively, of men, not women."[7] How much worse do the economy, the environment, our education system, and global conflicts have to get before women step in and step up to leading equally, side-by-side with men? It's time for American women to raise our voices, collectively, once again. Start by strengthening your own vocal cords. Then join the chorus.

Raise Your Voice:

- ✓ Polish communications skills
- ✓ Overcome fear
- ✓ Articulate your vision
- ✓ Grow Teflon skin
- ✓ Join the collective chorus

CHAPTER 9

Break the Rules

You can't break the rules until you know how to play the game.
— RICKIE LEE JONES,
American Singer and Songwriter, *Interloper*

In the spring of 1979, a young TV journalist stood in a chilly, concrete corridor in a major league baseball stadium. She was staring straight ahead, ignoring the men who were rushing past her through a door labeled *Detroit Tigers Clubhouse.* It might as well have read *Women, Enter at Your Own Risk.* For the other journalists on deadline—all men—the post-game sports reporting ritual of interviewing partially clothed and, yes, even naked athletes in locker rooms was as natural as scribbling quotes in their notebooks. Few had any interest in the emotions or sweaty fear that gripped the young woman who was practically hyperventilating as she tried to find the courage to walk through those doors and face whatever was waiting for her on the other side.

Why didn't that *Interloper* just walk away, avoid the conflict, and go back to TV news where she was more welcome? I can answer that question because I am that woman, one of the first female TV sports broadcasters to work in a major market in the United States. I was offered the groundbreaking opportunity in November 1978 by Mike Von Ende, the news director at WJBK-TV, the CBS affiliate in Detroit. The moment he offered me the job, I knew we'd be breaking an unwritten rule of that era: *women can't cover sports.*

A highly visible, on-camera job as a TV sports broadcaster was considered off-limits for women in the late 1970s and early 1980s. The locker rooms weren't the only obstacles. Sports fans were brutally skeptical, as well. If a male announcer made an on-air mistake, it was considered a slip of the tongue. If a woman made a similar mistake, there were instant howls that she didn't know what she was talking about. Just to make sure that the few women who managed to get sports jobs (most were at newspapers) understood they were "out of bounds," professional and college teams routinely refused women equal access to athletes. Post-game, locker room interviews have long been an essential part of covering sports. But the prospect of female reporters entering those sacred male sanctums was highly controversial, even among most male journalists. Some felt women had no business covering sports. Others were concerned that complaints about unequal treatment of female journalists would eventually lead to the locker rooms being closed to both genders. As one of his sports broadcasting peers angrily told my father after I had been hired, "You've got to stop your daughter. She's going to wreck it for all of us."

As I sat in Mike Von Ende's office listening to his job offer, I was well aware that a potentially precedent setting lawsuit on the issue was working its way through the federal courts. *Sports Illustrated* reporter Melissa Ludtke, backed by her employer, Time, Inc., was suing the New York Yankees and Baseball Commissioner Bowie Kuhn for refusing her equal locker room access during the 1977 World Series. Talk about leading the way by breaking the rules! Before I signed up for what I knew would be combat duty, I told Mike Von Ende, "Let me think about it overnight."

"How did your interview go today, Annie?" was the first thing my father asked me over dinner. "Great," I told him. "They offered me a job." Then I dropped the bombshell: "But it's not as a news reporter. They want me to cover sports." My father put down his fork, looked me in the eye, and said, "Really?" He paused only a few seconds before telling me, "You take it." "But Dad, if I do, I'll have to get into this whole locker room issue," I warned him.

Vince Doyle understood as well as anyone the furor that a woman fighting for locker room access would trigger. At the time, my father was the sports director at WWJ radio, the major news/talk station in Detroit, the immediate past president of the Detroit Sports Broadcasters Association and a highly respected dean of the local sports scene. But he didn't hesitate in his advice, telling me, "Absolutely, you have to go in those locker rooms. You'll have no credibility as a sports reporter if you don't." I took the job. One of the first things I did was meet with the general managers and athletic directors for Michigan's major professional and college teams. They were all cordial, but several reacted as Tigers General Manager Jim Campbell did when I requested credentials for locker room access. Campbell pulled the cigar out of his mouth, leaned across his desk and jabbed the cigar in my face as he snarled, "Over my dead body you'll go in our Tiger clubhouse."

Just months later, after the U.S. Supreme Court refused to re-consider a decision by NY federal Judge Constance Baker Motley who ruled that the Yankees had violated Ludtke's constitutional rights, teams all over the country were faced with a defining moment: Allow female reporters to enter their locker rooms or keep male reporters out, too.[1] The Tiger's GM was constantly popping Tums on Opening Day, 1979—as one columnist reported—but when confronted with federal law, he changed his mind and announced that women reporters would have equal locker room access "on a trial basis." Jim Campbell survived the season and the world didn't come to an end.

Sports locker rooms in the late 1970s and early 1980s offered rich lessons for the few female journalists who dared break the rules and insist on entering those male sanctums. At the time, American women were breaking new ground on nearly every professional front. It took just as much gumption and chutzpah to be the lone woman lawyer in the courtroom, surgeon in the operating room, police officer on the squad, or factory worker on the assembly line as it did for me to enter a locker room. Sometimes we seek challenges and at other times they find us. I took one of the most daunting jobs of my career because the doors to sports journalism needed to be opened to women. And I knew if anyone could do it, I could. It wasn't until decades later that I realized what a valuable leadership crucible I had waded into. Learning how and when to strategically *break the rules* is a skill women leaders must master earlier than most men.

Be a Game Changer

Ask any *Interloper* if she ever broke any rules, particularly early in her career, and chances are you'll hear some great stories. Women who helped open professional doors of opportunity in the 1970s and 1980s were breaking rules left and right. We couldn't shy away from controversy or healthy conflict. By the time *Insiders* were coming out of school and beginning their careers, however, the U.S. work environment and social attitudes about women's places were changing dramatically. And *Innovators,* such as 24-year-old graduate student Nicole Marble, can barely believe the stories of the blatant discrimination and sexual harassment that their more seasoned professional sisters once routinely faced. "I never felt because I'm a woman, especially a young woman, that I wasn't taken seriously," Marble told me. "I don't see many barriers anymore."

As a result, *Insiders* and *Innovators*, in particular, often underestimate the importance of knowing how and when to strategically break the rules. "Young women today don't know how to fight," is the way *USA Today* sports columnist Christine Brennan puts it. The founding president of Women in Sports Media, Brennan has blazed a wide trail during her over four decades as a highly-visible and often outspoken journalist.

"I've fought for women in sports media throughout all of my career. I'm astonished at the void of women today who have the fight, the savvy about working the system and the sense of purpose that 'we're all in this together.' The void is as big as the Pacific Ocean—whether its sports, business or politics." Brennan points to the lack of outrage about the increasing numbers of crude and hostile comments posted on the internet under columns, particularly those written by female journalists. "What is allowed to be said about women would never be allowed to be said about African Americans or a particular religious or ethnic group," Brennan says. "I feel strongly that if you are not going to be advocates, if you're not going to make your voice be heard, then you will have limited success."

There are opportunities everywhere to be a catalyst for change by engaging in strategic rule breaking. All that's required is the courage and leadership savvy to act. One area crying out for large numbers of women to become game changers is the good old work/life conundrum. As long as work cultures continue to favor men with stay-at-home wives, women will struggle with the push/pull conflict between personal priorities and professional goals. For nearly ten years, I have observed how a highly-regarded Washington, D.C. *Insider* and mother of two young boys has successfully negotiated staying in a job she loves while achieving the flexibility she craved to enjoy her parenting years. She preferred not to be quoted, but she is passionate about the need for women to lead culture change within their own organizations. So, she was happy to share what she has learned about how to make it work. Here are her recommendations:

Begin with the right attitude. "Go into a discussion with your management about a flexible work schedule with the attitude that you will do whatever it takes to make the situation work. My validation that this can work is that over nine years, no balls have ever dropped."

Earn your stripes before you ask to re-write the rules. "You have to have a track record with your company and have earned their trust in the level and quality of work you do. It's unrealistic to expect you are going to get accommodations before you've proven yourself over a period of time."

Be flexible. "Your work demands and home life may dictate regular adjustments. What works the first year may change the next. Family years are times of constant transition. Schedules can always be re-evaluated and tweaked. There is no one-size-fits-all solution."

Hold your company accountable for its public image. "Is your company winning awards for being family friendly, but the internal reality is that people are made to feel as if they are cutting deals under the table, can't talk openly with HR about best practices in other parts of the company, or fear they will be slow-tracked if they take advantage of flexible work programs? Don't be afraid to point that out. Help your employer find ways to live up to the spirit of their public claims."

Encourage transparency. "The knee-jerk reaction from management is nearly always, 'If I do this for you, I'm going to have a line out the door.'" My response is, 'You have to take it on a case-by-case basis. Don't be afraid to try with one because of what may or may not come down the line.' And don't keep breakthroughs you achieve secret. Share information with others on how you made it work. Help management become comfortable with seeing flexibility as a highly effective and creative way of getting work done without losing top talent."

Even today, when half of all U.S. workers are women and four in ten mothers are either bringing home as much (or more) than their spouses or are the sole breadwinners, women continue to shoulder the majority of all family caretaking, not to mention having primary biological responsibility for re-populating the human race. Work cultures designed decades ago for white, middle-class men with stay-at-home wives no longer work for the majority of the new American workforce. We need game changers willing to use their hard-earned influence to work individually and collectively within their organizations and our society to achieve systemic change. And don't allow the change to be about special accommodations for women. The focus should be on *family* and *life* flexibility for men and women.

One of the best stories I ever heard of a woman playing the leadership game her own way belongs to *Influential Insider* and banking executive Sandy Pierce. Just a few hours after giving birth to her third child, Pierce received a phone call in her hospital room from her boss. "I thought he was calling to congratulate me. He wasn't," Pierce recalled about that morning over a decade ago. "He never said one thing about my son. He simply wanted to know when the bank could announce my next big promotion." Pierce, who today is CEO of Charter One Financial, Inc, was stunned. "I was so teed off that I wanted to resign on the spot," she told me. Instead, she kept her cool and told her boss, "I'll have to think about it." That's when she decided to break the rules for navigating the executive fast track.

"I called him at five the next morning to inform him that he couldn't make the announcement because I wasn't going to take the job. I then gave him the names of several other excellent candidates for the position. I showed no emotion, telling him that they were all terrific people. I then said breezily, 'I have to go now. I'm breast-feeding.'" Sandy Pierce's unexpected response stopped her boss in his tracks. And that was just the beginning of her going rogue. A few days later, when she returned to work, Pierce asked to see the CEO. "When I walked in, I had my resignation letter in my hand and told him, 'You can either accept my resignation or find me another position within our bank. I will not work for that (expletive deleted).'" Point made. To his credit, the leader confronted with Pierce's ultimatum wasted no time in finding a new position—and a new boss—for a future chief executive officer.

Pierce loves telling that story to audiences of professional women. They inevitably roar with joy over the clarity and courage with which she broke the rules in order to manage the changing rhythms and priorities of her life. The youngest of ten children and the first in her family to attend college, she believes to the tips of her red high-heels that "It's important to know when you have to back away from something. I did it several times in my career. But taking a side-step and charting your own course doesn't have to mean giving up or walking away," Pierce says. And she encourages those who work for her to follow her lead.

"It's a risk [to lead culture change]," says *Insider* Miriam Muley who has held senior marketing positions at several Fortune 500 corporations. "When you've worked so hard and gotten so far, you just don't want to jeopardize it. That's the real distinction of a leader: someone who is willing to help right the wrongs in an organization. I don't mean doing it blindly. You have to do it in way that leverages your business savvy and understanding of the politics of the organization, while still being steadfast in achieving your mission." Strategically breaking the rules—not just for yourself but to achieve systemic change that benefits others—is leadership in action.

First, Master the Game

Every woman who has dared push the edges of gender boundaries for cultural change knows there's little room for error. Believing you can play the game your own way before making sure you have what one executive called the necessary "table stakes" behind you is a critical mistake. It's essential that aspiring leaders earn the respect of those above, below, and beside them before they start trying to change the game. You also need to make sure you've built relationships with influential allies who believe in you and can provide valuable guidance when you start venturing into uncharted waters.

Sandy Pierce had already built a strong reputation within her company; had developed relationships with key allies, including the CEO; and had earned her stripes as a top performer when she turned down a major promotion and took a side-step on her company's fast track, after the birth of her son. She knew that working for a boss who had no interest in her life beyond the office would be stifling. Pierce had earned the power to break the rules when she needed to. She had the courage to take the risk. And she acted strategically, planning her own path to the top rather than allowing others to chart all of her moves. She mastered the game before she started breaking the rules.

The same was true for me. Before I stepped across the threshold of my first locker room, I already had nearly ten years of experience under my belt as a TV news street reporter. And, growing up as Vince Doyle's daughter, sports was part of our family DNA. I'll never forget the Sunday evening that I watched my mother pile every piece of sports equipment she could find—baseball mitts, basketballs, football helmets, even ice skates—onto our dining room table. My Dad made the mistake of walking in and asking, "Hi Isabel, what's for dinner?" She pointed to the table and growled, "That's what's for dinner. It's what we have for dinner every night!" Vince Doyle's kids might not have been great athletes, but we knew a lot about sports. Nevertheless, the morning after I accepted the TV sports job at Channel 2, my Dad walked into our kitchen and dropped a huge pile of magazines and newspapers on the table in front of me. It was dozens of back issues of *Sports Illustrated*, *Hockey News*, *Basketball Weekly*, and the industry bible, the *Sporting News*. "Start reading," he told me simply.

Expect the Heat and Take It

If you think the second leadership practice, *Raising Your Voice,* is tough, wait till you see what happens when you start breaking the rules. Sometimes, the consequences are immediate and open. Other times, they are covert, even subconscious on some people's parts, and it may take you a while to sense them. Not everyone will appreciate your leadership when you start straying from the beaten path. So you'd better be ready to take the heat. I learned this lesson during my first season covering the Detroit Tigers.

Locker rooms after games, particularly after wins, can be noisy, crowded places with music playing, athletes joking with one another and reporters going from locker to locker to interview players. Several months into the 1979 baseball season, I was starting to get my sports "sea legs," and the players were beginning to accept me as a professional.

One afternoon, my cameraman and I were doing an interview with Tiger catcher Lance Parrish. Lance was standing at his locker and I was facing him with my back to the rest of the room. Suddenly, a loud voice sliced through the racket yelling, "This is a fucking *man's* locker room." Every conversation in the room suddenly stopped. I turned around to see Kirk Gibson, a hot-tempered rookie who had just joined the Tigers after graduating from Michigan State University. Gibson had been a star college athlete, pursued by teams from both the National Football League (NFL) and Major League baseball. He was hot stuff and had the arrogant attitude that often comes with it.

Gibson was strolling across the locker room heading toward the showers. He was wearing a white terry cloth towel slung across one shoulder—and nothing else. Every eye in the room was on him as he repeated his message in a loud voice. "This is a fucking *man's* locker room. Get the fucking *pussy* out of here." Gibson wasn't looking at me, but I was the only female anywhere around, so there was no question that I was his target. I turned back to Parrish whose face was beet red. One of the best catchers in the major leagues at the time, Lance was a classy, low-key, gentle giant who led with his actions and few words. He looked me in the eye and said simply, "He doesn't speak for all of us."

I stood my ground, refusing to allow a hot-head rookie to intimidate me, and did a few more interviews. But I was embarrassed and fuming as I left the locker room. That evening, I called my father to tell him what happened. "Dad, I don't have to take this. I think Jim Campbell [Tiger GM] and Sparky Anderson [Tiger Manager] should know what happened. What do you think I should do?" "You do absolutely nothing. Don't go running to management to protect you. You're being tested. You have to face the heat and prove you can take whatever they throw at you," he told me. I didn't always understand my father's advice, but I trusted him. I let the incident drop and simply ignored Gibson the next few times I saw him.

A few weeks later, I learned how wise my father's advice had been. For all of his attitude, Gibson was one of those great competitors who consistently came through with big plays in key situations. I was covering a game when he pulled off a classic Gibby move, hitting a come-from-behind, game-winning home run. Afterward, there was a huge scrum of reporters squeezed around his locker all trying to get a quote from the game-winning player. I started pushing my way through the pack to get my mike close enough to pick up Gibson's comments and, I hoped, to give my cameraman a clear shot of his face, rather than the back of other reporters' heads. When he spotted me, Gibson stopped the interview, looked at me, and said, "Anne, you don't have to push your way through all of these smelly guys. Just hang on a minute and I'll talk with you." He finished answering the other reporters' questions then stepped away from the group and said to me, "OK, what do you want to know, Anne?" I had an exclusive, one-on-one interview with the star of the game.

What's the insight I learned from that experience? Two things. First, when you start breaking rules and blazing new trails, you're going to be tested. Expect that. Leaders are always reminded, "If you can't take the heat, get out of the kitchen." The best response I've ever heard to that line came from presidential candidate Hillary Clinton who told reporters wondering if she'd wither in the increasing heat of the campaign, "I'm very comfortable in the kitchen." Second, when those tests come, recognize them for what they are: potential springboard moments that can lift you to a higher level. Even if you fail, they are still valuable "mirror moments" that often reflect back important insight about what you need to work on before you're ready for the next step up. That's why it's so important to have mentors and allies you can turn to for wise counsel. By following my father's advice and not running to management to complain (or whine!), I not only passed Gibson's test, I earned a few credibility points with other players who watched how I handled the pressure.

I covered Kirk Gibson for five years. He was one of the greatest competitors I've ever known—one of those "big-play athletes" who wants to be up to bat when the game is on the line and consistently deliver under pressure. We never talked about the "pussy" incident. There was no point.

I had passed his test. Once you take the leadership step of breaking rules, don't be surprised when you start feeling the heat and your tests come. Welcome them. If you keep walking through the fire, just like tempered steel, you'll come out stronger on the other side.

Resist the Herd Mentality and Think for Yourself

Breaking the rules can also mean making a daring decision in a high-stakes time of crisis. Barbara Barrett was not yet 30 years old and a new member of the Civil Aeronautics Board (CAB) in Washington, D.C., when she came face-to-face with a defining moment. The year was 1983. The Soviet Union had just triggered an international crisis by shooting down a Korean airliner over the Kamchhaka Peninsula. The CAB needed to take immediate action to diplomatically signal the United States' strong displeasure with the Soviet action. The risks and stakes were high. And the CAB's response had implications for potentially hundreds of thousands of global air travelers. The decision fell to Barrett. "Normally, I would not have been the pivotal decision maker," she told me. "However, the crisis occurred when more senior CAB members were travelling and unreachable. Turnaround time was critical."

With a presidential announcement to the world news media looming within the hour, Barrett and the CAB management team deliberated a key piece of the U.S. reaction. The consensus of Barrett's colleagues was in one direction: toward *immediately* grounding flights and dishonoring tickets. Should she go along with that political consensus or delay implementation of a presidential directive in order to protect the travelling public?

What did Barrett do? She listened to input from the entire management team, yet thought for herself. "I heard them all out, but I felt the right answer was to protect travelers by delaying implementation of their recommendation until passengers, airlines and travel agents could make other flight arrangements." After a full discussion and robust questioning, she thanked the team and asked to confer privately with a CAB executive in whose judgment she had the utmost confidence. "I said to him, 'You and I usually agree on issues. In this case, however, I come to a different conclusion. I want you to give me your best professional reasoning behind that recommendation. Walk me through your thinking.'" He did. Barrett was not persuaded. She bucked the group, including much more seasoned advisers and resisted the pressure to go with the political response. Her practical solution (announcing that flights would cease and tickets would be dishonored in the future) was equally effective at making the point to the Soviets.

"The solution I advocated carried serious political risk because it could appear as though the CAB was selecting only a mild rebuke. But the other option would have stranded unsuspecting, innocent airline travelers all over the world," Barrett said. "We found a way to follow the President's direction *and* do the right thing to protect the public and confidence in the airline system, rather than what might have been safer or more politically expeditious." Over 25 years later, Barrett is still cautious about sharing all the inside details of the high stakes, international incident, but is very comfortable with the outcome. "I think that everyone on that team would say, in retrospect, that it was the right decision at the time. When faced with a tough decision, I focus on the overall mission. I keep asking myself, 'What are we really trying to do here?'"

How does a 30-year-old leader have the courage and strength to take command, think for herself and go against the unified advice of even more senior colleagues? A look back at Barbara Barrett's childhood provides plenty of clues. She grew up helping her former cowboy father run their family's modest riding stable in Pennsylvania. When her father died, Barrett, at age 13, became the sole support of her mother and five brothers and sisters. "At that point in my life, the mission was to stay in business, keep the horses healthy and have customers enjoy their ride." Barrett didn't let anything stop her from accomplishing that mission, not even college football players twice her size. Even as a teenager, the future, global leader didn't hesitate to tell anyone who was abusing a horse to "Get off and walk back."

Barbara Barrett had a head start on thinking for herself and resisting group think in order to do what she believed was right. She's a remarkable leader whose career has included serving as Deputy Administrator of the Federal Aviation Administration, U.S. Ambassador to Finland, president of the International Women's Forum, teaching leadership at Harvard's Kennedy School and, coming full circle in her life, CEO of Triple Creek Guest Ranch in Montana. An instrument-rated pilot, she is the first civilian woman to land in an F/A-18 Hornet on an aircraft carrier and is certified for space flight as an astronaut. She also happens to be married to Craig Barrett, CEO of Intel. The two of them met at the top of a mountain they were each hiking alone.

Barrett's a believer that everyone's formative years are pivotal. "I've heard it said that the harder your teen years are the more successful your adult years will be. And the easier your teen years are the less likely you are going to have smooth sailing in your adult life," she says. Regardless of whether you were tested by fire at a young age or are just beginning to push your personal limits, every leader needs to develop the confidence and courage to think for herself so that she is ready to break the rules, if necessary, when opportunity knocks or crisis strikes.

Small Rule Breaking Can Lead to Big Change

Opportunities to be a catalyst for change are all around you. Small actions can make a big difference. And that's how you build your leadership muscles. Numerous repetitions with smaller challenges will prepare you to be fit and ready when the big ones show up. Even in times of personal pain, taking a risk to make a difference that's bigger than yourself often pays unexpected dividends.

After the death of her young son in a car accident, the Honorable Hilda Gage, a pioneering appellate court judge who became the first woman chair of the National Conference of State Trial Judges, sought solace at her temple. "I went to services every day for months. At that time, it was all men. The women didn't go. The men embraced and welcomed me," Judge Gage (recently deceased) recalled. But something started to bother her. "There was a prayer that they said in Hebrew every day. I finally asked someone, 'What does that prayer say?' I was told it meant, 'Thank you God for not making me a woman.'" Rather than letting that daily insult eat away at her, the grieving mother took action. "I went to see the rabbi's wife. "The two of us had stickers made up in Hebrew that read, 'Thank you God for making me a Jew.' We put them over the line in every single prayer book in our temple." Two women's quiet act of breaking the rules by changing one offensive word in prayer books used by hundreds, perhaps thousands of worshippers over the years had a huge impact. It also helped heal a mother's broken heart. "I was more peaceful about my son after that," Gage remembered.

Here's another example. While I was writing this chapter, a 22-year-old *Innovator* who had just graduated from Chicago's Loyola University suggested that she would love me to speak to her professional business fraternity, Alpha Kappa Psi, during my book tour. "Our chapter is nearly all women. We've had a lot of trouble getting men to become members," Rabecca Heithoff, a social networking expert with a degree in public relations and advertising, told me. "But I thought you said it was a fraternity, not a sorority. If you are all women, why aren't you called 'sisters' instead of 'brothers?'" I asked her. "It started as a male fraternity many years ago before women were allowed to join," she explained. "Even today, we're all called 'brothers.'" Did being called a brother ever bother her, I wondered? "It did in the beginning," Rabecca acknowledged. "But after about a year I got used to it. And none of the other women in our chapter ever seemed to mind."

What a perfect opportunity, I thought, for an *Innovator* to gain some valuable rule-breaking experience by insisting that it was high time for Alpha Kappa Psi to admit the obvious and acknowledge their fraternity now includes *sisters.* I encouraged her to take the issue on. "Rabecca, what do you think would happen if you and the other members of your campus chapter simply broke that ridiculous, outdated rule and called your members sisters and brothers? Do you think the national organization would kick out all of the dues-paying members who rocked the boat?" "Well, if they did that would mean the end of our chapter because it's practically all women," she told me. "You have a leadership opportunity right in front of you," I told her. "It's staring you in the face, waiting for the right person—female or male—to come along and say, 'This is ridiculous.' Women are not brothers and they shouldn't be demeaned by calling them male names."

As one of seven children, I learned long ago that brothers and sisters can be allies just as bonded and powerful as a band of brothers. There's a very simple test that I apply when considering whether to make an issue of a gender question. Flip the situation around and imagine how men would react if they were told they had to be called *sisters* in order to be part of a professional networking organization. Can you imagine the outrage? "They wouldn't tolerate it for an instant," Rabecca realized immediately. "They'd consider it an insult to their masculinity."

At this writing, the Web site of Alpha Kappa Psi (http://www.akpsi.org) still reads "Network with other brothers, stay up-to-date with news . . . and much more." But the reaction of the young, highly educated, and ambitious woman to my probing gave me hope that the consciousness of *Innovators* is on the rise. "I can't believe how I'm reacting to the issues you're raising. This is really stirring up a lot of feelings I didn't know I had," Heithoff told me. "I'm going to talk about this with my fraternity *sisters*."

There is still plenty of embedded sexism left in American culture. Don't underestimate the impact you can make through the power of words. They shape and reflect attitudes. Today, we commonly use the phrase "he or she" to acknowledge that human beings come in two genders. Yet it wasn't that long ago that grammarians (mostly male, no doubt) insisted that "he" was a gender-inclusive pronoun. It took collective rule breaking by thousands of writers, reporters, and speakers to change our language. When the *New York Times* and the *Associated*

Press finally broke down and started using "he/she," even the grammarians were forced to catch up.

Don't Get Too Far Out on a Limb

Breaking the rules nearly always involves some level of risk. To be effective, leaders must use this tool strategically. Sometimes, that means not getting too far out in front of those you're counting on to follow you. "Going out on a limb is just an exercise in risk taking that may not be rewarded if you don't enlist others to participate with you," advises *Interloper* Patty DeDominic, founder of PDQ Personnel Services, Inc. and CT Engineering, which she eventually sold to Select Staffing Inc. This highly-respected California leader and entrepreneur learned the "out on a limb lesson" during an executive leadership course at Harvard. "At the time, I believed the only way you really make a difference is by going way out there and calling everybody out," DeDominic told me. She changed her mind after listening carefully to her instructor, a professor at the Kennedy School of Government where he often taught leaders from emerging democracies. "If leaders in developing countries get too far out ahead of their supporters, they could get shot or have a military coup. Leadership isn't always quite that dangerous, but any leader can still get 'shot at' whether they're out on a limb or not," DeDominic learned. "It was an epiphany for me to realize that believing with all your heart that something is right and needed doesn't always mean it's the right thing to do at that time."

An individual *Achiever* can charge off on her own. A *Leader*, on the other hand, must often build consensus around her vision and solutions first.

Te Toca

There is an expression in Spanish that I love. "Te toca" translates literally as "it touches you" and is a way of saying, "It's your turn." Its full meaning, however, is more profound. It's a lovely and simple way of saying that a challenge or opportunity has your name on it. *This one's for you.*

Our culture doesn't raise women to take risks the way we encourage boys and men to do. If you believe you have what it takes to lead, don't leave it to your role models and sheroes—be they Hillary, Sarah, Michelle, Sonya Sotomayor, Oprah, or your most inspiring mentor—to do all the heavy lifting to move women forward. We need women at every level who are courageous enough to veer from well-worn paths, to take calculated risks, and to venture where few have gone. This inevitably means questioning "the way we've always done things" and inspiring others to join you in pushing the edges of possibility. When opportunities knock for you to be a change agent, do you turn away because breaking the rules is just too hard? Or do you open the door and take a risk? Remember, well-behaved women seldom make history. Te toca.

Break the Rules

- ✓ Be a game changer
- ✓ First, master the game
- ✓ Expect the heat
- ✓ Think for yourself
- ✓ Don't get too far out on a limb
- ✓ Te toca

CHAPTER 10

Claim Power

The thing women have yet to learn is this: Nobody gives you power. You just take it.
— ROSEANNE BARR, American Comedian, *Insider*

Barbara McQuade remembers very clearly the moment she made up her mind to become the U.S. attorney for the Eastern District of Michigan. "It was the day I didn't get the criminal chief job," she told the *Detroit Free Press* a few days after she was sworn in as the first female to lead the U.S. Justice Department's 115-attorney office in Detroit.[1] Rather than internalizing her frustration and getting angry over not landing a senior position, McQuade used her disappointment as fuel to turbo-charge herself, over the next two years, into the top job. More than two dozen lawyers were competing for the prestigious and powerful position. When it came time for the interviews, McQuade was the only one who showed up with a detailed blueprint of how she would reform the office. She even gave a draft of her plan to the selection committee members ahead of time so they could ask better questions of all the candidates. "What she did was virtually unheard of," said one member of the committee, after the 45-year-old mother of four clinched support from the nomination committee for the presidential appointment. Along with a host of other complex cases, McQuade's office is now responsible for the federal government's prosecution of Umar Farouk Abdulmutallab. The Nigerian national is charged with trying to blow up a plane landing in Detroit on Christmas Day 2009—just a few days before McQuade stepped into the powerful position she sought and claimed.

Don't Wait to be Chosen

Leaders can't sit around and wait to be chosen. They have to "power up" themselves. Men grow up learning that lesson. By the time they reach adulthood, most men have years of experience elbowing their way through the competitive male hierarchies they routinely encounter. They also have thousands of role models from throughout history and contemporary life to emulate and imprint the notion that the "natural order" is for men to aspire to and assume power. By comparison, most women are unseasoned rookies at the power games played every day in primarily-male work environments.

The way women relate with one another has been characterized by social behavior researchers as much closer to a web of intersecting, cooperative relationships. We've also been socialized for centuries to defer to men, often unconsciously. And our mental images of powerful foremothers, female historical figures, and contemporary examples of women in command are in scarce supply. Claiming power in mixed gender groups is counter-intuitive even for many high-achieving women. Donna Brazile, a nationally respected political strategist and syndicated columnist, gave a personal example to *Oprah* magazine of how women often unconsciously take a backseat. "Years ago at an important political strategy meeting, I found that a place hadn't been set for me at the table. I moved toward the line of chairs ringing the room until I thought: 'Hey! No man would do that!' So I pushed aside a place card and sat down. If you want a seat at the power table," Brazile advises, "take one."[2]

Yes, more of us than ever are earning seats at the tables of influence. But as long as we wait to be *chosen* for leadership roles, based on merit, we'll remain in our present "team member" positions, while men will continue to muscle their way to the top. The willingness and ability to *Claim Power* is a skill women leaders must add to their repertoire and keep practicing until it becomes second nature.

"Power exists. Somebody is going to have it, so why not you?" asks Kim Campbell, the first (and to date) only woman prime minister of Canada and founding member of the Club of Madrid, an invitation-only organization of former heads of state and government working to strengthen democracy in the world. Campbell recognizes power for what it is: capital for making a difference. "I love power," she told me. "I want it. I'm power hungry. Not for myself but because when I have power I can accomplish things. I can serve my community, I can help open doors for deserving people and I can influence decisions. If you think you would exercise it ethically, don't disdain power. You must embrace it as the essential currency for making things happen."

For centuries, the words *power* and *masculinity* have been synonymous, while *femininity* and *power* were considered a virtual oxymoron. While women have always had power, it was primarily confined to private life. No wonder we're still on a steep learning curve when it comes to visualizing ourselves in command. This chapter is a guide through the cultural labyrinth that women must still negotiate on our paths to power. To master this practice, you'll need plenty of confidence, courage, and role models. And just as important as claiming power is using it—frequently—once you have it.

Are Leaders Born or Developed?

The answer to the age-old question "Are leaders born or developed?" is: both. "The idea of taking charge, being the one out front is something that I believe is driven from within. It's a need. Leaders are born," says auto industry CEO Kathleen Ligocki. "People can be groomed to become better leaders. They can learn important skill sets. I don't believe at all that it's gender related. A lot of girls have it when they are very young, but then lose it because we are socialized so differently than boys."

Women leaders have been around for centuries. However, because opportunities have been so limited for us to achieve positions of authority in paid, predominantly male environments, women with the drive and skills to lead have tended to funnel their abilities into family, church, or civic organizations. Not everyone who feels the *need* to be in charge, however, has the skills, savvy, and experience to lead well. Our most visible examples are politicians who aspire to higher levels but aren't ready. What about women *Achievers* who sense they are ready? "Don't shy away from leadership," Ligocki advises. "You'll learn on the job just like the guys do. Raise your hand and say, 'Pick me.'"

I would add one further point to her advice. Take a very realistic look at the opportunities and paths in your present work environment for women—at every level and in every function—to develop their leadership skills. Start at the top. How many women are on the board? If less than one-third of your directors are female, their influence is limited, and your company may be doing little more than checking the female box. How many women hold officer and senior executive positions? When was the last time those percentages increased? What mentoring and high-level networking opportunities are in place to give women equal access to influential allies and powerful sponsors who are still predominantly men? How many male leaders in your organization believe their teams are diverse if they have merely one woman and perhaps a person of color among their predominantly white, male lieutenants? How many executives have promoted several women and minorities to their leadership teams? Do you have an influential male champion who will openly advocate for your advancement when opportunities arise?

If you are getting a queasy feeling in your stomach as you think of the answers to these questions, you may want to ask yourself whether you are in the right place. Investing your energy and time in an organization that values female *Achievers* but is still wearing cultural blinders about *why* increasing the number of women *Leaders* is a strategic advantage is a dead-end street. It may be time to take another kind of risk and look for more fertile leadership pastures.

On the other hand, perhaps your work environment is one where you can see multiple paths for high-performing women and individuals of color to develop and strengthen their leadership skills. If so, raise your hand and go for it. Don't wait for someone else to recognize your leadership potential. Ask for more responsibility. Volunteer for stretch, high-risk assignments that will broaden, deepen, and hone your leadership skills. And when you get them, be sure to negotiate a raise and title that reflect your increased responsibilities. *Women Don't Ask: Negotiation and the Gender Divide* is an excellent resource for strengthening your negotiation skills.[3] "Recent changes in workplace culture are making it essential for women to exercise far more control over their careers than in the past," write authors Linda Babcock and Sara Laschever. "At the same time, ongoing changes in the roles women play at home force them to manage a clamor of conflicting commitments in their lives. In the midst of so much rapid-fire professional and personal change, negotiation is no longer optional. It's become a basic survival skill."

Ambition, the drive to be the one in charge, and the courage to claim power by asking for what you want are not unfeminine. They are the qualities of winners and leaders—regardless of gender.

The Courage to Take Command

"You've got to have the confidence to be comfortable with command positions and want to be the one in charge. If you are not in charge, you are one of the team," says Air Force Brigadier General Barbara Faulkenberry. "To truly shape an organization and take it or an issue in the direction you believe it should go, you've got to be the leader. Standing up and saying, 'Give me the stick. I can make this work' is the key."

Once we understand the cultural muck we must slog through to even begin visualizing ourselves as leaders with power, how do we find the courage to go for it? For answers, I turned to Faulkenberry and other women officers in the Armed Services whose job it is to teach leadership.

"The opportunities that I have had and my success in many command positions almost surprises me," says Faulkenberry, an *Insider* and navigator who graduated from the Air Force Academy in 1982. "The military prepares you about 75 percent for the next step, with experiences, training and development. The system gives you responsibility and perches you on the end of the limb. If you believe in yourself and your ability to handle and master the other 25 percent, you jump out into leadership positions you've never done before. And sure enough, you excel." Faulkenberry believes women don't go after leadership opportunities as they should. "It's either lack of confidence in themselves or no one has ever told them that they can do it. Women need to hear, 'Yes, you can do it,'" she says. "But how do you get that confidence," I asked? "You get it," she advises, "from a mentor, a coach, strong role models, or from a system, like the military, that says, 'Yes, we believe in you.'"

In the fall of 2009, Command Sergeant Major Teresa King became the first woman ever named commandant of the army's elite training school for drill sergeants. According to a *New York Times* profile of King, the eighth of twelve children who grew up near Fort Bragg, North Carolina, "It was the sight of a commanding-looking female soldier in a stylish red beret at the fort that inspired her to enlist while still in high school. Within three years, she was sent to drill sergeant school, graduating as one of five women in a class of thirty."[4] It was a female role model—someone of her own gender she could identify with—who set Sgt. Maj. King on the leadership path to heading the rigorous school that trains drill sergeants for the entire Army. Once she enlisted, however, it was King's belief in herself, her tenacity, and her performance (at age 48, she scored a perfect 300 on her recent semi-annual physical training test) that led her to excel as a leader. "When

I look in the mirror, I don't see a female," King told a reporter "I see a soldier." The vanity plates on her black Corvette read "NOSLACK."

Another great place for girls and women to build confidence and learn that it's OK to be a star and compete openly for leadership positions is sports. Faulkenberry and King, as well as a high percentage of the other women leaders I interviewed, were athletes and believe playing sports is one of the best ways for women to develop an appetite for winning and the necessary edge to lead. "Early in my career, I already had some racquetball championships under my belt and could beat everybody. That led to respect in the male-dominated military world I was competing in," Faulkenberry said. "Sports is a great place to build confidence, which is absolutely key. Your confidence in yourself has to be greater than those who lack confidence in you and tell you 'No' or 'You shouldn't.'"

As a pre-Title IX *Interloper,* I never played on an organized team until I joined a women's softball league in my mid 20s. I played first base and, at the end of the season, I was named Most Valuable Player by my coach Barb Zeek. That award meant more to me than much more prestigious honors I received years later. Growing up, I was a tomboy who loved to play catch with my brothers and the neighborhood kids. But I never learned how to "throw like a boy" until I was an adult and learned from my first coach. Over the years, I've wondered what kind of athlete I could have been if I'd had the chance to play on teams growing up. Or better yet, if I'd had a coach such as Tennessee's Pat Summitt, Rutgers' C. Vivian Stringer, or the University of Connecticut's Geno Auriemma pushing me to give more, to compete harder, to take command, and to *want* to win. A subtle but significant example of Claiming Power is UConn's decision to drop the traditional "Lady" designation from their women's basketball team. In December 2010, the Huskies shattered a sports record that had stood for nearly 40 years: 89 consecutive wins by a Division I basketball team, set in the 1970s by UCLA's legendary men's teams. As of this writing, the Huskies have won 90 in a row—by consistently taking command on the court.

If you played competitive sports, claiming power may feel more comfortable to you than to women who were not athletes, either by choice or because they lacked opportunities. I'm a strong believer that *anything* women do to claim our own physical power and strength—be it running, backpacking, swimming, yoga or body building—builds confidence. But playing competitive sports and joining the military aren't the only ways to develop the confidence required to take command. Here's the advice of Beth Brooke, global vice chair of public policy for Ernst & Young, who has been named several times to the *Forbes* list of *100 Most Powerful Women in the World.* "Part of the magic is understanding your strengths and your weaknesses and leaning continually into your strengths. Then, lean into opportunities rather than stepping back from them for fear that you may not have every qualification imaginable. For young women, I also think it's important that they build confidence by putting together a string of small successes every day. Building confidence through small successes, being well prepared, and pushing to make a difference, I'm convinced, will lead the next generation of women into leadership positions in unprecedented numbers," says Brooke.

Finding Your Authentic Power

When it comes to claiming and using power, it's simply harder to be powerful and feminine than powerful and masculine. Women leaders must operate within a narrower bandwidth. Acceptable behavior for women has expanded a bit, culturally, but there is still a very big difference in the amount of room male and female leaders are "allowed" to operate within—by both genders. Texan Marsha Clark, president and CEO of Marsha Clark & Associates, is an *Interloper* and organizational development expert who has spent the last decade guiding high-level women on how to effectively—and just as important, *authentically*—walk that narrow band. Before opening her consulting practice, Clark worked for EDS for nearly 21 years, rising from an entry-level secretary with a college degree to a corporate officer. Clark invited me to sit in on several mini-sessions of "Power of Self," a twelve-month, women-only leadership program that she developed and has been teaching since 2000. I was fascinated by the attitudes that surfaced and the discussion that was generated by an exercise Clark calls "Powerful Women Are, Powerful Men Are, Powerless Women Are, Powerless Men Are."[5]

Participants are given a sheet of paper and asked to write down the first words that come to mind when they think of each of the four groups. Clark conducts the exercise quickly to get unfiltered, uncensored, top-of-mind responses that reflect gut reactions. Things start getting interesting when Clark asks people to begin sharing their responses. Using a colored marker, she writes them down on a large flip chart and keeps writing until everyone's gut reactions are recorded for all to see. She then circles words that appear on several lists. For example, "strong" and "confident" showed up on the lists for both powerful women and powerful men. But the similarities in the lists were few and the differences abundant. Clark has done this exercise with several thousand high-achieving individuals, primarily women. Here are the top words that repeatedly appear whenever Clark leads the exercise:

- Powerful women are *strong, smart, decisive*
- Powerless women are *scared, abused, victims*
- Powerful men are *leaders, smart, dominating/aggressive*
- Powerless men are *weak, wimpy, lazy*

The exercise is a great way to quickly reveal unconscious, yet ingrained, attitudes and biases that we all carry within about women, men, and power. It can be done with mixed gender groups, but Clark has discovered that people are more honest when they do the exercise with only members of their own sex. What are the insights that she wants participants to gain? There are two. "It's important to recognize that deeply-held beliefs or assumptions, whether at the conscious level or not, impact our relationships with people of our own gender as well as those of the opposite gender," Clark says. "When we bring our unspoken attitudes from the unconscious to the conscious, almost to the 'self-conscious' level, we can make different choices about how to engage with others." Her second point is that the significant contrasts between the lists reflect very different, culturally implanted attitudes about how men and women become powerful or powerless. "The words used to describe powerful women reflect *inside out* power, while those used for powerful men are primarily about having *power over* others," explains Clark. "In the case of powerless women, the words that recur over and over—*scared, abused, victim*—reflect the notion that powerlessness is being thrust upon them by a larger system. Something being done to them. But when it comes to powerless men, the words reflect a bias that they are choosing to be powerless," says Clark, who is quick to acknowledge that her database is strongly influenced by women's responses.

One of Clark's primary objectives is for every individual she works with to discover and hone her *authentic* leadership style. "What I strive to do in my programs is to continue to help women develop and optimize their leadership opportunities *and* to hold onto themselves. By that I mean, "Don't conform to someone else's definition or version of leadership. Truly become grounded in your own style of leading. It's as much about the *being* as it is about the doing," says Clark.

If your leadership development has required you to conform to or model yourself after someone else's idea of how leaders look and act, you may be on a very slippery slope. It's easy to lose yourself along the way. You can only play another's role so long. Eventually, it just *feels* wrong. In the worst-case scenario, those you hope to lead will also sense that something just doesn't feel right. Just as there is plenty of room for tremendous differences in style among great musicians, athletes, writers, and thinkers, so it is with leaders. Yet we have just begun to explore the possibilities for effective, new ways of leading that women are beginning to bring to the art.

Finding authentic ways to claim our power is a fresh frontier awaiting women *Achievers*. That's one of the reasons I'm a believer in the value of women-only training programs, such as Clark's "Power of Self," the White House Project's "Run Girl Run," Wellesley's Centers for Women, The Girl Scouts, and the hundreds, perhaps thousands of other outstanding avenues that now exist for females of every age to discover their unique abilities and leadership styles. I'm not knocking mixed-gender leadership training. I've benefitted tremendously from leadership training I received at the Ford Executive Development Center, Harvard's Kennedy School of Government, and Duke's Fuqua School of Business. For the past four decades or so, it has been essential for ambitious women to adapt to male behavior and work environments. We've gotten very good at that. Every high-achieving *Interloper, Insider*, and *Innovator* worth her salt must become multilingual when it comes to gender behavior. And women of color have had to master the ability to change cultural gears, as well, shifting from the behaviors and expectations of white professional environments to those of their personal lives, which are often very different. The rules morph instantly when the sex of the leader changes—even today. When you are ready to begin searching for your authentic leadership style, look within.

Putting Your Power to Work

"It's not enough to have power if you let pass the moment when the power is needed. Sidelines are for cheerleaders and hecklers. The future lies with those who get in the game,"[6] says African American columnist and author Rochelle Riley who writes frequently on cultural and social issues. Getting in the game is what claiming power is all about. One of the biggest deterrents holding high-achieving women back from leadership is our ambivalence about power. Researchers are beginning to look at gender differences between how women and men view power. Are they cultural, hormonal, or a little of both? That's the billion dollar question. It doesn't really matter why we approach power differently. The important thing is for each of us to pay attention to what's keeping us from claiming our power and putting it to work. *Twenty-first Century Women's Leadership*, a study done in 2007 by the Research Center for Leadership at New York University's Robert E. Wagner Graduate School of Public Service, explored this question with a group of very high-level women from the private, nonprofit, and public sectors. One-third of the participants were women of color; their ages ranged from 50-67. Participants "considered the influence of gender on perceptions of leadership and jointly engaged in reflection about their experiences," according to the report. The women leaders were asked to closely observe their own behaviors in their work environments and discuss them with the group.

What was the primary finding of the research? "While ambition was identified as a critical element of the leadership trajectory, fueling accomplishment and driving results, the participants spoke of the conflicts aroused by ambitious women. The group coalesced around the idea that in every sector, women are concerned about the exercise of responsible power," wrote study authors Shifra Bronznick and Didi Goldenhar.[7] An unnamed woman executive quoted in the report summed up one of the group's conclusions about women's widespread ambivalence. "We want to know what the impact is going to be, as opposed to just having power for power's sake. We have a desire to be more intentional about what the outcome is going to be when we exercise power."

Finding Purpose in Power

Perhaps what's needed next, suggests Deborah Wahl-Meyer, are training manuals on teaching women how to put their power to work in ways that are personally meaningful. "We've trained women to be competent, to be tough, and to know they can hold their own in very competitive male environments. But there's a lot of discussion going on among my peers about how many women in high, executive positions are not getting fulfillment out of 'the game.' You get to a certain point and you wonder, 'Is it worth it?' We're still struggling with how to use our power in a fulfilling way," explains the 40-something Wellesley graduate and *Insider* who has held senior executive positions in several industries.

She is now a vice president and chief marketing officer for Pulte Homes, a *Fortune* 500 building corporation. "Most women I know don't want to use their power. Women need to learn how to get personal fulfillment out of wielding power and influence for positive change—and to have some fun with it, which is what I see men able to do thoroughly."

That's why "Discovering Your Purpose" is the first on my list of seven Practices women *Achievers* must master to make the leap to leadership. If you find yourself having trouble with the practice of *Claiming Power,* go back to chapter 7 and review your personal passion and purpose. That's where you will find meaning for *why* you want to lead and the motivation for overcoming any ambivalence you may feel about becoming a powerful woman.

Ambivalence and the Biological Power Clock

Caroline Kennedy, daughter of President John F. Kenndy and Jacqueline Kennedy Onassis, gave us a textbook example of ambivalence about power a few years ago. She was born into power, moving into the White House at age three. She has been soaked in the Kennedy family business of politics, governing, and the media spotlight her entire life. I suspect she's comfortable with power and knows how to use it. Yet she never openly aspired to leadership until she boldly announced her interest in being appointed to the U.S. Senate seat that Hillary Clinton vacated in early 2009 to become secretary of state.[8] My first reaction to Kennedy's political power play was "Where has she been for the last few decades? Does she really think she can stroll into the United States Senate just because she's the closest thing America has to royalty?"

Then I had a new thought. "What about that pet peeve of yours, Anne, about how we devalue women's work?" The professional world routinely embraces men's military and sports experience as valuable credentials directly transferrable to leadership. Many a man has leveraged both—not to mention acting careers—on his way to political office. Yet we place little or no professional value on the skills developed through the essential and difficult work of parenting—where women have always taken the lead and still do most of the heavy lifting. The same goes for the millions of hours of unpaid volunteer work that countless women donate to nonprofit boards and community organizations. Our culture places little value on the leadership skills women have been honing for centuries in those arenas. As for Kennedy, let's not underestimate the strength of character and empathy that comes from being tested by fire in the many ways she has, which few other of our national leaders have experienced.

So what made such a private woman, who had focused her primary energies on her three (now nearly grown) children, consider *powering up*? What made her take the risk, stick her neck out, raise her hand, and say to the world "Choose me." Was it the urging of her uncle, the now deceased Senator Edward Kennedy, who had just been diagnosed with a fatal brain tumor? I suspect it was something deeper. Something uniquely feminine, which I call our biological *power* clock.

We're all familiar with our reproductive biological clocks. What if women also have a biological *power* clock, which doesn't kick into gear until after we've satisfied nature's biological demands, as well as our own parenting desires? The rhythms of women's lives are very different than men's. Think of the women you know who have gone back to complete college or earn advanced degrees after their children were raised. Listen to Kennedy's response when asked why she threw her hat in the ring. "I really felt it was a crucial moment, and if I had something that I believed in, then I really owed it to myself to express that," she told *Time* magazine. "I recently turned 50, so I figured, I'd better get going—what am I waiting for?"[9]

Caroline Kennedy heard the call to leadership. And she had the political muscle and inside track to win the coveted appointment. But just as suddenly as she entered the race, she pulled out, eliminating herself. We've heard barely a peep from her on the national scene since. When I see Caroline Kennedy, I see a brilliant, highly-educated (she holds a law degree) parent, community leader, and engaged citizen who does not need or seek power for personal affirmation. I see a woman who could bring a depth of unique experience, empathy, and commitment to essential human priorities. I'll always wonder what made her back away. Caroline Kennedy moves in a different galaxy than most people. Her path to power would hardly have been traditional if she had pushed ahead and made the leap to the U.S. Senate. But she would not have been out of her league. Look at the audacious leap Barack Obama made from first term U.S. Senator to president of the most powerful nation on earth. And there's no reason why she couldn't have done what all the guys do: learn on the job. New York voters would have decided soon enough whether she was up to it.

Women's leadership is in its infancy and we need many more role models of women claiming power. Not for ego, but because women's skills and human perspective are still essentially missing in action at the highest level of decision making. Each of us should aspire to contribute to the world at our highest level of capability. I wish Caroline Kennedy had not backed away from her most significant step to claim power, which has been hers for the taking for decades. The choice was hers. But her aborted foray into the fire is a powerful clue that she has mixed feelings. Jacqueline and President John F. Kennedy's only daughter may have just begun to hear the ticking of her biological *power* clock. I hope she listens. I can't think of anyone more perfectly positioned than Caroline Kennedy to show women *Achievers* that there is more than one path—and timetable—to leadership.

Cultural Differences

It's also important to recognize that there are major cultural differences among women regarding strength and power. African-American, Hispanic, Asian, and Caucasian cultures have given their daughters very different messages. "Black women were always raised to be strong. I think that's a cultural difference between black and white women in America," says *Interloper* Beth DunCombe, a 1974 graduate of Georgetown Law School who was one of the few African Americans *and* women in her class. "Growing up, I never heard anyone say that women can't do something.

So when they told me I couldn't be a litigator because women don't do that, I did it anyway."

One of the best books I've read on this subject is *Our Separate Ways: Black and White Women and the Struggle for Professional Identity.*[10] Authors Ella L. J. Edmondson Bell and Stella M. Nkomo wrote, "Black women haven't been socialized to be submissive, docile or fragile. For them this is one of the enduring legacies of slavery, and a result of another century and a half of race, gender and class oppression. Historically, they have often assumed the role of family provider in addition to family caretaker, carrying both male and female gender roles in the household."

Hispanic women *Achievers*, part of the fastest growing demographic group in the United States, are contending with their culture's machismo, which has long expected women to be submissive. "Latinas are just breaking into the professional world. There are not a lot of role models in our communities of women with authority and careers. We're still dealing with social stereotypes within our culture and lots of discomfort with a woman's power," said Edith Castillo, a Washington D.C.-based manager of multi-cultural marketing for AARP. The daughter of Mexican-American immigrants who had very traditional ideas about women, Castillo grew up in a poor, Orange County, California neighborhood. During high school, she was an excellent student and hoped to attend UCLA. Her parents wouldn't even allow her to apply because it would have meant living away from home. But that didn't stop Castillo. She lived at home, graduated from college and went on to become a congressional staffer on Capitol Hill. "When it comes to Latinas leading," says *Innovator* Castillo, "we're breaking our own barriers. Women of my generation are the trailblazers."

Run for Office

Running for office is one of the most visible ways for women of every cultural, ethnic, and economic background to claim power. It requires moving out of our comfort zones, knocking on unfamiliar doors, and asking people who barely know you to entrust you with authority to impact their lives. As I mentioned earlier, it is also one of the most effective ways to speed the cultural mindset change required for women leaders to be seen as the norm rather than exceptions to male rule. "When women enter political races, the candidates are not the only ones who stand to win. Simply watching women run for office has been shown to galvanize female citizens, making them more interested and actively involved in the political arena," according to *Benchmarking Women's Leadership.*[11] "Since children model their dreams on what adults and society show them to be possible," the researchers reported in the 2009 study, "the increased visibility of women on the campaign trail teaches girls that they, too, can make a difference in politics when they grow up. It also teaches boys to respect and accept women as leaders actively participating in public life."

The White House Project, which helped fund the *Benchmarking Women's Leadership* study, is a New York-based non-partisan organization working to increase the number of women running for office—and winning. They've launched an ambitious initiative to train over 36,000 women candidates by 2013. At this writing, more than 15,000 women have gone through their "Debate Boot Camp and Run, Girl Run" training programs. Actress Geena Davis, who played President Mackenzie Allen on *Commander-in-Chief*, the 2005/2006 TV series about the first U.S. woman president, is an ardent and vocal advocate of women running for office. "It's all about numbers," Davis told me. "We're making progress, but it's not enough. I want my daughter and the next generation of girls to grow up knowing they can lead." I met Davis during an event with WHP founder and president Marie Wilson, who recruited Davis to serve on the organization's national board. "I'm desperate for women to encourage and support one another to stop deferring their own dreams and take the next steps to get where they want to go," says Wilson. "In our political leadership training, we insist that everyone becomes part of a smaller group and no one leaves until she commits to what she will do to support other women in the group. It's about encouraging, with the *courage* in that word, to take the next step. We will only move if we move together."

American women are on the verge of a tremendous surge into political leadership. Culturally, women still need that extra nudge to raise their hands and stake a claim on political power by running themselves and actively supporting other female candidates for office. I needed that nudge, too. Yet once I walked out onto the edge of that psychological high diving board and took the plunge into the political waters, I was absolutely astonished at the support that materialized all around me. I felt the wind at my back, urging me forward, and had no trouble raising campaign funds. It's urging you, too. As Marie Wilson puts it, "Men wake up in the morning and say, 'I think I'll run for office.' Women rarely do that. They need to be invited, encouraged, recruited."

Let's help each other over the hump. One of the best ways to practice claiming power is to run for office. Come run with me.

Passing Power Forward

Another great way to put your power to work is to empower someone else. Nearly two years ago, just before I was to give a speech before a group of businesspeople, I met a woman who was wearing a very unusual, intriguing pin. I complimented her on it, and she told me how much she loved it. After my speech, the same woman came up to me, handed me the pin and said she wanted me to have it. "Oh no, I couldn't take your pin. I know it's very special to you," I said. She insisted. But there was a string attached to her gift. "You must promise me that one day you will give this pin to another woman," she said. "I'm giving it to you with the understanding that you will pass it forward." "How long can I keep it?" I asked. "You will know when it's time," she said.

There is something almost magical about the pin. Every time I put it on, I felt empowered by the woman who gave it to me. But as much as I hated to give it up, that day finally arrived. I knew for several weeks exactly to whom the pin should go next. I was searching for the right opportunity to give it to her. That moment came during a breakfast gathering of the Women Officials Network, a group of elected leaders, judges, political appointees, and people committed to increasing the number of women in elected office. The woman I had in mind would be there.

Originally from Peru, Blanca Fauble is a bilingual, stunningly capable dynamo who *gives* and *gives* and *gives* to others. She volunteered to run my campaign for the Auburn Hills City Council and did an extraordinary job. At the time of the breakfast, she was going through one of those life and career transitions that most of us have experienced. They are always tough and it is easy, particularly for women, to forget how strong our wings truly are and how high we are capable of soaring. Before the breakfast began, I asked the organization president, Judge Joan Young, if I could take a few minutes to present the pin. She urged me to use the opportunity to encourage every other woman in the room to find ways to pass her power forward, as well. The "pinning" turned into an emotional, memorable moment, not only for two "sisters," but for every person in the room.

The next step, which I dream of achieving in my lifetime, is for women throughout the world to come together into a powerful, collective feminine force field. That transformation will begin when we learn how to share our individual power and begin to collectively collaborate to achieve common goals. We must be the wind beneath each others' wings. Otherwise, none of us will reach the heights we could achieve together. You don't need a magical pin to lift another person. We become most powerful when we empower others. Claim your power. And then pass it forward.

Regardless of your generation, you are never too old or too young to run for office. California Congresswoman and now House Minority Leader Nancy Pelosi didn't begin her congressional career until she was 47. Delegate Madeleine Bordallo (D-Guam, 2003-present), a non-voting member, is the oldest woman elected to the U.S. House of

Representatives. She was 69 when she was seated in 2002. At the other end of the generational spectrum, Senator Olympia Snowe (R-ME) and former Representatives Susan Molinari (R-NY, 1990-1997) and Elizabeth Holtzman (D-NY, 1973-1981) were all 31 years old when they were first elected to national office.

Confidence in one's self, role models, and the courage to raise your hand and say "Let me lead" are the secret ingredients mentioned over and over as essential for more women to begin aspiring to and claiming power. There will always be people who tell you "No" or "You shouldn't." When they do, that's the time to remind yourself—over and over, if necessary—of my father's wise words: "Never eliminate yourself." Never allow others' lack of confidence in you to deter you from pursuing your passion and purpose for leading. Claim your power.

Claim Power

- ✓ Don't wait to be chosen
- ✓ Learn to take command
- ✓ Find your authentic power
- ✓ Find purpose in power
- ✓ The biological power clock
- ✓ Run for office
- ✓ Pass power forward

CHAPTER 11

Drink at Dangerous Waters

Leaders grow by jumping into the refining fire of a crucible and coming out changed. Leadership is a performing art that can only be learned through action.

— MARY O'HARA DEVEREAUX,
Author, *Navigating the Badlands, Interloper*

Imagine a jungle watering hole. Predators and prey, allies and enemies, strong and weak, every creature is dependent on the same water source in order to survive. For all but the top of the food chain, each risks danger every time it ventures out of the safety of its jungle comfort zone and returns to the nurturing waters. To survive, the animals have no choice but to risk drinking with others, who can turn to deadly enemies as soon as their thirst is quenched and their stomachs growl. "Drinking at dangerous waters" is a powerful metaphor that San Francisco-based futurist Mary O'Hara Devereaux writes about in her highly regarded book on global business strategy, *Navigating the Badlands: Thriving in the Decade of Radical Transformation.*[1] Patty DeDominic a California entrepreneur who donated $500,000 and pledged to match another one-half million to the Los Angeles chapter of the National Association of Women Business Owners (NAWBO), first introduced me to Devereaux' work. DeDominic took a leadership course on "Women and Power" at Harvard where she learned first-hand from Devereaux the leadership lessons of jungle watering holes. "If you think in terms of public life or the business of the world as a jungle where animals have to drink at the only water that's available, it becomes clear why leaders have to learn to drink at dangerous waters if they're going to make a significant difference," DeDominic explained to me. "In order to make wholesale change for the good or stop major wrongs, people who used to be competitors have to go in and collaborate in order to accomplish a goal."

I love the analogy. In today's increasingly global and diverse world, as leaders, we must intentionally and repeatedly move out of our comfort zones. There are as many ways to begin this essential practice as there are people on the planet. To me, it begins with making the effort to truly get to know and deepen relationships with people who don't remind you of yourself. Perhaps their race, religion, gender, ethnic heritage, generation, social class, or values are very different than your own. Everyone has something to teach us. Some more than others. But it's very difficult to recognize talent, learn from, and become advocates for people with whom we seem to have little in common, *unless* and *until* we build trust across differences.

Drinking at dangerous waters also means going to places you've never been. Listening with an open mind to people you disagree with. It means taking calculated risks and trying things you've never attempted. Engaging the world in new ways. At times, it even means working with rivals or individuals with whom you aren't comfortable. "In order to get peace in the world, for example, those who used to be at war have to learn to work together," says DeDominic.

Seek Collisions

"Seeking collisions" is another way Dr. Devereaux puts it. "Leaders must confront and manage their own stress and fears about letting go of old ideas and outworn roles and seek collisions by learning to connect to new and different kinds of people who can help them change and grow," she writes in *Navigating the Badlands*. "Leaders need to choose pathways that will provide surprising encounters with outsiders, who can often see possibilities invisible to insiders."

Drink at Dangerous Waters, the sixth of the seven Practices that I believe distinguish female leaders from *Achievers,* is not so much a skill as it is a mindset—that eventually becomes second nature. Think of it as a commitment to interact in more courageous, open ways with people and unfamiliar opportunities that cross your path. In this chapter, you'll learn the value of leading yourself and others into unfamiliar waters—over and over. Of course, for most of us, there's nothing truly *dangerous* about embracing new people, new ideas and new experiences. We are nearly always enriched. The only danger for a leader is becoming complacent, smug, and too settled in your own ideas, your vision of how things should be done, and with your own all too cozy comfort zones. Let's take a look at this leadership practice in action.

Engage in the World

When I was 11 years old, my mother inherited a little money after her mother's death. As the parents of seven children, Mom and Dad had a long list of ways to spend it—everything from their first new furniture to back-to-school clothes. But instead of using it for normal family expenses, they decided to take a trip they would remember forever: to Europe. They made another important decision that paid long-term dividends for our entire family. They took their two oldest children with them: my brother Danny, who was in eighth grade, and me. My five younger brothers and sisters (Mary, Tom, Irene, Vinny, and Teresa) stayed with relatives while we were gone.

I was with my Mother when she met with my sixth grade teacher to explain that she was pulling me out of school from October to December for a family trip. The teacher listened to my Mother's explanation of how we'd be taking an Italian ocean liner from New York to Genoa and would then be driving through Italy, Austria, Germany, France, Spain, and Portugal before returning home from a port in Lisbon. My teacher at St. Vincent's grade school thought all that was very interesting. But she also wanted my Mother to understand that "I can't guarantee your daughter will pass to the seventh grade if she misses so much of her schoolwork." We left with a huge pile of text books and homework assignments I'd need to complete while I was gone. Pretty much the same thing happened with my brother's eighth grade teacher.

Fast forward a few weeks. My father was driving our VW Beetle somewhere in Italy. Danny and I were in the back seat starting to work on our school assignments. I will never forget my mother turning around, looking at us, and saying, "Put away those books and look out the windows!" We never opened another school book on the entire eight-week trip. And yes, Danny and I both passed to the next grade.

What did I learn at age 11, because of my parents decision, that I wouldn't have learned sitting in a classroom in Elkhart, Indiana? I got an early introduction to dramatically different cultures. The moment we passed through border checkpoints, the money changed, the food changed, and the language changed. It was decades before the euro became the continent's common currency. Few people spoke English. And there were no McDonald's, Starbucks, or even jars of American peanut butter in the stores. World War II, which was just another piece of history I'd read about in school, became very real as Danny and I walked past the remnants of bombed buildings in Milan and explored concrete pillboxes on beaches in France.

I also learned that you don't need to speak the same language in order to communicate across cultures. My mother's French was pretty good. But it was often my Father's sign language and humor that helped us leap across language barriers and make human connections in six different countries.

And I saw poverty up close. It wore the face of a gypsy girl about my age who was scavenging with her family on a dump on the outskirts of a small Spanish town. I was looking out the window as we drove slowly by and the girl and I made eye contact. She and her family followed us to our hotel and were waiting with open hands as we got out of the car. My parents gave them money. The girl, who was just my height, was watching me and shivering in the November evening cold. I took off my sweater and gave it to her. The experience was all the reminder I've ever needed of the advantages I was born with.

My parents' willingness to take two of their children on a major adventure into unfamiliar cultural waters gave Danny and me an early peek at the rich diversity the world has to offer. But even my younger brothers and sisters, who didn't get to go on that enriching trip, have often talked about the impact it still had on them. Because of the pictures we brought home and the stories we told, all of Vince and Isabel Doyle's children learned they could, should, and would explore the world. Global travel became part of our family culture. My mother's lessons in engaging with the world didn't end with that trip. Whenever she encountered foreigners visiting the United States, even in the grocery store, she went out of her way to get to know them. She often invited them to our home, and they would reciprocate by inviting her to visit them in their country. More than once I heard her warn them, "If you invite me, don't be surprised if I show up on your doorstep." And she meant it. Even as a 70-something widow, she traveled alone to the tip of South America, the only passenger on an Italian freighter.

Leaders Travel

"Great leaders travel," Kim Campbell, the former prime minister of Canada, told me. She was quoting the work of Harvard professor Howard Gardner, who has written multiple books about leaders and intelligence.[2] "Gardner doesn't just mean having a passport and getting out of your own country," Campbell explained. "He's talking about the importance of getting out of your own reality, so that you see the world in a broader way." Those opportunities are infinite and all around us.

One of the best ways I've found for getting out of my own reality is through the International Women's Forum (IWF).[3] Committed to advancing leadership opportunities for women across careers and continents, IWF is a global network of women leaders with chapters in every state and 24 countries. Twice a year, it sponsors global conferences. I've attended several on three continents. In May 2007, as I mentioned in the Introduction, I was privileged to participate in an unprecedented gathering of women leaders in the Mideast. Entitled "Building Bridges, Breaking Walls," the conference was hosted by the leading business, political, academic, and cultural women of Jordan, under the patronage of Queen Rania Al Abdullah. Topics included *Arab Women: Myths, Misperceptions and Realities*; *Islam, Democracy and Modernization—Are They Compatible;* and *Faith, Identity and Co-Existence—The Challenges and Opportunities for Peaceful Co-Existence in Today's World.*

Six months before the conference opened, it was nearly cancelled because renewed violence between Israel and Lebanon, two of Jordan's close neighbors, created some of the worst unrest in years in the Middle East. My family and quite a few friends questioned the sanity and safety of my traveling to that part of the world at that time. I felt the risks were low and the dividends high. I wasn't alone. "We were hoping for up to 150 women leaders from around the world to accept our invitation," Reem Abu Hassan, president of IWF Jordan told me. "Not even in our wildest dreams did we dare imagine that nearly 600 women from 45 countries would travel here to open their minds and hearts to this unique opportunity."

Jordan is one of the most progressive countries in the Arab world. I was repeatedly struck by the willingness of our hosts to "create collisions" among the thought leaders in the room by not backing away from sensitive issues. There was an open microphone and questions were uncensored from an audience without a shy bone in it, including from a strong contingent of IWF Israeli women. Gender inequity was singled out as one of the major obstacles to development in the Arab world. Conference attendees were reminded, however, that misperceptions between East and West abound, that the quest for equality for U.S. and European women is only a few decades ahead of progress in the Mideast, and stereotypes about Arab and Muslim women have grown dramatically in the last ten years.

Surrounded by an astonishing gathering of some of the brightest lights of the most accomplished generation of women in the history of the world, I felt like a kid in a candy shop. I sought out Jordanians, Egyptians, Israelis, South Americans, Africans, Russians, Europeans and Chinese. All spoke nearly flawless English and were eager to build personal connections with other women from all corners of the world. I asked each if there was any message she wanted me to carry home to American women. The answers were nearly always about the responsibility that women in the United States have to help lift our global sisters.

We are citizens of the most influential nation in the world. The United States is now home to the largest cohort group of highly-educated women *Achievers* on the planet. But we're fooling ourselves if we think we are far ahead of women everywhere else. "I have met a lot of American women who are high achievers and I admire them a lot. But I do not see America as a country with many women in top jobs," Chinese IWF member Ophelia Cheung, chairman and managing director of Cheung-Macpherson & Co, who lives in Hong Kong and served on the country's Women's Commission, told me. "In China, the position of women is quite high," she reminded me (one of the unexpected benefits of Communism, which required men and women to do similar and equal work). "Both of our nations are globally influential," Cheung said. "I would suggest that the women of America and China join hands and make use of our influence to help lift other women in our own countries and the rest of the world."

In this age of the Internet, e-mail, personal Web sites, Skype, inexpensive global travel, and a very flat and increasingly smaller world, the opportunities to "create collisions" for ourselves, to build global relationships, to seek "surprise encounters," and to see the challenges we face through fresh eyes have never held more promise. *Traveling* in multiple ways is the behavior of leaders.

Become Socially Multilingual

You don't have to travel to the other side of the world in order to begin drinking at fresh cultural waters. You could begin by taking a close look at your own circle of friends. How many of them are of a different race, social class, or religion than you? How many were born in another country or speak English as a second language? Four years ago, I had this same conversation with myself. I live in southeast Michigan, 30 miles north of Detroit, the biggest African-American city in the United States. Our community also has the largest Arab population in the world outside of the Mideast. I have many multi-cultural "acquaintances" and have gotten to know a few Arabs. But when I evaluated who my real *friends* were, who I regularly intersected with at social gatherings and who invited me to their homes, I realized that I wasn't venturing far from my social comfort zone on a regular basis. The loss was mine.

So I did something about it. I registered for Leadership Detroit, a one-year program, sponsored by the Chamber of Commerce, which brings together leaders from all over the region. It was one of the most diverse work groups I've ever been part of. There were nearly equal numbers of men and women; whites were just one of the many ethnic groups, which included quite a few African-Americans, as well as Asians, Hispanics, and an openly gay man. The conversations in our once-a-month, day-long sessions included plenty of opportunity for healthy cultural collisions. The program expanded and diversified my professional network. I couldn't help but notice, though, how easy and natural it felt to begin cultivating friendships with the white women in our class and how much harder it was to build the bridges necessary to get across gender, racial, and cultural differences. Today, several years after graduating from Leadership Detroit, I could call upon any member of my LD Class. But I'm discouraged to admit how few of those diverse acquaintances have developed into deeper friendships. Despite the best intentions of everyone who took the class, our circles rarely overlap, unless we make a special effort to gather. We're working on that!

"When you don't socialize together, don't belong to the same organizations, and don't see each other outside the work environment," says African-American *Interloper* Dr. Glenda Price, president emeritus of Marygrove College, "you truly don't know each other. You don't establish the same levels of comfort, of trust, of mutual respect and expectation as when you know an individual from personal experience. So there's no foundation for becoming allies and advocates for one another, let alone true friends."

It's not easy to develop authentic, trusting relationships across the many social and cultural lines that differentiate groups of people. It takes repeated effort. But for leaders, there is no time to waste. In our lifetime, the world has gotten dramatically smaller and more diverse. People are venturing beyond their own borders, intermingling, and intermarrying in greater numbers than at any other time in history. CNN, the Internet, Facebook, even sports, such as World Cup Soccer, are just a few of the powerful social forces that are creating daily opportunities for new cultural collisions.

The United States is changing more rapidly than most realize from a predominantly Caucasian, English-speaking country to an ethnic nation. We've all read the statistics: Hispanics are our fastest growing population group. They're projected to contribute 45 percent of the nation's growth from 2010 to 2030, and 60 percent from 2030 to 2050.[4] Over 35 million Americans, 12 percent of U.S. residents over the age of five, now speak Spanish at home. Our Black population is expected to double its size by 2050 to more than 62 million. Asian and Pacific Islander populations are also increasing. The slowest growing group is non-Hispanic whites who, according to the U.S. Census Bureau web site (www.census.gov), "would contribute nothing to population growth after 2030 because it would be declining in size."[5]

In addition to the dramatic changes under way in our cultural diversity, women's presence and influence in public and professional arenas is accelerating. In the summer of 2010, *Newsweek* magazine published an article entitled "Women Will Rule the World."[6] Loaded with the latest statistics on women's steady gains in the workforce, it predicted that the recovery from the Great Recession, which began in 2007, would be female led. In many developing nations, it is women, just as here in the United States, who are earning the majority of college and graduate degrees, as well as starting most new businesses. "On a global level," *Newsweek* reported, "women are the biggest emerging market in the history of the planet—more than twice the size of India and China combined. It's a seismic change, and by all indications it will continue."

We're also on the verge of a seismic generational shift in the workforce. As the 78 million American baby boomers (born 1945-1964) begin retiring in huge numbers, 60 million New Millennials (born 1978-1994) will just be hitting their stride, as workers, consumers, voters, decision makers, and culture shapers.[7] "The world is no longer operating from a frame of reference of plain vanilla," says Kim Casiano, president and CEO of San Juan-based Casiano Communications and a member of the Ford Motor Company board of directors. "If you come from a background where you realize that things are not black and white, you're going to be a lot more innovative, a lot more flexible. Individuals who feel there is only one way to do something, who don't have the sensitivity to adjust to people who are different, whether it's culturally different or emotionally different, are going to be at a disadvantage in the non-vanilla world we're entering."

This is an area where *Innovators* have an important edge over even some of the most accomplished *Insiders* and *Interlopers.* "Most of my peers are definitely more multi-cultural than women from previous generations," says *Innovator* Maloni Goss, an associate director of strategy with Chanel in New York City. Goss, who earned her MBA from Columbia University is the daughter of a highly-accomplished *Interloper*. Her mother, Carol Goss, is the president and CEO of the Skillman Foundation and was recently profiled in *Fortune* magazine's "Visionaries" series.[8] Maloni understands the head start she and her peers have on the art of drinking at dangerous waters. "Traveling more than my mother was able, having friends from all over the world and just really understanding all different cultures and speaking different languages is not uncommon among my friends. My generation has had so much more exposure to all different types of cultures," says 29-year-old Goss. "When you talk about being socially multi-lingual, I think we're good at it."

The Diversity Prediction Theorem

At the 2009 World Economic Forum in Davos, Switzerland, the global consulting firm Ernst & Young released *Groundbreakers: Using the Strength of Women to Rebuild the World Economy.* The pivotal report, which I've referenced several times, is packed with evidence and the latest research on the need for "building more inclusive societies and more diverse leadership."[9] One of the most compelling pieces of research in the report is the diversity prediction theorem (DPT). It was developed by Scott Page, an economist and professor of complex systems at the University of Michigan and Lu Hong of Chicago's Loyola University. Page and Hong studied the impact a group's diversity has on its ability to solve complex problems. What did they find? It turns out that a group's diversity is just as important as the ability and brainpower of its members. "The diverse group almost always outperforms the homogenous group—by a substantial margin," Page reported. "This is always true. It isn't a feel good mantra; it's a mathematical fact . . . When solving complex problems, you want diverse minds. You want people who categorize things in different ways."

But leveraging the benefits of diversity isn't as simple as merely putting very different people together. In his landmark book, *The Difference: How the Power of Diversity Creates Better Groups, Firms, Schools and Societies,* Dr. Page makes the case that diversity must be managed well (led, actually!) in order to reap its benefits. Here's how he explains it in his book, using a metaphor he calls "the bicycle test."

> *A group of empirical social scientists wants to determine whether bicycling or running is a faster form of transportation. Our intrepid social scientists venture into the depths of various Glendales, Glenbrookes, and Glenviews, and gather up one hundred five-year-old children. They divide these children into two equal-sized groups. They ask each child in the first group to run as far as possible in ten seconds. Perhaps the fastest child runs sixty or even seventy yards, and the slowest covers only twenty. Being good social scientists, they plot the distances that these children travel and*

compute an average of around forty yards. They place the other fifty children on bikes and ask them to peddle these bikes as far as they can in ten seconds. Again, the social scientists plot the data and find the average distance to be about forty yards. However, the variance in distance is enormous. Those children who know how to ride bikes travel well over a hundred yards. Those children who don't know how to ride bicycles fall down and skin their elbows and knees. (We can assume that our social scientists have a ready supply of bandages.)

If we look at the data, biking appears no better than running, and we might conclude that bikes are no better than feet. But if we look at the situation more carefully, we see that riding a bike requires training and experience. And we might expect that as people acquire those skills, the bicyclists will dominate the runners. This parable of the bicycle test is important because we're just beginning to have widespread diverse interactions. Globalization is a relatively new phenomenon, so is serious interdisciplinary research, and so are multiethnic teams. It may take some time to learn how to exploit diversity's benefits.[10]

Beth Brooke, global vice chair of public policy for Ernst & Young, was the driving force behind the development of the *Groundbreakers* report, which featured Page's fascinating research on the extraordinary innovation that diversity can trigger. Brooke championed the release of the report at the prestigious World Economic Forum in an effort to develop traction around a conversation, which she says "isn't happening," on the need for diverse leadership. "We cannot rebuild the global economy ignoring one half of the world's population as we have consistently done for years," Brooke told me. "To achieve better outcomes, we need people who can look at familiar things in new and different ways. That comes about by engaging individuals with very different perspectives, different social programming, different appetites for innovation and risk," she said. "It's also important," Brooke is convinced, "because there are a lot of biases in the world. You have to bring different perspectives to the table and then openly and consciously start to address some of the unconscious bias that exists in both women and men." Clearly, Beth Brooke is a leader who understands the value of continuously "seeking collisions," learning to "ride the bike" and isn't afraid to drink at dangerous waters.

During the July 2009 confirmation hearings for Sonia Sotomayor, the first Hispanic and third woman ever named to the U.S. Supreme Court, her critics raised a fuss about a comment she'd made in a speech a few years earlier. "I would hope that a wise Latina woman with the richness of her experiences," Sotomayor had told an audience, "would more often than not reach a better conclusion than a white male who hasn't lived that life."[11] I was fascinated by the umbrage—real or feigned—that Judge Sotomayor's critics took over her comment. How dare she suggest, they argued, that the experiences of a Latina woman, which are dramatically different than those of western white men who still predominate throughout our court systems, could bring fresh perspective and wisdom to judicial decisions?

Here's how I see it. For centuries, white males have been considered "the norm." Everyone else—whether women or racial or cultural minorities of any group—has been measured against white male templates. In order to succeed and achieve influence, women and minorities had to become "culturally multi-lingual"—i.e., able to smoothly move back and forth between their own cultural group's behaviors and values and those of the predominant majority. The only ones who haven't needed to do much adjusting—until now—have been white males. The time has come for men, particularly leaders, to begin drinking at diverse waters, as well.

Talent, wisdom, and valuable life experience come in all shades, all genders, and all generations. The more multi-cultural you become, the less intimidating those dangerous waters will seem and the more skilled you will be at navigating them.

Take Calculated Risks

I'm not sure when I first learned to take risks. But I will never forget the first time I took a big one—without my parents' safety net to catch me. When I was a junior in college, I returned to Spain, the country that had touched me deepest, perhaps because of the gypsy girl I have never forgotten. I attended the University of Madrid and rented a room from a Spanish family who had a daughter, Ana, my age, and a 15-year-old son, Joaquin. My original plan was to stay for three months; I had prepaid my room and board. But by December, I knew that I wanted to stay for the entire year. I wrote to my parents telling them how much I loved Spain, how quickly my language skills were improving, and what a mistake it would be for me to return home by Christmas, as planned. I was running out of money and was counting on my parents to send some, even if it meant paying them back. (All of my brothers and sisters and I paid our own way through college.) I waited, a little desperately, for their response, carefully putting aside the three pesetas (about 10¢ at the time) I needed each day for the subway roundtrip to school. Food was secondary.

I know you *Innovators* have a hard time imagining how "unconnected" we truly were back then. There was no Internet, of course. Cross-Atlantic telephone calls were prohibitively expensive and letters were very slow. The fastest way to communicate—in a pinch—was to send a Western Union telegram. I remember exactly where I was standing when Señora de Aleman (my Spanish mother) knocked on my bedroom door and called, "Ana, ha llegado un telegrama para tí." I ripped it open and stared at the very short but clear message from my parents. The telegram read:

"Dear Anne,

Glad you love Spain. We have six other children. Come home.

Love, Mom and Dad"

I was dumbstruck. From the time I was in high school, I had earned my own spending money and even bought some of my own clothes. At that point, I had already paid for my freshman and sophomore years of college with money from summer jobs and student loans. My parents gave me money here and there, as they could. Knowing how much my Mother and Father valued global travel and learning about other cultures, I was sure they would find a way to help me stay in Spain. When they closed that door, I wasn't sure what I was going to do. But I was certain of one thing: I wasn't going home. My immediate solution was to cash in my return airline ticket and use that money to live on. I also put small, classified ads in the local paper, *El Sol*, offering to give private lessons in conversational English and earned money that way. And my Spanish family helped, too. By that time, I was no longer just another foreign student renting a room. I had become a member of the family. My Spanish sister, Ana, offered to let me share her room so that another paying student could rent the private bedroom. I stayed a full year, finally managing to get home the following summer on a cheap student ticket from London.

More than three decades later, I am still in touch with my Spanish family and have visited Ana, Joaquin, and their families in their homes. Now, we are passing our cross-Atlantic connections on to another generation. Joaquin's daughter, Laura, spent a summer in Chicago with my sister, Irene, and her family. Then, Irene's son, Zak, was invited for an extended, language-polishing visit to Madrid. While he was there, he went to Huesca in the north of Spain to meet my *sister* Ana and her mother, Señora de Aleman Mur, who welcomed a stranger from America into her home more than 30 years ago. If I had done the safe thing decades ago and used my original ticket to return home as planned, I would have never been "adopted" in the way I was and would have missed nine months of enriching cultural collisions. My decision to take the calculated risk of cashing in my return plane ticket led to a rich, lifelong friendship with a family on the other side of an ocean. Little did I know that it would also be the ace I would play to score one of the most memorable interviews of my broadcasting career.

Find Common Ground

During my five years covering sports, I had to return repeatedly to locker rooms and press boxes that often felt as dangerous, for a female reporter, as a jungle watering hole. It wasn't just *places* that were uncomfortable. People can be pretty intimidating, too. None more so than superstar athletes. Reggie Jackson, the famed New York Yankee slugger and now a member of the Baseball Hall of Fame, was one of the biggest names in sports during the time I was working for the CBS affiliate in Detroit. When the Yankees came to town, everybody wanted an interview, or at least a few words, with Reggie. My station was no different. Naturally, they gave the assignment to the rookie—me. It was my first year covering major league baseball, and my chances of getting an interview with the prima donna of the New York Yankees were slim to none. It was a test. Or maybe a joke.

But I had plenty to prove and wasn't about to eliminate myself! So, I started doing my homework, reading everything I could find about Jackson. "What could I possibly come up with that he hasn't already been asked a thousand times?" I wondered. Then I discovered that his maternal grandmother was Castilian and that Reggie Jackson spoke fluent Spanish. At the time, Latin American players were relatively rare on U.S. teams; the Yankees, however, already had several. Jackson, I discovered, had been helping the Latin players with the language barrier.

The moment of truth came a few hours before the game that I was assigned to cover between the Tigers and the Yankees. Credentialed journalists are allowed to go out onto the field and talk with players during batting practice, usually about an hour before game time. When I walked out onto the field, Reggie Jackson was easy to spot. Of course, I knew what he looked like. But he was also alone, standing—or perhaps I should say posing—just behind the batting cage, watching another player hit balls to the infielders to shag. His chin was on his muscled, right forearm that was resting on the steel frame of the batting cage, just a little above his shoulder. He looked cocky. Unapproachable. Like a man who knew all eyes were on him. I swallowed hard, told myself "It's now or never," and walked up to him, followed by my wary cameraman.

"Hello Reggie. My name is Anne Doyle with Channel 2 here in Detroit," I began. "Could I ask you just a couple of quick questions?" I might as well have been one of the tiny gnats that were flying around the field that summer evening. Jackson didn't acknowledge in any way that he had heard me or even that there was a human being who had approached him. He never turned his head. I was conscious that other reporters milling around the field were observing, probably anticipating my forthcoming humiliation. A lone woman sports reporter encroaching on men's territory and about to be taught a lesson by a future Hall of Famer could be entertaining.

That was when I went to Plan B. I tried again, this time in Spanish. "Señor Jackson, me llamo Ana Doyle. Me hablaría usted un poco en español? (Mr. Jackson, my name is Anne Doyle. Would you speak to me a little in Spanish?) Reggie Jackson barely moved a muscle, but he turned his head slightly to look at me. I kept talking and said something like "Tengo interés en saber su opinión acerca de los jugadores latinos. Hablaría usted conmigo por solo unos minutos?" (I'm interested in your opinion about the Latin players. Would you talk with me for just a few minutes?) Jackson turned toward me, nodded at my cameraman, and responded, "Ningun problema, señorita. Que quiere saber?" (No problem, Miss. What do you want to know?) Much to the astonishment of the other journalists and players who witnessed the encounter, I got my interview. We put the story about Jackson's thoughts on the increasing number of Latin players coming into the league on the air that night—with English subtitles.

Did I risk embarrassment in front of my colleagues if Reggie had scorned even my best laid plan and refused to talk with me? Sure. But think of what I would have missed if I had eliminated myself and hadn't even tried. The lesson I learned from that experience was the importance of making the effort to seek common ground, particularly when you are trying to overcome resistance. That requires listening to people, paying attention to what motivates them, and investing energy in figuring out what makes them tick. By the time I walked up to Reggie Jackson, he had been interviewed thousands of times. Summer after summer, in baseball parks all around the country, every sports reporter who ever picked up a pen or a microphone wanted to talk to one of the most famous athletes in the country. After a while, it was just the same old stuff to Reggie. If I had not done my homework, I would never have gotten that interview. On the surface, it's hard to imagine that an African-American male sports superstar and an Irish-American female, rookie sports broadcaster could have anything in common. But we did. He talked to me because I had discovered something unique about him that few people knew, and I offered him a chance to show off his Spanish. My discovery of common ground that Reggie Jackson and I shared, and my willingness to try to connect with him there, if only briefly, opened the door to a close encounter I will never forget.

Seeking common ground is also the magic ingredient necessary for learning how to begin unlocking the possibilities your network may hold. "Networking," one executive *Interloper* told me, "is kindergarten when it comes to building relationships." Leaders must learn how to leverage their relationships to get things done. Asking favors of people, reciprocating by doing favors for others, connecting people for mutual benefit, strategically linking with individuals who share your goals in order to accomplish more than you could alone are all ways to put your network of contacts and acquaintances to work. It may feel a little uncomfortable and dangerous at first. It all begins by seeking common ground.

Look at the alliance between billionaires Bill Gates, the founder of Microsoft; his wife, Melinda; and Berkshire Hathaway founder Warren Buffett. It was their shared passion for using their wealth to make a difference in the world that brought them together. Buffett has committed to donate the bulk of his $47 billion fortune to the Bill and Melinda Gates Foundation, which focuses on fighting global poverty and disease. Now, they're targeting other billionaires (how's that for common ground?). As of this writing, they have convinced 16 others, including Facebook's Mark Zuckerberg, to commit to the Giving Pledge to donate at least half of their holdings. Their goal is to convince America's 400 wealthiest individuals to give half of their combined $1.2 trillion net worth to charity, which would raise over $600 billion—twice the annual amount Americans currently donate.[12] That's the power that's possible when leaders leverage their relationships. How are you putting yours to work?

Collaborating with Rivals

Another element of drinking at dangerous waters is the ability to work and even collaborate with rivals. The best example I've ever witnessed of this leadership skill in action is the alliance between President Barack Obama and Secretary of State Hillary Clinton. They're an odd professional couple. During the 2008 U.S. presidential campaign, one of the most polarizing in recent history, the two senators fought toe-to-toe, sometimes bitterly, for the Democratic nomination. Neither gave an inch during the debates. When Senator Clinton seemed to be building momentum, after winning three of four primaries in the spring of 2008, she publicly suggested that the two join forces as a Clinton/Obama ticket—with her at the top. Obama and his camp were insulted by the suggestion that he concede and went on to defeat Clinton for the nomination.

Although she won eighteen million primary votes, once Obama had prevailed, there was never any doubt that Hillary would have to be a Democratic "team player" and endorse the party's Obama/Biden presidential ticket. It must have been a very bitter pill for her to swallow and she had to do it with the eyes of the world upon her. She did it, though, hitting the campaign trail once again, stumping for her former opponent, and watching from the sidelines as her fiercest rival was elected the 44th president of the United States. It was fascinating political theater. But what happened next surprised even Washington, D.C. insiders and revealed plenty about the character of two of the world's most influential leaders. When President-elect Obama offered Clinton the position of secretary of state, one of the prime spots in his Cabinet, he was taking a page from President Abraham Lincoln's "team of rivals" leadership playbook. "I thought he was kidding, but he was very persuasive," Clinton told the news media after she accepted.

Collaborating with rivals is a two-way street. It requires effort and nearly always includes some risk for both parties, as *Time* magazine pointed out in a November 2009 cover article, "The State of Hillary."

"It is a cliché to say that by naming Clinton (Secretary of State), Obama brought his most popular potential opponent into the tent," columnist Joe Klein wrote. "The conventional wisdom . . . is that he thereby succeeded in neutering her. But by naming Clinton, Obama also gave her great power, which cuts both ways. How will Clinton use her power? How will Obama react if and when she does?"[13]

From my perspective, Obama demonstrated the confidence and intellectual curiosity to risk constructive conflict by inviting a strong, independent voice into his inner circle. Clinton showed she was woman enough to swallow her pride and put aside her differences with her nemesis in hopes of accomplishing greater goals they both shared. Those are the skills of seasoned leaders unafraid to drink at dangerous waters. They require emotional maturity and personal confidence. Qualities that take years to develop. Regardless of how the collaboration between former rivals Barack Obama and Hillary Clinton unfolds, there is plenty to learn from watching two power players dance together on the global stage.

If you find yourself having trouble working with a rival, go back and re-read chapter 7, *Discover Your Purpose.* Reconnecting with your personal passion to make a difference beyond yourself is often all the antidote leaders need to overcome the inevitable obstacles that get in their way—including present and former rivals.

Avoid Toxic Waters

There's an unwritten rule that women are held to a higher moral standard than men. There's no point in arguing whether or not that's fair. It's where we are in our cultural evolution. Because women are still so few in number at leadership levels, we're scrutinized more carefully than men. Expect it. And as you venture into unfamiliar waters, watch out for toxic, poisonous, polluted waters that have enticed and destroyed many an accomplished leader. Guard your integrity, your reputation, and your authenticity at all costs. Nothing is worth risking your good name.

No one understands that better than *Insider* and Enron whistleblower Sherron Watkins. She was vice president of corporate development at the Texas energy company when she challenged and eventually exposed criminal behavior by Enron's senior executives, leading to one of the most devastating business scandals in recent history. "Safeguard your own reputation. Always consider your actions as if you were going to be judged alone," Watkins advises. "It's very easy to fall into group think and say to yourself, 'If I were running the company, I wouldn't do this, but it's what's expected of me at this corporation,' Those are the small steps leading toward the edge of the cliff. Even small little lapses in ethics or integrity are really the seeds of destruction."

We see examples every day of companies and very successful people who lose their moral compass. You need look no further than the Gulf of Mexico and the unethical and illegal shortcuts (ordering safety alarms on the oil rig turned off) that so-called "leaders" of BP took for the sake of a bulging bottom line. Wall Street banking executives brazenly paid themselves obscene bonuses—from taxpayer bailout funds—even after their high-risk business practices nearly crashed the U.S. economy in 2008-2009. An astonishing number of powerful politicians—former senator and presidential candidate John Edwards, former South Carolina Governor Mark Sanford, former New York Governor Eliot Spitzer and former President Bill Clinton, just to name a few recent examples—have risked their families, their careers, and their reputations for sexual excitement.

There haven't been enough women in positions of power to know if we will be equally susceptible to corruption. We do know, however, that most whistleblowers are women. And Catalyst (www.catalyst.org), the leading nonprofit organization working globally to advance women in business (primarily Fortune 1000 companies), has found that corporate boards with women directors are significantly more likely to develop ethical standards and governance policies than all-male boards.[14]

We also know that when a female leader makes a misstep, she will fall faster and harder than a man. We had a blatant example of this phenomenon several years ago in Detroit, during what came to be known as the city's "sex, lies, and texting" scandal. Mayor Kwame Kilpatrick and his chief of staff, Christine Beatty, were both charged with multiple felonies for lying under oath—to hide their affair—during a whistleblower trial. Beatty, a 41-year-old *Insider* and single parent with two young children to support, had little choice but to resign immediately from her powerful position. Even Kilpatrick, her boss, former lover, and partner in the crimes in question, told the news media after her resignation, "She had to go."

And that was just the beginning of her troubles. At one point, a local magistrate ordered Beatty to begin wearing a tether because she had violated her probation by flying to Atlanta for a job interview. Kilpatrick, on the other hand, brazenly refused to resign and continued to enjoy the fruits of his office: collecting his paycheck, living in the mayoral mansion, driving city-owned luxury vehicles accompanied by a posse of city-paid bodyguards, and traveling out of state without court approval. The drama played out in juicy, daily headlines. The *Detroit Free Press* even won a Pulitzer Prize for its investigative reporting that broke the scandal wide open.[15]

I have never met Christine Beatty and have little sympathy for the mess a once powerful and admired woman leader got herself into. But I was so incensed by the blatant double standard playing out in the local media that I wrote an Op Ed for the paper. "Where is the outrage," I wrote, "over a once admired and highly accomplished woman leader of our city being discarded like yesterday's newspaper and ordered by a judge to be tethered like a criminal, while the male leader who faces even more serious felony remains firmly seated on his powerful throne?"

My column touched a nerve. Dozens of readers posted reactions online and dozens more emailed me directly. Most of the comments were from women. Nearly all shared the feelings of this reader. "What great insight you gave into the Beatty crucifixion, without supporting the deeds that got her into trouble in the first place. It really opened my eyes to how women associated with powerful men are not only exploited by them but are then left alone to handle the fallout. Thanks for giving voice to the silent seething we feel at the injustices." Eventually, Kilpatrick, once a rising political star with national potential, went to prison, as did Beatty. And in December, 2010, U.S. District Attorney Barbara McQuade (remember her from Chapter 9?) announced a 38-count indictment against Kilpatrick and several of his associates for extorting millions during his corrupt mayoral reign. He could face up to 30 more years in prison.[16] Arrogance, hubris, and loss of their moral compasses caught up with both flawed leaders. The woman, however, fell long before the man.

There is no "girls will be girls" social leniency for high-profile women who compromise their integrity and reputation. Nor should there be. Don't risk yours. The fastest way to destroy a promising career and eliminate yourself from leadership opportunities is by losing your moral compass. Societies throughout the world have long counted on women to be civilizing, humanizing forces. That's not going to change soon. Integrity, trustworthiness, honesty, authenticity, humility, empathy, character—never let those virtues out of your sight. The higher you rise and the more powerful or influential you become, the greater your exposure to what I think of as "toxic waters." They are as lethal for a leader as a poisoned watering hole is for jungle mammals.

Drink Deeply

Future leaders will come from a richer talent pool than the world has ever tapped. They will include many more women, younger leaders, and individuals from every imaginable cultural and ethnic group. Each generation of American women *Achievers* in the workforce today can play a significant role in unlocking the capabilities of those groups. "Gut instinct can be very useful if it is a reflex based on all of the experiences we've had. But if our experiences are minimal and our curiosity is zero, then relying on our gut instinct is a pretty dangerous thing," former Canadian Prime Minister Kim Campbell told me. Whether you are an *Interloper, Insider*, or *Innovator*, I can think of no better advice with which to finish this chapter than the words Campbell asked me to pass forward: "Inform your gut! Get out there. See the world. Experience things outside your own reality so that the reflexes and instincts that you develop about the world are based on some understanding of the complex realities."

I'm an Optimist Club member and am inspired every time our chapter recites together the Optimists Creed, which is a list of promises we make to ourselves and one another. My favorite line reads, "Promise yourself: to give so much time to the improvement of yourself that you have no time to criticize others."[17] Seek new ways to continuously refresh your thinking and inform your gut. Model that behavior for those you mentor. Look for unfamiliar waters that hold the most intrigue or new possibilities for you. Start with a few sips. Then drink deeply.

Drink at Dangerous Waters

- ✓ Seek collisions
- ✓ Leaders travel
- ✓ Become socially multi-lingual
- ✓ Take calculated risks
- ✓ Find common ground
- ✓ Collaborate with rivals
- ✓ Avoid toxic waters

CHAPTER 12

Get Back in the Saddle

You have to have the ability to persevere because you're going to get knocked down a lot. The winners are the ones who say, "I'm going to pick myself up. I'm going right back out there. And no one is going to stop me."

— MARY PETROVICH, CEO, AxleTech, *Insider*

Everyone gets knocked off her horse now and then—no matter how well you ride. What distinguishes a leader is how quickly she gets back in the saddle and charges back into the fray. Sarah Palin, who has become a formidable political force playing by her own rules, has this ability in spades. Rather than lick her wounds and retreat to Alaska after she and John McCain lost their 2008 Republican bid for the White House, Palin regrouped. She didn't waste a lot of time ruminating over what went wrong. Instead, she stunned the political establishment, as well as her supporters and opponents, by calling a Fourth of July news conference to announce she was resigning as governor of Alaska to "free myself up." Nobody knew at the time what Palin's ambitions or next moves would be. Plenty of political strategists and media commentators gleefully predicted her ascending star was about to crash and burn.

How wrong they were. At this writing, she's a formidable political force with over two million Facebook followers and presidential ambitions. Palin's father, who probably knows the unpredictable politician as well as anyone, provided the first hint of what was to come, telling reporters, "Sarah didn't retreat. She reloaded." In other words, she didn't waste a lot of time bemoaning her vice-presidential loss. She got right back in the saddle.

There isn't a leader alive (or dead!) who hasn't suffered setbacks, endured criticism, and made mistakes. Women, however, tend to internalize and waste time blaming ourselves for negative experiences much more than men. As one executive told me, "If a woman puts on her pants and discovers they're too tight she'll tell herself, 'I've gained weight.' Most males will think, 'The cleaners shrunk my pants.'" That's why *Get Back in the Saddle* is the sixth leadership Practice that women, in particular, must master. In this chapter, I'll walk you through the qualities and skills we all need to overcome the inevitable setbacks everyone encounters on a leadership journey. Perseverance, tenacity, mental strength, backbone, resiliency, guts—those are the building blocks. In action, saddling back up requires standing up to critics, learning from mistakes, having good clean fights, recognizing and welcoming defining moments, and knowing "when to hold 'em and when to fold 'em." Before you are ready to lead others, you must walk through a few red hot crucibles yourself. Adversity, losses, course corrections, embarrassing missteps, and difficult transitions are all part of the refining fires that test and temper us. The first step is to welcome the struggle.

Welcome the Struggle

How many times have you heard: "Never, never, never give in;" "It's not over till it's over;" or "Show me a good loser, and I'll show you a loser." Sports, politics, business, and war, which have shaped our cultural images of leaders and champions for centuries, all celebrate examples of underdogs fighting on against the odds to victory. From Winston

Churchill to baseball's Yogi Berra and football's Vince Lombardi, mantras of leaders and champions have always been about never quitting and overcoming obstacles. We need memorable quotes from famous women leaders, as well, about the importance of prevailing through life's struggles. They're coming. As increasing numbers of women move into prominent positions, their words will inspire us and become part of our leadership lexicon, too.

Life tests everyone. The essential lesson for leaders is to recognize that struggles and setbacks are as valuable as successes. "All experience, good and bad, makes you who you are. We'd all like to sift our negative experiences, but we wouldn't be the person we are if we hadn't gone through them," says Kym Worthy, the courageous Wayne County prosecutor whose leadership and tenacity during a high-stakes battle with former Detroit Mayor Kwame Kilpatrick led to his conviction and imprisonment. Throughout the drawn-out investigation and prosecution, Worthy was cool under tremendous pressure, which included death threats toward her and her family. When I asked the 51-year-old *Interloper* and Notre Dame Law School graduate about her strength during the very public showdown with the politically-connected Kilpatrick, she told me, "My mother died when I was seventeen. I was raped during law school. And I've lost a child, a daughter, only nineteen days old. When you get through experiences like that, you can get through any damn thing."

A very different, but equally inspiring example of how struggle strengthens and prepares us for future challenges, comes from *Insider* Thear Sy. A 37-year-old senior executive with Accenture, a Texas-based global management and consulting firm, Sy's work is demanding and often requires travel, which she enjoys. But that's just the half of it. She is also married, the mother of three young sons, and was expecting her fourth child when I first interviewed her. I was struck by the sense of serenity she exuded and astonished when she described her life as "very busy, but stress free." Sy credits her husband, also a consultant with Accenture, for her peace of mind. "Without that kind of support, my life would be very stressful," she acknowledged. But not until I asked about her childhood did I understand the source of Sy's inner strength and grace under pressure.

"My family went through the war in Cambodia from 1975 to 1979. After that, we were in various refugee camps for two years in Thailand, Indonesia, and the Philippines," Sy explained. "By the time we finally arrived in Dallas in 1981, I was eight years old. I didn't speak any English and never went to school prior to starting my education in third grade. That experience has certainly helped me to take things in stride without making a big deal out of issues." Like Kym Worthy, Thear Sy has learned not to fear adversity and refuses to be limited by what she calls "life happening." "I believe going through trials and tribulations and being stretched *absolutely* helps you to become a stronger and better leader," Sy told me. "It also changes the way you think about the world, about yourself, and what you're capable of."

Once you recognize that struggle is essential for growth, the skills and strength you need to overcome whatever life or opponents throw at you become a lot easier. Let's start with the mental strength required to face the heat.

Face the Heat

If you're a high-achieving woman, you've already had a lot of success. Feels great, doesn't it? But be prepared for what's next: the higher you go and the more visible and influential you become, the greater your chances of facing increased criticism of your ideas and challenges to your authority. Leaders welcome both. When you are prepared, they are golden opportunities to show you know your stuff and what you're made of. "Don't expect to be treated politely," says organizational development consultant Nancy Badore. "Don't be unprepared even for dirty tricks."

Neither Badore nor I are suggesting, however, that you completely ignore negative feedback. There's often a grain of truth hidden in even the most mean-spirited criticism. Don't turn a deaf ear. But don't swallow criticism hook, line, and sinker, either. Acknowledge it, evaluate it, and then decide what to do with it. Ask yourself, "Is there any truth to this? Am I in denial about something in my behavior that others see and I don't?" Better yet, ask your allies. Keep in mind, however, that most people don't like to give critical feedback. Even bosses, mentors and friends are often reluctant to point out our faults. You have to actively *solicit* frank, honest feedback—especially if you've been given clues about behaviors that may be undermining your effectiveness. Once you've gleaned everything useful from criticism, let the rest of it go. Immediately.

Badore advises her clients to handle their critics as comedians do hecklers. "The best comedians learn to rebut, hold their ground, stay cool, and top hecklers," she says. "It takes preparation and a certain amount of grit. Strive for the day when people who counter you bring out that tiny little crinkle of pleasure because you know you're about to engage in a debate that you're ready for and that's worth winning."

The 2010 elections provided compelling examples of sexist personal attacks on women leaders and fresh insight on how to handle them. Former EBay CEO Meg Whitman was referred to as a whore during the California gubernatorial campaign by an associate of her opponent, now Governor Jerry Brown.[1] And 28-year-old *Innovator* Krystal Ball, a CPA and a democratic candidate for Congress from Virginia, was humiliated when her opponents posted racy photos of her, taken six years earlier at a costume party, on the internet.[2] I cheered when Ball ignored political advisers who told her to lay low. Instead, she came out swinging. "Siobhan (Sam) Bennett, from Women's Campaign Forum, helped me to realize that the way to combat this was to take it head-on, to confront it," Ball told her supporters and the news media in a statement that was closer to a battle cry than a press release. "The tactic of making female politicians into whores is nothing new. It's part of the whole idea that female sexuality and serious work are incompatible . . . But I realized that photos like the ones of me, and ones much racier, would end up coming into the public sphere when women of my generation run for office."[3]

Ball didn't win, but after she stood up to the sexist attacks, she received an outpouring of encouraging emails and financial support for her campaign, particularly from women she called the "Sisterhood of the Travelling Pantsuit *(Interlopers)*." "They will not watch the tide of everything they fought for washed away by the public exposure of female sexuality. They are stepping up to protect young women like me, to support us and to help us grow up."

A 2010 study of voter attitudes has found that hard-edged, sexist attacks on women candidates are much more damaging—among both male and female voters—than gender-neutral criticism of their positions on issues. Sponsored by the Women's Media Center, the WCF Foundation and Political Parity, the research also determined that the most effective response is for women candidates to immediately counterattack. Celinda Lake, a Democratic pollster who conducted the survey, told *USA Today*, "I was stunned at the magnitude of the effect of even mild sexism. Right now campaigns tend to be silent and try to tough it out, and this really opens up a whole new strategy of responding."[4] What's the lesson for all of us? A woman who strives to inspire others to follow her vision can't lose her nerve when the heat gets turned up.

The Likeability Factor

There's a Catch-22 every highly competent woman eventually faces. "Unfortunately, research has revealed that assertive women are less well-liked than those who are not assertive," reported Linda Babcock and Sara Laschever in their highly regarded 2003 book *Women Don't Ask: Negotiation and the Gender Divide.* The authors quote multiple studies that show "For women who want to influence other people, research has found that being *likeable* is critically important—and that women's influence increases the more they are liked . . . In contrast, whether or not they are liked does not affect men's ability to influence others."[5] The researchers cite multiple other studies that confirm their findings, including the work of sociologist Cecelia Ridgeway. "Women seeking to assert authority can mitigate the legitimacy problems they face by combining their assertive, highly competent behaviors with positive social 'softeners' [friendly, cooperative, confident but non-confrontational, and considerate]," Dr. Ridgeway reported. "Using such techniques, highly competent women can overcome others' resistance and win influence and compliance."

In other words, don't underestimate the importance of strategically playing your "likeability" cards. "The positive consequences of such techniques are not trivial," Ridgeway found. "They allow very competent women to break through the maze of constraints created by gender status to wield authority."[6] Even today, women who exhibit the same tenacity, guts, and mental toughness that our culture expects of male leaders, nine times out of ten are criticized for coming on too strong. What that really means is that we're coming on too strong *for a woman*. We've committed the social faux pas of making people uncomfortable by crossing a gender line. Stand up to the heat anyway.

The only way we're going to change the social limitations female leaders are still up against is by increasing the number of women willing to push the edges of expected gender norms. And do it collectively, as a focused female force field. That's what we did in the 1970s and 1980s when huge numbers of American women muscled our way into previously all-male professions. It wasn't easy. Ask any female doctor, judge, journalist, coach, politician, factory worker, or businesswoman over 50 if she was ever criticized for "coming on too strong." If all those trailblazing *Interlopers* had backed down when the heat was turned up, American women wouldn't be where we are today. The career, family, and lifestyle choices that are mainstream today—for men as well as women—were considered radical in the 1960s and 1970s. *Insiders* and *Innovators* would have faced much rougher roads than those you've traveled so far. Face the heat, fight back when you are the target of gender-biased attacks. But remember: there's still plenty of truth to that old "steel magnolia" approach. Play your likeability cards strategically.

Over the past few decades, Hillary Clinton has faced the heat and glare of the global spotlight as publicly and intensely as any leader I've closely observed. She has repeatedly refused to be deterred by gender-biased criticism, which men rarely encounter. As First Lady, her unconventional approach caused outrage, particularly when President Clinton broke precedent and named his wife to head the President's Task Force on Health Care Reform. She was reviled on many fronts and suffered a very public defeat when her herculean effort failed. Once President Clinton left office, Hillary ignored howls of "carpetbagger," running for and winning a New York senate seat. Criticism of one of the most remarkable women leaders of our time reached fever pitch when she dared to run for president. Political pundits had a field day attacking her. "Let's face it, the only reason Hillary Clinton is running for president and the only reason she became a U.S. senator is because her husband messed around," opined Chris Matthews, host of MSNBC's *Hardball.*[6] (For a fascinating behind-the-scenes read on the gender politics of what Salon political reporter Rebecca Traister calls "the election that changed everything for American women," I highly recommend her book, *Big Girls Don't Cry.*[8]) *Interloper* Clinton has faced withering heat and a never-ending chorus of critics for most of her professional life. Yet, in 2010, for the ninth consecutive year, she was named the "Most Admired Woman in America" in Gallup's annual poll. She hasn't finished writing her legacy, but our secretary of state has earned her place in history by taking the heat and modeling the leadership art of *getting back in the saddle* over and over and over.

As Huffington Post founder and thought leader Arianna Huffington likes to say, "Nothing fortifies your opponent like signaling your willingness to surrender." Face the heat. Next step: learn to have good clean fights.

Have Good Clean Fights

A work culture of "terminal niceness" is counterproductive, says Xerox CEO Ursula Burns. During an employee "all-hands" meeting shortly after she was named head of the company in early 2010, Burns urged the Xerox family to start acting more like a *real* family. "When we're in the family, you don't have to be as nice as when you're outside of the family," she told employees. "I want us to stay civil and kind, but we have to be frank—and the reason we can be frank is because we are all in the same family." *New York Times* reporter Adam Bryant, who was working on a profile of the new CEO, was in the audience that day. In his February 20, 2010, article entitled "New Xerox Chief Tries to Redefine Culture," Bryant reported that "nods of recognition rippled across the audience" when their new CEO tackled the company's "too nice" culture. "We know it. We know what we do," Burns told the employees, referring to company meetings where people don't speak up and challenge presenters. "And then the meeting ends," she continued, "and we leave and go, 'Man, that wasn't true.' I'm like, 'Why didn't you say that in the meeting?'"[9] Sounds familiar, like a lot of work cultures, doesn't it?

The adjective "bold" has often been used to describe Ursula Burns. The 52-year-old *Interloper* and mechanical engineer was never shy about speaking her mind. According to the same *New York Times* profile, her willingness to challenge Xerox leaders with tough questions brought Burns to the attention of senior management early in her career. On more than one occasion, when she was called into the office of a senior executive, she suspected she was about to be reprimanded or even fired. Instead, several Xerox executives, to their credit, became mentors and eventually sponsors offering rare opportunities for a talented and outspoken *Achievers* to begin polishing her leadership skills at a very young age. Today, the pioneering Xerox CEO is urging her 130,000 employees to "become more fearless and be more frank and impatient with one another to ratchet up performance."[10]

I couldn't agree more. The ability to fearlessly and effectively challenge colleagues, authority figures, and anyone within your circles of influence are marks of a leader. Earlier in this chapter, I talked about the importance of being able to *face the heat* when others confront and criticize you. The other side of that same coin is to *turn up the heat*—to frankly speak your mind and engage in healthy debate with people with whom you disagree. Asian-American *Interloper* Teri Takai calls this "the ability to have a good clean fight." Takai, who recently left a position in the cabinet of former California Governor Arnold Schwarzenegger to join the U.S. Department of Defense, learned this powerful skill during her mid-career years in the auto industry, telling me:

> *"I had a peer at Ford who was a great competitor of mine as we came up through the ranks. He was 6'4" and I am 5'2"." Over the years we became best friends. At one point, we were working side-by-side on a very large project. We would argue like cats and dogs, even in front of other staff members. In his mind, he was totally right. When I didn't agree with him, he would assume it was because I didn't understand his point. So he would start talking slower to help me understand. If that didn't work, he'd use the 'I'm going to talk louder' technique. I would get so irritated with him that I would finally say, 'Bob, it's not that I don't understand, it's that I don't agree with you. And I'm not going to agree with you, no matter how long we talk.' Then, we'd finish the discussion and go to lunch together. People couldn't understand how we could do that. I developed the ability to have good, clean fights by working with him."*

Remember the Teflon skin I encouraged you to start growing? It's essential armor that will protect you from making the mistake of taking differences of opinion personally. Even *Innovators*, who are often seen by *Interlopers* and *Insiders* as oozing with confidence, experience this gender difference. "I think as women we take things more personally than guys would," acknowledged 31-year-old Nicole Navratil, a managing director with BBMG, a New York consumer marketing and branding consulting firm. "Guys are more off the cuff. Their attitude seems to be, 'Hey, I'm not thinking about how it's going to make him or me feel. I'm just going to go with it.' It's better for them professionally. Women over-think things and get too emotional."

There's no better boot camp for starting to grow that armor and learning how to fight fairly with people you'll need to see again than growing up in a large, very vocal family. My six siblings and I fought so often as children that our mother finally had enough. We still talk about the day she lined up her seven squabbling offspring and made us watch as she stenciled "Jesus Said Love One Another" in large, block letters on the white woodwork in our dining room. Just to make sure her message made an impression, she had each of the four oldest (me included) climb up on a stepladder and take turns filling in the letters with bright green paint. My father wasn't thrilled when he came home that night and saw the new decorating touch. But those words remained in our dining room as long as we lived in that house.

If you didn't grow up practicing "good clean fights" with a rowdy bunch of siblings, it's never too late to start. Leaders have to be able to hold their own and engage in frank back-and-forth discussions in sometimes very tough environments. Practice with a friend or professional ally. Start engaging in "healthy disagreements" in real situations: in meetings or large group discussions. If you agree to publicly disagree ahead of time with your ally, it will be easier for both of you to jump right in and stir up a lively debate. The more you practice in "safe environments," the better prepared you'll be to speak up and hold your own when the stakes are high.

"When I start to feel myself getting emotional about a work issue," Takai told me, "I've taught myself to catch the emotion, step back, and try to listen in order to understand the other person's point of view. After doing this a few times, particularly with a friend with whom you feel safe, you realize that's the way you have to approach professional disagreement and challenges. If you don't feel personally attacked, you can speak forcefully without feeling (or coming across as) bitchy." As my mother frequently reminded us, "You don't have to be disagreeable to disagree."

Elizabeth Warren, the Harvard Law School professor who came to national prominence during the 2008-2009 U.S. financial crisis, repeatedly demonstrated the skill and tenacity of "good clean fighting" while serving as chair of the Congressional Oversight Panel for TARP (Troubled Asset Relief Program). Warren also led the charge for financial reform legislation, which became law in 2010. Listen to the words she used to describe the political fight required to establish the new Consumer Protection Bureau.

> *"They (Wall Street banks) fought us every single inch of the way. They announced in August of last year that the consumer agency was dead. And why was it dead? Because they were going to kill it. They were quoted in the New York Times. They were that sure of themselves. The lobbyists came out and said, 'We will kill the consumer agency.' They announced it. And they re-announced it. They announced its death over and over and over. If you check the papers, the agency was still dead as of February of this year. But we didn't give up. We scratched, and we bit, and we hung on. And today here's where we are. With a good, strong set of tools to change the consumer market."*[11]

No matter how passionately they may disagree, most people are reluctant to speak up and confront others, particularly in large groups. If you see things differently than others whose voices are dominating an important discussion, chances are you're not the only one in the room who feels that way. It's up to leaders to make sure that all sides of an issue are thoroughly considered. "Men count on women being more easily worn down, shouted down and put down, so they will fade away and allow males to fight it out amongst themselves for whose in charge," says one male executive friend of mine. Take a page from the leadership playbooks of Ursula Burns, Teri Takai, and Elizabeth Warren. When the debates begin, put your shoulders back, take a deep breath, and model for other women who are watching why fighting smart is an important part of the leadership practice of saddling back up. The more you do it, the easier it will get it.

Learn from Mistakes

"Women have a tendency to second guess ourselves, rethink mistakes and setbacks," says Susan Peters, vice president of executive development for General Electric. "That can be debilitating. You have to learn to get over it. A differentiator for women to move into leadership roles is the ability to say, 'That sucks, but I get it and I'm moving on.'"

I shudder when I think back on some of the foolish mistakes I made over the years. One of the most embarrassing occurred during my first year as a TV news and sports anchor. Thanks to a tip from a longtime family friend, I was the first reporter to learn that Greg Landry, the starting quarterback for our Detroit Lions NFL team, had been traded. Eager to prove myself, I insisted on getting on-air credit for breaking the story on our six o'clock news. Later that evening, when I was co-anchoring the 11 o'clock news, I was incensed that our sports anchor, Charlie Neal, didn't mention that I had broken the story. To my everlasting shame, I challenged him on the air as he finished his sportscast saying, "Charlie, why didn't you mention that I was the first to break the news about Landry being traded?" I can't remember exactly how he responded to my unprofessional ad lib. Charlie was pretty smooth, so I'm sure he batted the comment away like an irritating fly. I was so busy carrying a big chip on my shoulder and being angry that he hadn't given me credit, I barely heard his response. To this day, I regret that incident, which only lasted a few seconds, but revealed a lot about how much I had to learn. It took me a long time to forgive myself and let it go.

But the lesson was invaluable. I discovered how easily our emotions, particularly anger, can override professionalism. Like Teri Takai, I learned to monitor my emotions and guard against my tongue saying things I'd regret. "The best advice I ever received came from the Dean of the Business School at Wayne State University," Mary Kramer, publisher of *Crain's Detroit Business* and the first woman president of the prestigious Detroit Athletic Club, told me. "'Don't make it a morality play, Mary,' he said. There is hardly a day that goes by that I don't think about his wise words. When you have a clear sense of what is right and what is wrong, it's easy to get emotionally invested in outcomes. But if you really want to accomplish something, take the emotion out of it," Kramer advises. "Instead of righteous indignation, step back, check your emotions and figure out 'How am I going to get what I really want?'"

No matter how grievously you've been wronged, attacked, or offended, before you stick your foot in your mouth, count to ten, or maybe even 25. There's always plenty of time to speak your mind, but never enough to take back words you regret. "We are all flawed. You have to admit your mistakes and move on. You can't dwell on them," says Wayne County Prosecutor Kym Worthy, who says she doesn't mind sharing the missteps she's made along the way. As an elected official, Worthy was publicly embarrassed and openly criticized when the news media reported that she had fallen behind on her property taxes. "They never report the whole story," Worthy told me. "I had paid $6,000 of my $8,000 bill, so was only late with the remaining $2,000. But you can't let the fear of something personal coming out about you affect how you do your job. The bottom line," she says, "is not to live your life looking into the rearview mirror."

As long as we learn from our mistakes, each time we pick ourselves up and get back out there, we become stronger. The best coaches use mistakes to build confidence in athletes. "If you aren't persistent and resilient, you're not going to make it. That's what we teach kids in athletics," says widely-admired Big Ten softball coach Carol Hutchins. "We knock them down and teach them how to come right back and keep fighting. Once an individual realizes, 'You might knock me down, but you're not going to knock me out,' she becomes empowered." If you haven't failed recently—and I mean *really* failed—then you haven't tested your full capabilities. What are you waiting for? Stick your neck out. And when you make mistakes, which you will, don't even think about retreating and wallowing in your wounds. Pick yourself up, dust yourself off, and get right back into the fray. Just make sure you *learn* the lessons each mistake teaches, so you don't need to make the same ones over again.

Know When to Hold 'Em and When to Fold 'Em

Every list I've ever found of the essential qualities for success always includes *perseverance.* I think of it as the mental strength to hang in there and overcome whatever obstacles and difficulties life and other people throw at us. But equally important is the ability to recognize when you're pounding your head against a brick wall. *Getting Back in the Saddle* doesn't always mean to keep charging at the same obstacle that got you bucked off in the first place. Sometimes, the smartest thing you can do is pack up, jump on your horse and gallop off to greener pastures. Knowing *when to hold 'em and when to fold 'em* is an ability that will serve you well. Billie Jean King, one of the greatest athletes of our time, talks about this leadership behavior in her book *Pressure Is a Privilege*: "To enjoy life and make the best of it, try to recognize when it's time to try a different approach, and when it's time to just walk in a new direction."[12]

I've had to "walk in a new direction" many times in my life. I've voluntarily left high-profile, well-paying jobs in TV news, TV sports, and the auto industry. I've adopted a child—with only eight weeks notice—and gone through a painful and difficult divorce. I've buried my 22-year-old sister, my young son's 37-year-old father, and both of my parents. And, while working on this book, my life took an unnerving and unexpected turn when I received the bad news millions of women have faced: breast cancer. I was very lucky. Thanks to regular mammograms, we found my Stage I, noninvasive cancer early. Following a small lumpectomy, I went through eight weeks of radiation therapy and will be taking Tamoxifen for several more years. I don't think of myself as a survivor or particularly unusual. I'm just one of the millions of people who, every day, come up against difficult times, figure out the best way to handle them, and move on. We all face transitions. Some we choose. Others choose us. Whether you're struggling with major obstacles in your career, agonizing through difficult days in a personal relationship, torn over work/life balance dilemmas, or grappling with other issues that trigger major angst and foreshadow change, I urge you to welcome these inevitable periods of "white water" as important growth opportunities.

Women take breaks from traditional career tracks much more frequently than our male peers—often by choice. The rhythms and priorities of our lives are very different than those of most men. Perhaps you're an *Innovator* or *Insider* who dialed down to focus on children and serve as the COO of your household, or an *Interloper* stepping up to care for elderly parents. *Getting Back in the Saddle* is what women who hope to return to leadership tracks must do. Not long ago, the price for leaving the fast track was steep—it was nearly impossible for women to regain an upward trajectory after taking a break. That's changing as leading edge companies increasingly seek innovative approaches for retaining and re-engaging high-potential women today. But it's still an uphill slog.

One of the best books I've found on the topic is *Off-Ramps and On-Ramps: Keeping Talented Women on the Road to Success.* Author Sylvia Ann Hewlett, a nationally recognized thought leader on issues of gender and work, is the founding president of the Center for Work-Life Policy and the Director of the Gender and Policy Program at Columbia University's School of International and Public Affairs. "At the nub of the problem is the fact that women are not male clones, they are not merely 'men in skirts,' to use Shirley Conran's inimitable language," Dr. Hewlett writes. "A large percentage of highly qualified professional women have different needs and wants and find it extremely difficult to replicate the white male competitive model. They tend to have serious responsibilities on the home front [to children, to elderly parents], and they have somewhat different professional aspirations. We need to develop work environments where women can both take charge and take care."[13]

There are two very different mindsets that I believe shape how individuals deal with life passages. Some people—I call them *Explorers*—welcome change. They're the ones who are always scanning the horizon for the next mountain to climb. I'm one of them. When I run into resistance, my first instinct is to go around it. My brother, Tom, once told me, "Anne, you are the best quitter I've ever known." He meant it as a compliment. I've always known when it was time to leave. The challenge for me through the years has been developing the patience to determine when it's better to persevere and "hold 'em." I've had to work at this. It's important to evaluate whether problems we're up against are worth fighting our way through before we throw up our hands and "fold 'em."

Perhaps you identify more with people I call *Settlers* They have a very different mindset. *Settlers* are builders who put down roots. They tend to be loyal; sometimes too loyal. Tenacity and perseverance are some of their greatest strengths. Change is more difficult for them. Their challenge is to recognize—earlier rather than later—when it's time to stop pounding their heads against brick walls. They need to learn when to "fold 'em." Whether your natural instinct is to hang in there when the going gets tough or to cut your losses early, I've learned that there is a time for both.

Today, when there are over 1,000 women journalists covering sports in the United States, people often ask me, "Why did you leave TV, Anne?" I've never regretted that decision. It wasn't easy to make, but the day came when I realized I had run into a cultural brick wall that stood between me and what I planned as my next career step: covering sports for one of the national networks. In the early 1980s, ESPN was little more than an ambitious start-up; CNN was in its infancy; and Fox Sports, MSNBC, and multiple other sports channels didn't exist. ABC, NBC, and CBS were the TV "big dogs." Their idea of women covering sports was Phyllis George or Jayne Kennedy, former beauty queens whose primary role was to decorate the all-male sports shows. I didn't realize at the time that it would be decades before significant numbers of women would make serious inroads into sports journalism. I was simply impatient, ambitious, and didn't want to keep doing the same work in the seventh largest TV market, hoping for national opportunities to open up. So I finished my contract with WJBK-TV in Detroit, submitted my resignation, and moved to Atlanta. I had no job and no clue what I was going to do next.

I'm not suggesting that as a career strategy. My transition in Atlanta was very difficult. While trying to figure out my next career move, I took a part-time job as a news editor for the southeast bureau of United Press

International (UPI). I worked the graveyard shift—all alone—writing and editing news wire copy from 10 p.m. to 6 a.m. During a weekend trip home, I injured my back while body surfing in Lake Michigan. I couldn't sit for two weeks. My only choice was to do my UPI shift on my knees in front of my computer. I needed the money. During that difficult, self-imposed transition, I remember standing in line at a 7-Eleven store. While watching the cashier checking out the person in front of me, I thought to myself, "Well, there's a job I could do."

Confidence and self-esteem are often the first things to start slipping away during difficult transitions. I know. I've been there. During our Great Recession that started in 2007 and still isn't over as I write, hundreds of thousands, perhaps millions, of skilled professionals who thought their careers were on very solid ground lost their jobs. "It's astonishing to me how fast things are happening in the business world today. People who once felt very secure now feel the ground moving beneath their feet," Terry Barclay, CEO of Inforum, a women's professional alliance and the Inforum Center for Leadership, told me. "Everybody gets hit with body blows at some point, but some recover faster than others," she's observed. "The ability to pick yourself up and change—quickly—is a major differentiator."

Difficult as they often are, transitions—if managed well—nearly always lead to new and often greater opportunities. Those years in Atlanta, while hardly the highlight of my career, served as refining fires. The move was a risk. I knew only one person there, my best friend Mary Allen. But it opened new paths I could never have predicted or imagined. Once I got over feeling sorry for myself, doors opened. I met my future husband, Mike Farrell, a charming Irishman. Coca-Cola became one of the first clients for my corporate communications business, giving me an insider's view of one of the most famous global brand blunders and recoveries: the introduction of New Coke and resurrection of Coke Classic. Most importantly, I met and became close friends with CNN executive Ann Williams. My friendship with her would lead to the unexpected and joyful opportunity to adopt our son, Kevin, who was born in Atlanta.

And when my brand-new husband's work brought us back to Detroit, another door opened. Ford Motor Company offered me an opportunity to put my journalism and corporate communications skills to work at one of the most respected companies in the world. None of those experiences would have been possible if I had not gotten right back in the saddle and taken the risk to move to Atlanta, after hitting a wall at the New York networks.

Here's another example of how I learned why "knowing when to fold 'em and when to hold 'em" is so valuable. When my son was 11 years old, I took an early retirement from a leadership position at Ford. By then, I was a single parent and the sole support of myself and my son. As much as I loved my work, the global travel and financial rewards, not to mention all the cool vehicles, as Kevin approached those critical adolescent years, I wanted more flexibility and control over my schedule—as so many women, particularly mothers, often do. My decision to request an early retirement forced me to embark on another difficult transition. I was only 53, but I didn't want to take another full-time, fast track job.

"Too often people think to themselves, 'I'm an accountant or I am an engineer or homemaker,' without thinking how the skills and abilities they developed doing that work are transferrable to many other arenas," says PhD Glenda Price, whose career has taken her from hospital laboratory professional to faculty member, dean, provost, and college president at four higher education institutions in three regions of the country. "We get hung up on the need to have professional goals or a life plan. I've never had a life plan. I don't want a life plan. My life has evolved and it's been wonderful. I don't know what the next steps are, but I know they will be just as wonderful."

Because of my unusual career path, I learned long ago to think of myself in terms of my skills and strengths—writing, public speaking, strategic thinking, managing information and empowering others—rather than positions I've held. That's one of the reasons I decided to write this book, which gave me the flexibility I craved while my son was in high school. Writing it was one of the hardest things I've ever done—other than parenting. It's lonely work that took me nearly three years. At times, I felt as if I was swimming in circles in the middle of the Pacific Ocean with no idea which way shore was. At other times, I felt the exhilaration of meeting and talking about leadership with several hundred fascinating and highly-accomplished women who agreed to be interviewed and trusted me to pass along their hard-earned wisdom. On the days that I felt discouraged, I reminded myself that my struggle was self-created, that there was no "folding 'em" this time. I had made a commitment. Finishing this book was also an exercise in personal discipline and a reality check of how well I could practice what I preach about the importance of perseverance.

Transitions never end. As long as we are alive and open to possibilities, fresh opportunities are all around us. I have no idea how my life would have evolved if I had stayed on my original career path. Looking back, I wouldn't change a thing. I've learned to roll with the punches and bend but not break, as the willow has taught us. I'm convinced that each time we successfully navigate a major life change, pick ourselves up after a defeat, or reinvent ourselves, we emerge stronger and better prepared for the next tests. When you find yourself facing pending change or a major crossroad, before you make your move, ask yourself the question Billie Jean King recommends: "Is this time to try a different approach? Or is it time to walk in a new direction?" Knowing the distinction will make all the difference.

Recognize and Welcome Defining Moments

Throughout this book, I've talked about defining moments I've faced in my life. Everyone has them. They are the times when you feel you're over your head in pretty deep water. You may hear that little voice inside whispering "Let's get out of here. This is too hard." People around you—some critics, others well-intentioned family or friends—may be saying "You're not ready," "Why are you taking this risk?," or "Be content with what you have."

All defining moments are opportunities that fall into one of two camps. One I call *Mirror Moments,* the other I call *Springboard Moments.* Mirror moments are those times when we are tested, but fail. They show us we're not ready. We have work to do. If we're paying attention, *Mirror Moments* always reflect valuable information about areas of ourselves that need polishing. *Springboard Moments* are just the opposite. They are those exhilarating times when we are tested and pass with flying colors. They spring us to a higher level. When you find yourself resenting critics, struggling to recover your confidence after a mistake or defeat, or slogging your way through difficult personal transitions, reflect on what every defining moment is: a chance to discover something about yourself you didn't know—either a shortcoming that needs fixing or a strength you had underestimated. Next time you see a defining moment coming, think of it as opportunity knocking. Open the door and let her in. Just don't forget to saddle up first.

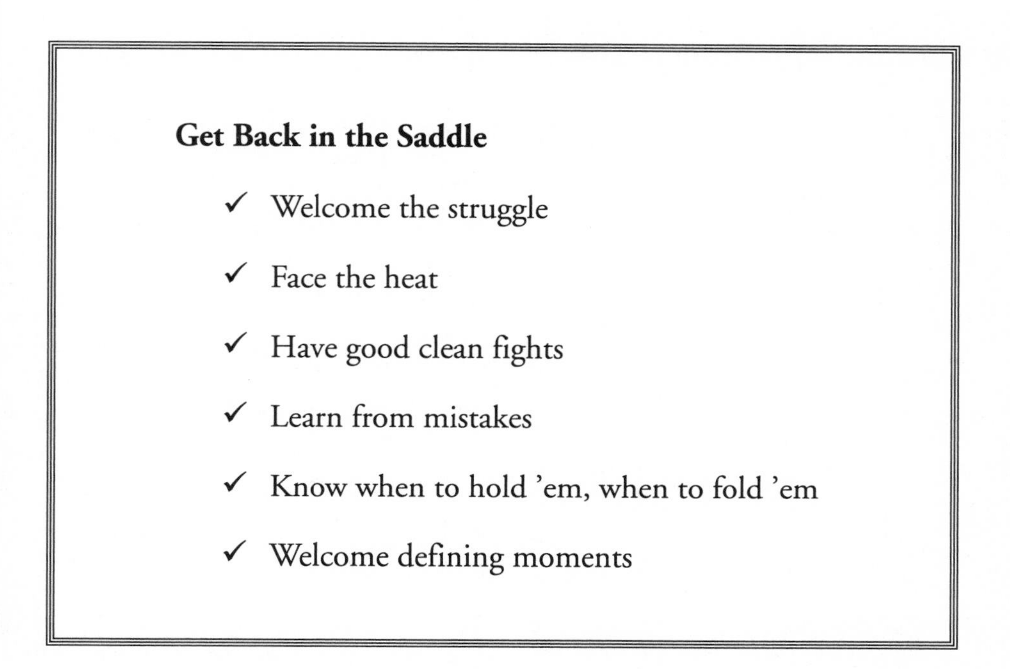

Get Back in the Saddle

- ✓ Welcome the struggle
- ✓ Face the heat
- ✓ Have good clean fights
- ✓ Learn from mistakes
- ✓ Know when to hold 'em, when to fold 'em
- ✓ Welcome defining moments

CHAPTER 13

Womaninity— Beyond the Girls and the Guys

If you're born a girl, grow up and live long enough, you can become an old female. But to become a woman is a serious matter. A woman takes responsibility for the time she takes up and the space she occupies.

— MAYA ANGELOU, Poet, Playwright, Author, *Interloper*

Womaninity is to masculinity as Ms. is to Mr. You won't find *womaninity* in a dictionary or in Wikipedia. It's a new word I've coined to describe female adults who have learned to draw upon and become comfortable with all the strengths and uniqueness of our gender. *Womaninity* is much more than femininity, which multiple dictionaries define as Webster's does: "Weak; gentle; the softer and more delicate qualities apparent to a woman; the opposite of masculinity." I cringed as I read that definition. It's so limited, describing feminine behavior primarily in contrast to male characteristics. If we've been conditioned (as most of us have) to believe that masculine men are strong, then their gender opposite would be weak. If we believe that manly men are courageous and natural leaders, then feminine women would be cautious and more comfortable as followers. Right? So wrong.

Our learned concepts of feminine and masculine behavior, imbedded like powerful computer chips in our American mindset, create all kinds of confusion when it comes to leadership. "I think that 'femininity' carries a lot of baggage," says Dr. Terry Sullivan, president of the University of Virginia and a native Texan whose leadership style is as direct as her handshake. "I grew up in the South. Femininity there carried a real undertone of deception because you appeared weak but you weren't," she told me. "You might let the men seem like they were in control but the object was to stay in control." Even young *Innovators* are discovering that the line women in positions of authority must walk hasn't widened much. "You have to come across as nice and friendly. But you also have to be strong in your opinions without being bitchy," said 33-year-old Kelly Schilling, one of the youngest and few female senior vice presidents with Spysource, a Texas-based financial services software company. "It's this crazy tightrope!"

That "crazy tightrope" is widening—slowly. That's why discovering and fully developing our *Womaninity* is the seventh key to America's female *Achievers* becoming the *Leaders* we are ready to be.

What do you think of when you hear the word *womaninity?* Does it make you a little uncomfortable? Is it hard to say because it doesn't roll off your tongue with familiarity? Or does it resonate right away as it did with so many women I tested it on? "I totally get it. I am a person who embraces my gender, and I want my players to embrace the fact that they're strong women who are very good at what they do." That was the instant response of University of Michigan head softball coach Carol "Hutch" Hutchins, who is as passionate about developing women leaders as she is about instilling a winner's mindset in her athletes. "People like the masculine man. What's the female version of being a fully evolved human being? Our *womaninity*," she told me, "is every bit as important as men's masculinity."

Womaninity, I'm certain, is what Maya Angelou was getting at when she wrote "To become a woman is a serious matter." It's an adjective for women with the ambition to become a Supreme Court justice or a military general, but who have not abandoned their natural empathy for others and relationship orientation. It's a word that works when trying to describe women with the courage and tenacity to engage in open competition with men, while still trusting the value of their unique female perspective. It embodies the versatility of women who manage a multitude of demands, yet still engage in the world as ardent and—at our best—fierce protectors, nurturers, and, yes, mothers to the human family. Gone are the days when *Interlopers* needed to neutralize ourselves with navy blue power suits and look to men for leadership models. When *Insiders* felt the only way they could fit in with "the guys" was by distancing themselves from "the girls." Or when women felt they had to make an either/or choice between career and family.

Women throughout the world are shedding our "second sex" status. It's time to begin describing women not in comparison to what men *aren't* but as what fully evolved females *can be*. That's what *womaninity* and this chapter are all about.

I'll Start Wearing a Tie When . . .

If there was ever an ambitious, accomplished evolved woman leader who refuses to minimize her female side, it is Kathleen Ligocki. I've quoted her several times throughout this book, but here's my favorite story about her leadership style. A high-energy, global executive who speaks three languages, she's an *Influential Insider* with long red hair and a quick wit. Ligocki also has one of those voluptuous figures that's hard to hide—even beneath a St. John suit. I'm not implying for a second that she plays the sexual card in business environments. She doesn't. Yet she also understands that her *womaninity* is as essential to her leadership style as masculinity is to a male leader's. Even in her 20s, during her first week on the job in a testosterone-laden, manufacturing plant, Ligocki had the confidence and savvy to know she didn't need to model herself after men in order to succeed. When her tough, old-school plant manager told the first female member of his leadership team that "she'd have to wear a tie, just like everyone else in management," Ligocki didn't miss a beat. "When the men start wearing bras," she responded, "that's when I'll start wearing a tie." That was the end of the discussion and the beginning of Ligocki's path to leadership. Her refusal to model herself after men didn't slow her one bit, as she rose to hold multiple CEO positions in the fiercely-competitive global auto industry. Kathleen Ligocki understands how and when to play her *womaninity* card.

Brand New Territory

One of the challenges of our times is for women, collectively, to move beyond the limitations of *femininity* and evolve to the full possibilities of *womaninity.* In the scheme of cultural evolution, a feminine alternative to widely accepted masculine leadership behavior is brand new territory. Women have barely begun to get our leadership sea legs in the upper echelons where the guys still rule. Those of us who dare to raise our voices, break the rules, and claim power still run the risk of being scrutinized and dissected under an outdated social microscope. It will take decades to unearth and wash away all of the sexism still deeply embedded in our culture. Most of the time, it is hidden just beneath a "politically correct" veneer. It can flare up quickly, however, when ambitious women overstep the boundaries of America's gender comfort zones. Throughout this book, I have referenced "Sexism Sells . . . But We're Not Buying It." The disturbing video montage features clip after clip of blatantly sexist comments by well-known TV broadcasters including this classic: "Men shouldn't allow the vagina monologue to become a vagina dialogue." You can view the six-minute video on YouTube or www.womensmediacenter.com.[1] In 2009, I showed "Sexism Sells" to journalism and business students at Indiana University, where I had been invited to speak. The young women and men were stunned by the blatant misogyny of the TV news clips. While they watched the video, I watched them. Many shook their heads or winced in disbelief; several actually jerked in their seats, startled by comments made on national TV such as, "Men are depressed and it's their own fault. They are allowing women to take over the world."

Afterward, I probed the nearly 100 college juniors and seniors on what they thought. They had plenty to say. The overwhelming reaction of both male and female students was astonishment. Most said they "had no idea" such backward attitudes about women were awaiting them in the workforce.

Discovering what I mean by the leadership practice of *Womaninity* begins with recognizing two truths: First, our gender is a strength to be embraced and developed rather than an obstacle to be overcome. Second, it's time women *Achievers* realize that we will never truly be "one of the guys," nor should we aspire to be. If those two principles ring true to you, then you are ready to tap the power of your own *womaninity.* It has taken me several decades to finally accept that deep cultural change requires a long time to take root. Just as it took decades for people to get used to seeing women surgeons, judges, police officers, ministers, TV news anchors, and construction workers, our society needs time to become very comfortable with women in leadership positions. Instead of wringing our hands and commiserating about the obstacles we face, let's get on with the task at hand. Leadership is the next frontier for women. Each of us must do our part—individually and collectively—to help move the needle by expanding society's expectations of how "womanly" women act. We're modeling expanded female behavior styles for others to follow, which offer new options for moving beyond being simply "one of the girls," without modeling ourselves after "the guys." The good news is that the strengths, collaborative approach, and expanded perspective that women are bringing to leadership are beginning to be recognized and valued as never before. Courageous, extraordinary females who are taking the heat and leading the way have begun to forge a new leadership template. A woman's template.

Tapping the Power of Womaninity

This chapter is about four strong threads that weave their way through the fiber of a woman who has learned to tap the strength of her *womaninity.* The threads take years to spin. The first is becoming truly relaxed in your own skin. That includes understanding the intuitive strengths of our feminine gender. Second is learning to be a platonic peer, friend, and professional ally to men. The third is joining the Sisterhood, which is the magic ingredient to achieving collective power. Fourth is thinking like a woman, which includes trusting the validity of "women's intuition" and stepping up to our mothering responsibilities to protect, nurture, and guide the human family. Let's take a look at how stretching your wings beyond society's present expectations for women is another essential step on the path to becoming the leader you've long suspected you were born to be.

Relaxed in Your Own Skin

For centuries, women have been culturally pressured to walk a narrow band of acceptable female behavior. Too often that meant "knowing our place," playing second fiddle to men, and using our sexuality to get what we wanted. It also meant hiding our ambition or risk being judged *unfeminine.* Today, we're on the verge of creating another norm for ascending adult women. It is a model that gives us the freedom to lead with our instinctive strengths, rather than patterning ourselves after male behavior. It means trusting our judgment and leaning into the full power of our feminine side without misplaying the sexuality card. The days of trying to "macho up" and lead like a man are nearly over. Whew! That tactic didn't work very well, anyway. Trying to squeeze ourselves into male templates was always a Catch-22. But many of us tried (including me), only to be repeatedly reminded that if we were measured against purely male standards, we would always come up short. Expanding the possibilities for how leaders look and act is up to us. It has to begin with being truly comfortable with the bodies we were born into. *Interlopers, Insiders*, and *Innovators* have very different comfort levels in this area.

For many *Interlopers* of my generation, femininity felt like a sticky goo that labeled and limited us. We tried to crawl out by neutralizing ourselves in the workplace. Emotionally, we wrapped ourselves in flak jackets of pure professionalism and controlled our softer, lighter sides that might betray us as not "having the cojones" to handle the positions we aspired to. Physically, we modeled men's professional dress with conservative, power suits paired with buttoned-up blouses and scarves tied like bows (simulated ties) at our necks. By the time *Insiders* arrived on the scene, women didn't need the "armor" of navy blue suits to ensure they wouldn't be automatically asked to make the coffee and take the meeting notes. It helped, of course, that department stores finally caught wind of an exploding market in professional women's attire and began stocking entire floors with new possibilities. Today, there's a whole new twist to how women are dressing for work. Form-fitting and often revealing clothing have become all too commonplace in professional environments. "I think what's missing today is the understanding of the impact clothing has on what people think of you," says *Interloper* Barbara Whittaker, one of the first (and few) African American women who rose to executive positions at GM. "My generation got the message (about not sending confusing signals with our dress), perhaps too far. I think it got lost in the business casual thing. But you don't see men making this mistake. It's the young women who are falling into it."

What happened? Susan Douglas, author of *Enlightened Sexism: The Seductive Message that the Work of Feminism Is Done*, thinks she knows. Chair of the Department of Communications Studies at the University of Michigan, Douglas makes the compelling case that American pop culture has embedded an insidious, counter-feminist message into young women's consciousness. For the last two decades, Douglas says, American movies, TV, and music videos have bombarded young people in particular with the mantra that "it's through sex and sexual display that women really have the power to get what they want. And because the true path to power comes from being an object of desire, girls and women should now actively choose—even celebrate and embrace—being sex objects." In other words, says Douglas, the cultural drumbeat to young women goes like this: "Of course you can be career-driven, as long as you are also a sex kitten."[2]

Women who drink this dangerous cultural Kool-Aid *and* aspire to positions of authority are making a critical mistake. ESPN sideline sports reporter Erin Andrews was the talk of the country for a few weeks in 2009 after a pervert peering through a peephole in her hotel room door taped her dancing in the nude and posted the video on the web. Her stalking was a crime. She didn't deserve that. But long before millions of people downloaded the embarrassing video, the beautiful, svelte *Innovator* was well-known among sports fans (primarily male) as the "sexiest sportscaster on TV." She earned that title, not only with her looks and figure, but by routinely dressing in form-fitting clothing and stiletto heels to cover sporting events. You'll find dozens of examples of what I'm talking about on the Internet, simply by searching for photos of Erin Andrews. Months after the peephole scandal had calmed down and her stalker had been arrested, Andrews accepted an invitation to compete on the TV show *Dancing with the Stars*. Her revealing costumes left little to the imagination. If Andrews' goal, and that of other women who lead with their sexual "assets," is to become an entertainer, she's on the right track. Madonna built her empire on sexual provocation, and Lady Gaga has turbo-charged herself to a spot on *Time* magazine's 2010 list of "100 Most Influential People in the World" the same way. But if Andrews' driving purpose is for a long career as a broadcast journalist, she's sending confusing signals and heading down a dead-end path. Looks will only take a woman so far, says *USA Today* columnist and ABC commentator Christine Brennan. "My advice for anyone—male or female—who has asked is always the same. Rely on your brains and your talents," Brennan told me. "Looks can come and looks can go. What will sustain you is your talent, your expertise and your brain. It's all about what you bring to the table."

How a woman dresses is a pretty valid Rorschach reflection of how she feels about herself. "I am probably much more comfortable being a woman in the last seven years than I have in my entire career," admitted California *Interloper* Joan LeMahieu, president of Mountain Winery. "Now I wear more feminine clothes even in business settings." When I first started working in TV news, it really bothered me how much attention viewers paid to what I was wearing. Many even wrote letters to my station suggesting that "Anne Doyle should add more color to her wardrobe" or "Your new anchorwoman should wear more make-up." Eventually, I accepted the fact that how I present myself through my clothing and personal style sends powerful signals about who I am or what I want others to know about me. My son, Kevin, has given me plenty of feedback over the years in this department. He once said to me, "Mom, you either look like the president or a barn lady [We live in the country and have horses; he's right that "barn lady" is definitely one of my "looks."]. Why can't you dress like the other mothers picking up their kids at school?" I'm comfortable with my professional style, which has evolved—as I have—over the years. I'm still working on that "in between" look.

But growing comfortably into our own skin is a skill that is much more than skin deep and takes more than re-thinking our wardrobe choices. "Power is tricky when you're a woman. Too much and you're a bitch. Too little and you're a pushover. And then there's that elusive 'femininity' thing. Leave off the makeup, and you're a dog. Layer it on, and you're too pretty to be smart. Kids? Careful! Bring them into the picture, and you're pandering; leave them at home, and you're a bad mom."[3] That's the way journalist Lynn Sherr, writing a profile of Congresswoman Nancy Pelosi for the October 2010 issue of *More* magazine, described the "comfortable in your own skin" dilemma that women leaders deal with daily.

Barbara Whittaker acknowledges that it has taken her three decades to relax into a leadership style that reflects who she truly is. "In school, I machoed up a little bit. Eventually, you have to get to the place where you can be you. Where you can say anything you want to. I finally got to that point by watching a very close friend who is also a female executive. I watched how comfortable she is and said to myself 'I need to let go.

I'm not going to be as effective as I could be unless I do. I'm not going to bring to the party what I really want to unless I do.' So that's what I finally did. And I feel much better."

No one can teach us how to relax into our own skin. It takes time to ease into it, until it fits just right. While you're searching for that perfect fit, do what comes most naturally. And keep scanning your horizon for influential women whose personal style and leadership *presence* you like. Watch them. First impressions are huge. Pay attention to the signals you are sending with your dress and how you handle yourself. Others are always watching, usually when you don't realize it. The key is to develop your own style, based on your taste and natural strengths. I love the way British executive coach Peninah Thomson of Praesta Partners, one of the leading executive coaching firms in Europe, put it in an interview for www.fiftylessons.com: "Deploy your whole personality. It's a tool in your tool kit. If you are charming, be charming. If you are articulate, be articulate. If you are persuasive, use your persuasive skills. For women, becoming comfortable with their personal power and authority is sometimes quite a sticky bit."[4]

A sticky bit? We wouldn't describe it quite that way here in America, but we know exactly what she's talking about. Trusting the leadership strengths of our gender is just as tricky for women on this side of the Atlantic. Knowing how to effectively play your feminine cards without sending signals that can be misinterpreted is a skill that comes with developing your *womaninity.* I like the advice that Cynthia Pasky, founder, president, and CEO of Strategic Staffing Solutions, which employs more than 1,700 people in the United States and Europe, gave to an audience of college-bound high school girls. "When you walk into a room, you want people to respect you first," she told them. Liking you comes after that. Don't mix the two."

Getting comfortable in our own skin is something each woman does at her own pace, in her own style. It takes a long time to get it right. That's why another essential step in discovering the power of *womaninity* is to stop trying to be "one of the guys."

Not One of the Guys

If we've learned anything by now, it should be that a woman will never truly be "one of the guys." It's never going to happen. The smartest women have given up trying. Millions of *Interlopers* and *Insiders* spent decades trying to become "equity partners" in male circles of trust. Don't be surprised or take it personally when you run into reminders from men—be they subtle or blunt—that you're not one of their tribe. The recent economic downturn provided powerful lessons in what I'm talking about. Multiple women partners in law firms have told me that they and other women in their firms were stunned by the way "the men circled the wagons and took care of their own," as one lawyer put it. "When business was in short supply, the men brought their male colleagues in on work teams first, making sure all of them made their numbers. It was all the evidence we (the women partners) needed," she told me, "that we'd never be part of the male partners 'inner circle' no matter how hard we worked."

Trying too hard to be accepted as one of the guys always was and always will be a mistake. Yet seasoned professional women still slip into this trap. Leslie Murphy, a CPA who rose to leadership roles with Plante Moran and now serves on multiple boards, witnessed an incident recently at a social gathering of businesspeople. "I was with a mixed group of men and women professionals. There was a woman in the group who felt the need to tell a very off-color joke in hopes, I think, of impressing the men," Murphy recounted. "I watched the reaction of the others in the group. Frankly, they were all embarrassed. It was so inappropriate. At the time, I thought, 'What is going on here? What environment has she been in where that tactic has been successful?' This was a very accomplished woman. But I saw a person who isn't comfortable being a woman in a mixed crowd," Murphy said.

A female leader who is in touch with her *womaninity* is a true peer with men—but doesn't make the mistake of mimicking male behavior. Take it from a leader who helped navigate the uncharted gender waters of the world of fighter pilots (remember the Tom Cruise movie *Top Gun*?). "If you try too hard to be one of the guys, it can backfire," says Air Force Colonel and pilot

Dawn Dunlop. "I know a few women who tried to one-up guys in social settings or tell jokes that just ended badly. The men could always raise the bar to new levels," she said. "The women may have thought their behavior would help make them one of the team, but it actually caused more problems in the long run. It's always a mistake to try to be someone that you're not." Dunlop acknowledges that women can effectively bring a wide range of feminine behavior to the workplace. Each woman must make that choice herself, depending on her professional environment and personal style. "I've always found it simpler to err on the conservative side, keeping a clear gender buffer in behavior and actions between myself and male peers. I think this is especially true when you are the one woman and single data point for men in a work group. But it's still important for people to understand you are a woman, even when you're in a typically male role."

GE executive Susan Peters is deeply immersed in what it takes for leaders of both genders to be successful. As vice president of executive development, Peters has responsibility for the renowned GE Management Development Institute. It is as true as ever that women leaders are held to higher standards and need to go the extra mile to adapt to male environments. But Peters says it is no longer a one-way street. "Whether we like it or not, I think our current reality, even today, is that you have to be able to play ball with the guys," she advises. "I don't believe the future enables women to just be pure women. If they're going to lead, they have to be able to cross the culture divide [between men and women]. But it's becoming true both ways. In other words, the best male leaders are also capable of understanding and interfacing with women in a broader way." Sounds as if Peters is expanding the template for effective male leaders, too. But that's another book.

Some of the best insight about holding your own with highly ambitious men comes from women who have played competitive sports. Mary Petrovich, CEO of Axle-Tech International, a heavily male-driven engineering and manufacturing company, is a four handicap golfer who was MVP of her college softball team. "I know that a lot of women are intimidated by working with men, especially guys who try to out-muscle you," she told me. "I think of a guy I faced off with when a private equity firm bought our business. He wanted to be the CEO and spent a year studying the business. The private equity firm stuck with me as the CEO but they kept him on as an adviser. He was your classic blowhard. He was about talking big and making promises, pounding his fist and telling everyone how great he is. That's exactly what I'm not," said Petrovich. So how do you work with a rival like that? Petrovich wouldn't still be the CEO—which she is—if she hadn't been up to the test. "I've had to work with guys like that my entire career. I just let them go on," she advises. "When he's done, I show the group what I've got. My results. Pretty soon he starts quieting down. He starts realizing he's not getting any respect from the talent that's sitting across from him. The ability to be comfortable with men as peers is essential in environments that are very tough and, frankly, discriminating. You have to be good at working with the boys," advises this leader who has successfully passed many a male's test.

Recognizing that you'll never be one of the guys while still being able to work as a professional peer and, when necessary, go toe-to-toe with men are essential ingredients of *womaninity.* Once you stop wasting energy on trying to become part of the guys' inner circle, the next step is to join your own tribe.

Side with your Sisters

You may be aware that a few decades back, women were locked out of important, professional organizations such as the Rotary, Lions, Elks, Moose and Optimists. It was Judge Hilda Gage who presided over a precedent-setting lawsuit brought against the Elks Club in 1988 for refusing to allow women to become members. Gage, who went on to a distinguished career as the Michigan Court of Appeals, ruled that the Elks' "no-women allowed" policy was in violation of federal law. For ten years, the Elks challenged Gage's decision and kept their legal fight alive to block women from membership. They failed. Not only did Judge Gage's ruling stand, it opened a floodgate of professional networking opportunities for women in previously male-only service organizations throughout the United States.[5] Ironically, if it weren't for the support of other women—in the voting booths and in countless other ways—Gage, who recently passed away, told me, she might never have been a judge. In 1978, during her first judicial campaign, as she stood outside plant gates in the dark greeting voters as they arrived for work, she routinely faced men who refused to accept her leaflets. Many told her bluntly, "I wouldn't vote for a woman judge." Every step was uphill, but once in awhile she got an unexpected boost. During the campaign, she was invited to participate in a panel of candidates speaking at an Optimists Club luncheon. "It was very noisy during lunch. But when it was my turn to speak, I noticed that it was suddenly very quiet. I looked in the back of the room and all of the waitresses were standing with their arms folded, listening," Gage recalls. "They had stopped serving to listen to me and to make sure it was quiet for me to speak. That is what sisterhood can mean."

Gage's story is one of my favorite examples of the power of sisterhood in action. Men (primarily white, middle and upper-class men) still have a firm grip on the levers of power. They mentor, promote, and align with those they are most comfortable with, which nearly always translates into: other men. There's no point in wasting energy worrying or complaining about all the ways that male networks give men a major advantage in professional arenas. Staying within personal comfort zones is human nature; the leadership skill of "Drinking at Dangerous Waters" is one men need to work on, too.

If it's lonely at the top for men, it's even lonelier for women. And the higher you go, the lonelier it gets. Even in organizations and work environments with a track record of valuing and developing women's contributions, it can be a very isolating experience to be in a highly visible position of authority when nearly all of your peers are men. "There were many times during my career when I got to the most senior leadership positions that I felt very lonely," says Judith Mühlberg, who was always a few steps ahead of me during our years together at Ford. She rose from an intern in the Nixon White House to executive positions with Ford Motor Company and Boeing, earning her law degree along the way. "It often felt like that song, 'One Is the Loneliest Number,' because there were no natural opportunities inside for me to compare leadership tactics or even leadership anxieties with others." Mühlberg went outside for peer support she found through organizations like the Arthur Page Society (for chief communications officers of Fortune 500 companies). But external support isn't enough, says Mühlberg, who is now a Washington, D.C.-based consultant and adjunct professor at Georgetown University with two ambitious, *Innovator* daughters. She's hopeful that the next generation of women *Achievers* will have a greater capacity for developing strong networks early in their careers. "Women are at fault because we haven't traditionally extended ourselves to network with each other the same way men do," Mühlberg acknowledged. "Men engage in sports like golf and that becomes their network. Right now a lot of corporate cultures, in particular, use terms like diversity and inclusion. Yet they are more aspirational than they are reality. Reaching out to other women at all levels of your organization can be a very important way of creating a culture that is truly inclusive." Joining the Sisterhood is a great way to start.

There's a code among men of not betraying the Brotherhood. "American men want to be a 'man among men,' an Arnold Schwarzenegger–like 'man's man,' not a Fabio-like 'ladies man,'" says sociologist Michael Kimmel, a leading expert in gender studies and author of several acclaimed books, including *Manhood in America.* "Masculinity is largely a 'homosocial experience: performed for, and judged by, other men," Kimmel writes in his latest book *Guyland: The Perilous World Where Boys Become Men.*[6] Rare is the man who will buck the brotherhood and go to bat for a woman he's not romantically involved with. Yet to move up in competitive environments, that's exactly what it takes: powerful advocates going to bat for you. Facebook Chief Operating Officer Sheryl Sandberg, a 41-year-old *Insider*, former Google executive and Silicon Valley superstar, distinguished herself with her Harvard economics professor, Lawrence Summers, who served most recently as chief economic adviser to the Obama Administration. Summers became Sandberg's thesis adviser and eventually a powerful sponsor, hiring her to work with him at the World Bank and, later, as his chief of staff while he was Treasury Secretary during the Clinton Administration.[7] There are still not enough powerful women with the influence and connections of Larry Summers to mentor and open prestigious doors for other female superstars. But even when women are in positions to give a hand up to others, there's no such "femininity code" of taking care of your sisters. To the contrary, we're more likely to see other women as our primary competition for men's attention and for the limited "female spots" at the tables of power. The sooner you realize that women are always going to be outliers in male circles, the quicker you will understand why it's essential to cultivate a strong network of influential female allies. Many seasoned women leaders confided to me that one of their biggest mistakes was not looking around for other influential women to align with earlier in their careers.

In 2007, *Harvard Business Review* published "Women and the Labyrinth of Leadership," an article based on a book by the same name by researchers Alice Eagly and Linda Carli. They threw the glass ceiling metaphor right out the window, reporting that it's actually a complex *labyrinth* of twists and turns that women face at every step of their careers. "When you put all the pieces together, a new picture emerges for why women don't make it into the C-suites," Eagli and Carli reported. "It's not the glass ceiling, but the sum of many obstacles along the way." One of their key recommendations for navigating the labyrinth was for ambitious women and companies interested in retaining them to "shore up social capital." In other words, put in place "strong and supportive mentoring relationships and connections with powerful networks." The more powerful the "Sisters" become, the more interested our "Brothers" will be in cross-gender alignments.

Women's Leadership Networks

The good news for *Insiders* and *Innovators,* in particular, is that women's leadership networks are sprouting up all over. Early adapter companies like

Booz Allen, Johnson and Johnson, Deloitte, Plante & Moran, General Electric, and many others are leading the way. GE created its Women's Network in 1995. Since then, it has grown to more than 150 hubs around the world. Its annual, invitation-only, business-focused conference is now a hot ticket, not only with GE's high-potential women but also for female leaders at customer and supplier companies who vie for invitations. Topnotch speakers are a big draw, but it's the rare opportunity to meet and build working relationships with other powerful women throughout GE's global operations that make the conference a "don't miss" event. In its infancy, not everyone at GE, however, was a believer in the value of a women-only network, including *Insider* Charlene Begley, who became GE's youngest ever corporate officer at age 32. "I was reluctant at first because I spent my whole career trying to say 'I'm just as good [as the men].' I was not trying to be noticed for being young or being a woman, but just for what I accomplished. So I didn't want to be pulled in a room with a bunch of women and focus on being a woman." It didn't take long, however, for Begley, now president and CEO of GE Home and Business Solutions, to change her mind. "It was at my very first meeting that I realized how many women really needed to network with each other. To talk about some of the stresses they had in their life and to see that there are women who are also mothers who have big jobs in this company and can do really well. At that moment it clicked. I realized 'This is really, really important.'"

Not everyone is lucky enough to work in an organization that has a senior women's network as highly evolved as GE's. But the Sisterhood is everywhere. All you have to do is start looking. When you find women who have learned the importance of supporting and advocating for other members of our own cultural tribe, align with them. Show them the ropes. Open doors and help them rise. Share your network. Ask them to do the same for you. That's *womaninity* in action. "I am desperate for women to encourage each other—with the courage in that word—to take the next steps toward leadership," says Marie Wilson, founding president of the White House Project and a co-creator (with Gloria Steinem) of the original *Take Our Daughters to Work Day.* Her organization is working to develop women leaders at all levels, particularly in elected office from grassroots politics all the way to the Oval Office. "In our leadership program, we insist that no one leave our training until they have said what they will do to support other women in the group. It's essential to understand that we will only move if we move together," says Wilson.

NBC News correspondent Anne Thompson, a personal friend and colleague from our days together in Detroit TV where she honed her reporting skills, put it another way during a recent speech, telling 600 women leaders, "If there is anything I've learned over my years of covering change, it is this: power for change occurs when individuals set aside their differences and start thinking about themselves as part of a group. The strongest power is not with individuals but what we can accomplish as a group."

Think like a Woman

The final and perhaps most powerful thread that will connect you to the leadership practice of *womaninity* is your state of mind. Being told that you "think like a man" was once considered a compliment for a woman. It's not. Thanks to new research on how differently male and female brains process information, we now have scientific evidence of what we all knew anyway: men and women think very differently. Even more importantly, human behavior researchers have confirmed that the once mysterious "female intuition" is a very real and valuable skill. Today, it's been repackaged as "emotional intelligence." High-priced consultants have made millions teaching business leaders (mostly men) emotional intelligence skills that come naturally to women. Our intuitive ability (documented even in female babies) to read other people's emotions quickly and accurately, as well as strong verbal and social skills, are powerful leadership qualities. Trust them. Hone them. Stretch into them until they fit as well as your perfectly tailored suit.

Female leaders in professional environments still frequently find ourselves as one of the few or *only* women in the room. Chances are pretty high that we're going to see things a little differently than the male majority. Get used to it. A leader must have confidence in the value that she brings to the table. The more unique your perspective, experience and way of processing information, the more important it is that you raise your voice and speak up. Women's intellectual and emotional captabilities are valuable social assets that are badly needed in every public and private sector. There's no shortage of male thinking in leadership arenas. What we need more of are leaders who think like women—and are proud of it.

Mothering Leadership

There's another fundamental characteristic to thinking like a woman that goes to the core of who we are: mothering instincts. Whether or not you have children of your own, the drive to protect, nurture, and guide those in our care comes naturally to the female of nearly every species. Spiritual leader, lecturer, and best-selling author Marianne Williamson believes, as I do, that American women have neglected one of our most important mothering responsibilities. "The feminine archetype includes the keeper of the flame, the keeper of the hearth . . . There is no leadership more powerful than the leadership of a woman taking care of her children, taking care of a man if there is a man there and taking care of her family," Williamson writes in her book *A Woman's Worth.* "Now here's the mistake we've made," she says. "Now that women have—for good reason—moved out into the public world, we've forgotten our core leadership strength, which comes from our drive to care for the home and the children. What women now need to realize at the deepest level is that the earth is our home and the world's family is our family."[9]

Williamson, who lectures all over the world, tells the story of how fiercely female hyenas protect their young. "The females form a circle around their pups while they're eating or when there's a threat. They guard the pups even from male hyenas who would gobble up all the food," she said. "They feed the babies first!" Every five seconds, somewhere on our planet, a child dies of hunger, which adds up to 24,000 children every day. Female children are singled out for special horrors: sold into sexual slavery, sexually mutilated, or murdered by their own families to protect family "honor." "Surely, we can do better than female hyenas at taking care of ALL of our children," Williamson challenges. "The power we hold as American women is unmatched anywhere in the world. And our failure to use that power as effectively as we might on behalf of those who need us most is a situation ripe for change."

It's not just the children of the world who are crying out for mothering leadership. In their shocking yet inspiring 2009 book, *Half the Sky: Turning Oppression into Opportunity for Women Worldwide,* husband and wife team and co-authors Nicholas Kristof and Sheryl WuDunn proclaimed that the struggle for global gender equality is "the paramount challenge of the twenty-first century."

> *"The tide of history is turning women from beasts of burden and sexual playthings into full-fledged human beings," they wrote. "The economic advantages of empowering women are so vast as to persuade nations to move in that direction. Before long, we will consider sex slavery, honor killings, and acid attacks (on women) as unfathomable as foot-binding. The question is how long that transformation will take and how many girls will be kidnapped into brothels before it is complete—and whether each of us will be part of that historical movement or a bystander."*[10]

Moving beyond femininity to *womaninity* requires a woman leader to open her ears and eyes to the cacophony of calls for feminine values and strengths at the world's decision-making tables. Nature has it right. Female and male balance one another. Like yin and yang. When nearly all of the leadership positions are held by males, they are acting somewhat like single-parent fathers to society. No wonder the world feels so out of balance on so many fronts. As with any family, fathers and mothers bring diverse strengths to leadership, just as they do to parenting. They are different, complementary, and each tremendously important.

In January 2006, Ellen Johnson Sirleaf, the first elected black female African head of state, was sworn in as the president of Liberia. Nicknamed the "Iron Lady," the Harvard-educated *Interloper* was thrown into jail 20 years ago for her political activities and threatened with rape by her male cellmates. Today, she is evidence to the world of the strength, confidence, and authority of *womaninity* in action. In her inauguration address, President Sirleaf promised to "bring motherly sensitivity and emotion to the presidency" to her task of healing a nation emerging from two decades of brutal civil war. The people of Liberia call her "Mother" as a sign of respect. When asked about her historic role, one of the most respected women in the world told reporters, "I am going to be a leader and a president who happens to be a woman. But I am glad to be a woman because I believe I will bring an extra dimension to the task."[11]

The time is at hand for women "who take responsibility for the time and space they occupy" in the world to fully engage the skills and values we bring to leadership that men cannot. Fully embracing *womaninity* is a leap that women, collectively, have yet to take. Don't look to others for yours. Look within. But you'll only get so far acting alone. Remember the African proverb, "If you wish to go quickly, go alone. If you wish to go far, go together." Help your sisters.

Womaninity

- ✓ Relax into your own skin
- ✓ Forget being "one of the guys"
- ✓ Join the sisterhood
- ✓ Think like a woman
- ✓ Mothering leadership

EPILOGUE

Answering the Call to Leadership

Women aren't giving enough of themselves in a big way. We need to think beyond our boundaries and ask ourselves, "How can I give back to a better world?" Not everybody can do that, but there are lots of women who can—if they would just dare.

— SUSAN DAVIS, Chairman,
Susan Davis International, *Interloper*

The challenge for American women is no longer overcoming what has held us back. It is to embolden ourselves to step forward. The world is crying out for more leaders—at every level. The time is at hand for women -- collectively -- to answer the call to leadership.

Interlopers, Insiders, and *Innovators,* you have the education, the experience, and an unprecedented golden opportunity to be catalysts for the next stage of human evolution: the rise to leadership of a global feminine force field. You also have the responsibility. Because, as citizens of the most progressive and powerful nation in the world, we have been blessed and advantaged in ways hundreds of millions of our global sisters have not.

Reem Abu Hassan, a lawyer from one of Jordan's most prominent families, told me, "Anne, we were inspired when the first woman was named to your Supreme Court. We celebrated when one of your women stood her ground and ran for president. Don't underestimate the importance of each step American women take. You truly affect how women are viewed throughout the world." Our global sisters are counting on us to stand up, speak up, and rise up.

Individual leadership, however, isn't enough. Every woman for herself, as I have said throughout this book, is a losing strategy. *Powering up* will require women to get beyond our differences and recognize how interdependent we are. As a cultural tribe, we will rise or remain stalled together.

Leadership also requires continuously evolving through the stages and strengths that each generation of *Achievers* personifies. A fully evolved leader needs the courage of an *Interloper,* the influential savvy of an *Insider*, as well as the ambition and sense of unlimited possibility of an *Innovator.*

What do I mean by that? Natalie Randolph, a 29-year-old Gen Y high school science teacher from Washington, D.C. is, generationally, an *Innovator*. Yet when she recently accepted a position as the only woman among over 15,000 varsity high school football coaches, she became a bona fide *Pioneering Interloper,* breaking new ground for others to follow.[1] And the 1,102 Women Air Force Service Pilots (WASPS), who flew every type of military aircraft during World War II, were trailblazing *Interlopers.* For over 60 years, they remained outliers, their contributions nearly forgotten. Yet, when the 300 still-living WASPS were awarded the prestigious Congressional Gold Medal in 2009, the news media trumpeted their story around the world.[2] Finally embraced as national heroes, their new *Insiders* status has enhanced their ability to influence and inspire future generations of girls to spread their own wings.

Each generation of American women *Achievers* in the workplace today has a unique role to play in determining how quickly women will begin shaping our nation and engaging in the world equally with men.

Pioneering Interlopers: Give generously of your time and hard-earned wisdom to younger women who are searching for support and insight. This is no time to rest on your laurels or resent opportunities they have that we didn't. Our true legacy will be determined by how quickly we help turbo-charge future waves of women to rise faster and higher than we dared only dream.

Influential Insiders: You've achieved unprecedented positions of power thanks, in part, to the heavy lifting done by *Interlopers.* It's time to pay it forward. Your hard-earned influence is not to be hoarded. Your legacy will be determined by how willing—and effective—you are to invest in your global sisters' future by leading cultural change and lifting others with you as you continue to rise.

I'll-Do-It-My-Way Innovators: You are uniquely positioned to become the most influential generation of women leaders the world has ever known. Aspire to and claim leadership sooner rather than later. But don't forget that leadership is a team sport. You'll need the support and guidance of *Interlopers and Insiders*, or it will take you much longer than you believe.

Are you brave enough to bring your vision to the tables of power? Do you have the skills, tenacity, and moral compass to be a trustworthy and wise guide for those you are asking to follow you? When will you dare to give yourself—and other women—the green light to lead? "We are really ready to do something," Indiana University women's head basketball coach and Olympic gold medalist Felisha Legett Jack told me. She urges her athletes to "become phenomenal women." She is eager for other women to do the same. "I suggest that we grant each other permission to really go out there and be courageous enough to make a difference."

We are so close and yet so far from ascending to a place of true influence and leadership in the world. What will be the collective accomplishments that women of our times will leave on our culture, our values, our families, our workplaces, our country, and our aching planet? The human family is waiting. Hoping. Leadership is not for everyone. But, if you have heard its call, I urge you to answer. What are you waiting for? Dare to lead!

ACKNOWLEDGMENTS

More people than I could ever acknowledge have influenced my thinking for this book, which has been germinating for decades. Now I understand why author acknowledgments at the back of books are always so long. I imagine that most authors feel, as I do, that they couldn't have completed their task without a tremendous amount of help and support every step of the way.

First, I owe a debt of gratitude to the fantastic leaders who generously shared their time and wisdom by doing extensive interviews with me. I wish I could have quoted every one of you, because each of you contributed significantly to my learning. Next, I would like to thank my many friends who have not only tolerated my obsession with the topic of women's leadership and writing this book, but have engaged in thousands of conversations about it with me, while providing a steady and valuable stream of fresh articles, websites and books for my research.

I owe a special thanks to Laura Berman, my book whisperer. She was an invaluable guide and sounding board at a very critical time, when I felt I was swimming (or writing!) in circles, not sure which direction to head. She helped me fine tune my voice and pointed the way to the distant shore. To Pat Dalrick, for her excellent transcribing of nearly one hundred hours of interviews. To Marty Kohn, my outstanding copy editor, who also gave me valuable male perspective along the way. To graphic designer Nancy Cohen, for her fabulous cover and help with the internal formatting. To Ann Williams and my brother, Vince Doyle, whose artistic eyes at key moments made critical differences in the final "look" of this book. To Betsy Amster, Lynette Padwa, Dale Fetherling and Ruth Klein, seasoned publishing professionals whose encouragement and guidance at the very beginning of this project made all the difference in my ability to complete it. To Shirley Przywara, who enabled me to sleep at night, once I knew that your eagle-like proofreading eyes were reviewing every line of my manuscript.

To Linda and Barry Solomon whose steady encouragement and expert advice saved me from going over several perilous publishing cliffs. To Susan Shapiro, who generously gave me my first introduction to the world of book publishing—from someone who has done it all. To Steven Miesowicz, whose ongoing and unabridged insight into the rules according to men, kept me laughing when I needed it most. And to Blanca Fauble, whose support throughout the writing of this book has included managing my political election campaign, insisting on accompanying me to all doctor's appointments related to the treatment of my non-invasive, Stage I breast cancer and, now, leading the marketing efforts for Powering Up!

Finally, I want to express my deepest appreciation to all of my brothers and sisters, by birth and marriage—Danny, Tom, Irene, Vinny, Terry, Linda, Diane, Richard, Elizabeth and Dan—for all of your love, confidence and belief in me that gave me the courage and hunger to keep taking bites out of this elephant long before I believed myself that I could truly complete it.

FAVORITE MOVIES WITH GREAT WOMEN CHARACTERS

A Civil Action
Adam's Rib
Ahead of Time
Alien
A Dangerous Beauty
A League of Their Own
A Woman of Substance
African Queen
Algeria: Women at War
All About Eve
All About My Mother
Amelia
American Quilt
American Violet
Annie Hall
Antonia's Line
As Good As It Gets
Atonement
Auntie Mame
Babbette's Feast
Baby Boom
Bad Girls
Beaches
Bell Jar
Beloved
Bend It Like Beckham
Besieged
Between The Lines
Beyond Rangoon
Blind Side
Bound
Boxcar Bertha
Boys Don't Cry
Breakfast at Tiffany's
Bring it On
Broadcast News
Calendar Girls
Changeling
Chocolat
Claudine
Cleopatra
Clueless
Coco Chanel
Coming Home
Crouching Tiger
Dangerous Beauty
Daughters of the Dust
Deepa Mehta (Director) Films
Desert Bloom
Devil Wears Prada
Diary of a Mad Black Woman
Diary of Miss Jane Pittman
Divine Secrets of the Ya-Ya Sisterhood
Dream Girls
Dream Life of Angels
Eat, Pray, Love
Educating Rita
Election
Elizabeth
Elizabeth I
Elizabeth: The Golden Age

Emma
Entre Nous
Erin Brockovich
Evita
First Wives Club
For Colored Girls
Frida
Fried Green Tomatoes
Frozen River
Funny Face
Funny Girl
G.I. Jane
Girl Interrupted
Girl With the Dragon Tattoo
Girl Who Kicked the Hornet's Nest
Girl Who Played With Fire
Girlfriends
Gone With the Wind
Gypsy
Hairspray
Harold and Maude
Heavenly Creatures
Heiress
Hello Dolly
Hideous Kinky
Housekeeping
How Stella Got Her Groove Back
I Am Love
I Know a Woman Like That
Imitation of Life
In Her Own Right: the Life of Elizabeth Cady Stanton
In Her Shoes
Iron Jawed Angels
It's Complicated
Joy Luck Club
Julie and Julia
Kids are All Right
La Vie en Rose
Lady in Red
Lara Croft Tomb Raider
Legally Blonde
Little Women
Made in Dagenham
Mama Mia!
Maria Full of Grace
Mary Poppins
Mean Girls
Medea's Family Reunion
Memoirs of a Geisha
Mildred Pierce
Million Dollar Baby
Miracle Worker
Miss Congeniality
Miss Firecracker
Monster's Ball
Mrs. Brown
My Big Fat Greek Wedding
My Brilliant Career
Mystic Pizza
National Velvet
Nine to Five
Norma Rae
Not For Ourselves Alone: The Story of Elizabeth Cady Stanton and Susan B. Anthony
Notes on a Scandal
Places in the Heart
Postcards From the Edge
Pray the Devil Back to Hell
Precious
Pride and Prejudice
Real Women Have Curves
Raise the Red Lantern
Revolutionary Road
Ryan's Daughter
Secretariat
Secret Life of Bees

Sense and Sensibility
Set if Off
Shirley Valentine
Silkwood
Sisters
Sisterhood of the Travelling Pants
Sleeping with the Enemy
Songcatcher
Stealing Beauty
Steel Magnolias
Something's Got to Give
Sophie's Choice
Soul Food
Sunshine Cleaning
Space Between Us
Steel Magnolias
Terms of Endearment
The Burning Bed
The Color Purple
The Contender
The Dollmaker
The Golden Age
The Good Earth
The Good Girl
The King and I
The Sound of Music
The Queen
The Wizard of Oz
The Women
(1939 and 2008 versions)
Thelma & Louise
They Shoot Horses Don't They
Three Women
Thirteen
True Grit, 2010
Two Women
Vera Drake
Volver
Waiting to Exhale
Water
Whale Rider
Whales of August
What Ever Happened to Baby Jane
What's Love Got to Do With it?
White Orleander
Wild Hearts Can't Be Broken
Winter's Bone
Woman of the Year
Women
Women of Brewster Place
Women on the Edge of a Nervous Breakdown
Women on the Frontlines
Working Girl
Yentl
Young Victoria
See: www.womenandhollywood.com for updates!

U.S. INTERVIEWEES*

Anderson, Joan, author, *A Year by the Sea, An Unfinished Marriage, A Walk on the Beach*

Badore, Nancy, PhD, organizational development consultant, former Ford Motor Company senior executive

Barclay, Terry, president & CEO, Inforum: A Women's Professional Alliance

Barrett, Barbara, president and CEO Triple Creek Guest Ranch, former U.S. Ambassador to Finland

Barrons, Gerry, co-founder and former Executive Director, Detroit Women's Economic Club

Begley, Charlene, president & CEO, GE Home and Business Solutions

Beindorf, Jennifer, founder & CEO, Virtual Minds Agency

Benko, Cathy, chief talent officer, Deloitte co-author, *The Corporate Lattice: Achieving High Performance in the Changing World of Work*

Berkhemer, Betsy Credaire, president, Berkehmer Clayton Executive Search

Boland, Mary, senior vice president, Finance & Distribution, the Americas, Levi Strauss & Co.

Bolsinger, Lorraine, president & CEO, GE Aviation Systems, LLC

Brennan, Christine, sports columnist, *USA Today, ESPN*

Brooke, Beth, global vice chair, strategy, communications and regulatory affairs, Ernst and Young

Burnett, Patricia Hill, portrait artist, activist, founding president of Michigan chapter of N.O.W., Miss America runner-up 1942

Casiano, Kimberly, president and CEO, Casiano Communications; board member, Ford Motor Company

Castillo, Edith, senior manager, Multi-Cultural Markets and Engagement, American Association of Retired Persons (AARP)

Chappell, Beth, president, Detroit Economic Club

Chianese, Vanessa, manager, Brand Strategy and Consumer Insights, Mazda

Choi, Sarah, senior director, Levi Strauss & Co.

Chulick, Michele, associate vice president and executive director clinical services, University of Miami, Miller School of Medicine

Clark, Marsha, president and CEO, Marsha Clark & Associates

Corradini, Deedee, senior vice president Prudential Utah Real Estate, president Women's Ski Jumping-USA, former mayor Salt Lake City

Lin Cummins, senior vice president and corporate officer, Arvin Meritor

Davis, Susan, chairman, Susan Davis International

DeBoer, Kathy, executive director, American Volleyball Coaches Association, athlete, author *Gender and Competition: How Men and Women Approach Work and Play Differently*

DeDominic, Patty, business consultant and principal, DeDominic & Associates; founder and CEO, PDQ Careers Group

Deremo, Dotty, president and CEO, Hospice of Michigan

Dixon, Reverend Jane Holmes, pioneering female Episcopal bishop

Doyle, Lucy, college student

DunCombe, C. Beth, director, City of Detroit Building Authority; former president and CEO, Detroit Economic Growth Corporation; former partner Dickinson Wright

Dunlop, Dawn, Lieutenant Colonel, United States Air Force

Edwards, Ruth, PhD, principal, *Step Into Yourself, LLC;* author, *Step Into Yourself: Spiritual Affirmations for Embracing Change; Becoming a Black Woman*

Fakhouri, Dr. Haifia, founder and CEO Arab American & Chaldean Council

Fanroy, Michelle, senior vice president, Access One Consulting

Fareed, Charlene Green, PhD, senior consultant, Genesis Coaching & Consulting, Women's leadership Program

Faulkenberry, Barbara, Brigadier General, United States Air Force

Fernandez, Lisa, Olympic gold medalist (softball)

Friedman, Dr. Sonya, practicing psychologist, former CNN-TV host, Sonya Live, author: *Take it From Here, Smart Cookies Don't Crumble* and *Men are Just Desserts*

Gage, Hilda, the Honorable, Michigan Court of Appeals and former Chief Judge Michigan Circuit Court, deceased

Gallegos, Placida, PhD, professor, School of Human and Organization Development, Fielding Graduate University

Gladys, Niki, publisher, *The Nevada Appeal*

Gloria Garfinkel, head docent, Los Angeles County Museum of Art

Goss, Maloni, associate director of strategy, Chanel, Inc.

Gotthelf, Beth, shareholder, Butzel Long, environmental, energy and land practice

Grano, Megan, professional comedian

Hardy, Sue Kruszewski, former women's head basketball coach University of Detroit, University of Washington, Oakland University

Harsanyi, Fruszina, PhD, vice president, global public affairs, Tyco International

Heithoff, Rebecca, college student; video producer

Hollenshead, Carol, executive director (retired), Center for the Education of Women, University of Michigan

Hutchins, Carol, athlete; head coach, women's softball, University of Michigan

Jack, Felisha Leggett, Olympic gold medalist; head coach, women's basketball, Indiana University

Jackson, Danielle, senior staff manager, Marketing, Qualcomm

Jenkins, Carol, founding president, Women's Media Center, former TV news broadcaster

John, Karen, Olympic coach, United State women's softball team, associate director, National Fast Pitch Coaches Association

Kaiser, Catherine, senior vice president and senior finance manager, Bank of America

Kelly, Patricia, M.D. and Homeopath

King, Jean, trailblazing discrimination lawyer, inductee Michigan Women's Hall of Fame

Kramer, Mary, publisher, *Crain's Detroit Business*

Lawrence, Brenda, mayor of Southfield, MI; 2010 lieutenant governor candidate (D-MI)

LeMahieu, Joan, general manager, The Mountain Winery; former CEO, The Parade Company

Ligocki, Kathleen, CEO, Next Autoworks; former CEO, Tower Automotive

Litwin, Anne, PhD, president, Anne Litwin & Associates, Organization Development consultant; research fellow Fielding Graduate University

Marble, Nicole, graduate student; athlete

Mark, Florine, president & CEO, The WW Group, the leading franchise holder for Weight Watchers

McCarthy, Sharon, Abbot Laboratories, Manager, Global Training Compliance

Mendoza, Jessica, Olympic medalist, 2008 U.S. women's softball team; former president, Women's Sports Foundation; USA Softball Female Athlete of the Year

Meyer, Deborah Wahl, vice president and chief marketing officer, Pulte Homes

Miakinin, Elizabeth, founder and principal, E. Miakinin Associates; former engineering director, General Motors

Morella, Connie, former Congresswoman (R-MD); co-founder Vital Voices Global Partnership

Mühlberg, Judith, adjunct professor, Masters program, Corporate Communications and Public Relations, Georgetown University; board director, State Farm; former senior executive Boeing and Ford Motor Company

Muley, Miriam, CEO, 85% Solution Marketing firm; former marketing senior executive Avon and General Motors, author: *The 85% Niche: The Power of Women of all Colors*

Murphy, Leslie, president & CEO, Murphy Consulting, Inc, corporate and non-profit board member, retired group managing partner, Plante Moran LLP

Navratil, Nicole, chief operating officer, BBMG—brand innovation consultancy

Norlin, Cindy, director, Distribution Technology and Renewable Construction, engineer; DTE Energy

Nugent, Jane Kay, pioneering female vice president (retired), Detroit Edison

O'Connell, Marjorie, founder, O'Connell & Associates, global tax law firm, member American Bar Association House of Delegates

Orzech, Leslie, DMD, oral and maxillo facial surgeon

Page, Scott E. PhD, professor of complex systems, political science and economics, University of Michigan

Parker, Margot, senior executive, governmental affairs (retired) General Motors

Peters, Susan, vice president, executive development and chief learning officer, General Electric

Petrovich, Mary, CEO, Axle Tech International

Pierce, Sandy, CEO, Charter One Financial Inc.

Popp, Cynthia, TV director, *The Bold and the Beautiful*

Price, Glenda, PhD, president emeritus, Marygrove College

Reverby, Susan, PhD, professor of Womens Studies, Wellesley College

Riccio, Janet, executive vice president, Omnicom Group, Inc.

Rodriguez, Alba Contreras, business manager, Manufacturing, Vehicle Assembly Operations, Ford Motor Company; MBA student

Rom, Barbara, managing partner, Pepper Hamilton law firm, bankruptcy specialist, retired

Rosener, Judy, PhD, professor, Graduate School of Management, University of California, Irvine; gender and leadership expert; author of 1990 pathbreaking article in *Harvard Business Review,* "Ways Women Lead"

Rush, Andra, founder and CEO, Rush Trucking, Inc., largest Native American business in the USA

Schilling, Kelly, senior vice president, Enterprise Relationship Management

Schlichting, Nancy, president & CEO, Henry Ford Health Systems

Seger, Martha, PhD, economist, first woman named to the National Federal Reserve Board

Stancato, Shirley, president and CEO, New Detroit, Inc.

Stevens, Anne, former CEO, Carpenter Technology; former COO, the Americas, Ford Motor Company; named one of *Fortune magazine's* "50 Most Powerful Women in Business," 2005

Sullivan, Terry, PhD, president, University of Virginia

Sy, Thear, senior executive and partner, Accenture

Takai, Teri, chief information officer, U.S. Department of Defense

Talbot, Sue, trustee, Indiana University Board

Thompson, Anne, correspondent, NBC News

Van Slyke, Michelle Cervantez, vice president marketing, MBE/The UPS Store

Wanink, Billie Jo, founder and CEO, Office Furniture Supply

Watkins, Sherron, whistleblower, former vice president of Corporate Development, Enron Corporation

Whittaker, Barbara, president, BW Limited, former executive director, Global Purchasing, General Motors

Whitman, Marina, PhD, professor of Business Administration and Public Policy, Gerald R. Ford School of Public Policy, University of Michigan

Williamson, Marianne, spiritual activist, lecturer, founder The Peace Alliance, author of multiple best-selling books, including: *The Age of Miracles, A Return to Love, A Woman's Worth, Everyday Grace and A Course in Weight Loss.*

Wilson, Marie, founder and president emeritus, The White House Project

Woodward, Major General Maggie, Commander 17th Air Force and U.S. Air Forces Africa

Worthy, Kym, Wayne County Prosecutor, Detroit

Global Interviewees*

Adedeji, Dr. Olubukola, PhD, senior lecturer, Obafemi Awolowo University, Nigeria

Bethel, Keva, president emerita, College of the Bahamas, Nassau

Campbell, Right Honorable Kim, former Canadian Prime Minister, Paris

Cheung, Ophelia, chairman & managing director, Cheung-Macpherson & Co. Ltd, Hong Kong

Carral, Magdalena Cuevas, founder and partner, Carral, Sierra y Associados; government consultant and president, International Women's Forum, Mexico

Chitrapu, Sunitha, doctoral candidate and lecturer, India

Desjardins, Leslie, chief financial officer, Amcor, Global Packaging Corporation, Melbourne

Ginatta, Joyce, president, JJH Consulting, government official, business leader, received highest decoration from Ecuadorian National Congress, Ecuador

Gorenstein, Ruth Seidler, owner & managing director, Lerosh Investments, Ltd, Israel

Hassan, Reem Abu, lawyer, president, Jordan International Women's Forum, Jordan

Memela-Motumi, Ntsiki, Major General. Department of Defense, Republic of South Africa

Raber, Irina, prefect, Moscow Government, Russia

Walla, Kah, young leader, director general and elected official, Cameroon, Africa

Wisdom, Gail, director, Academia Limited of the Bahamas, Nassau

Youngman, Allison, senior partner, Stikeman Elliott, Barristers and Solicitors, Toronto; president, Canadian International Women's Forum

*** See Facebook Fan Page: Powering Up Women for photos.**

ENDNOTES

In addition to my own experience and reading, this book is based on the original field research I did with over 125 high-achieving women leaders who gave generously of their time to do recorded conversations. A complete list of those women, who each contributed in a significant way to this book, is included, along with a bibliography for further reading.

INTRODUCTION: SIZE MATTERS

Notes:

1. Ricardo Hausmann, Laura D. Tyson, Saadia Zahidi, "The Global Gender Gap Report, 2010," The World Economic Forum, October, 2010, *www.weforum.org.*
2. U.S. Census Bureau, October, 2009, *www.census.gov.*
3. Catalyst, "Women Corporate Executive Officers 2010," *www.catalyst.org*
4. Jenna Goudreau, "What Women Do With Their MBAs," www.Forbes.com, June 21, 2010.
5. Ernst & Young, "Groundbreakers: Using the Strength of Women to Rebuild the World Economy," 2009.
6. Catalyst, Women on Boards 2010," *www.catalystg.org.*
7. Hanna Rosin, "The End of Men," *Atlantic magazine,* July/August 2010, *www.theatlantic.com.*
8. Jessica Bennett and Jesse Ellison, "Women Will Rule the World," *Newsweek magazine,* July 6, 2010.
9. Dr. Julianne Maxveaux, president, Bennett College, *www.juliannemalveaux.com*
10. HeroinesCA, "A Guide to Women in Canadian History," *www.heroines.ca.*

CHAPTER 1: SO MANY ACHIEVERS—WHERE ARE OUR LEADERS?

Notes:

1. Nancy Gibbs and Michael Scherer, "The Meaning of Michelle," *Time magazine,* June 1, 2009, *www.time.com.*
2. Media Matters, "Tucker Carlson on Clinton," July 18, 2007, *www.mediamatters.org*
3. Jodi Kantor, Kate Zernike and Catrin Einhorn, "Fusing Politics and Motherhood in a New Way," *New York Times,* September 7, 2008, *www.nytimes.com.*
4. Dean Reynolds, "The Closer," CBS News and Washington Post, *www.washingtonpost.com.*
5. Zayda Rivera, "Who is Michelle Obama: Angry Black Woman or Supportive Spouse," *Diversity Inc., www.diversityinc.com*
6. Rebecca Traister, "Big Girls Don't Cry: The Election That Changed Everything for American Women." Simon & Schuster, New York, 2010.
7. Claire Shipman and Katy Kay, "Womenomics: Work Less, Achieve More, Live Better," Harper Business, New York, 2009.
8. Casey B. Mulligan, "In A First, Women Surpass Men on U.S. Payrolls," *New York Times,* February 5, 2010.
9. Dr. Mark J. Perry, "Women Now Dominate Higher Education at Every Degree Level," Carpe Diem, June 2, 2009, *www.mjperry.blogspot.com.*
10. "Women and the World Economy: A Guide to Womenomics," *The Economist,* April 12, 2006, *www.economist.com.*
11. Richard Fry and D'Vera Cohn, "New Economics of Marriage: The Rise of Wives," Pew Research Center Pubications, January 19, 2010, *www.pewresearch.org.*
12. National Auctioneers Association Championships, Greensboro, NC, July 2010. Gingell named First-Runner-Up in the Int. Jr. Championship, *www.she-sold-it.com.*
13. Ricardo Hausmann, Laura D. Tyson, Saadia Zahidi, "The Global Gender Gap Report, 2010," The World Economic Forum, October, 2010, *www.weforum.org.*
14. Lang, Ilene, "Targeting Inequity: The Gender Gap in U.S. Corporate Leadership," Testimony before the Joint Economic Committee, U.S. Congress, Sept. 28, 2010.

15. "Women in Management: Female Managers' Representation, Characteristics and Pay," U.S. Government Accountability Office report. Washington, D.C., Sept. 28, 2010.

16. Lang, Ilene, "Targeting Inequity" testimony. Ibid.

17. Lucie Lapovsky, PhD and Deborah Slaner, Larkin, "The White House Project Report: Benchmarking Women's Leadership," 2009, New York. *www.benchmarks.thewhitehouseproject.org.*

18. Ibid.

19. Linda Jean Carpenter, PhD and J.D.R.Vivian Acosta, PhD, "Women in Inter-Collegiate Sport: A Longitudinal, National Study, Thirty-three Year Update (1977-2010)," 2010. *www.webpages.charter.net/womeninsport.*

20. Benchmarking Women's Leadership, Ibid.

21. Christina Brinkley, "The Sex Effect: Empowering to Some, Trashy to Others," *Wall Street Journal*, May 29, 2008.

22. "U.S. Names First Female Four Star General," *CBS News,* November 14, 2008, *www.cbsnews.com.*

23. Benchmarking Women's Leadership, Ibid.

24. Paul Taylor, Rich Morin and D'Vera Cohn, "A Paradox in Public Attitudes – Men or Women: Who's the Better Leader?" Pew Research Center, Aug. 25, 2008, Wash. D.C.

25. "Women and the World Economy: A Guide to Womenomics," *The Economist,* April 12, 2006, *www.economist.com*

26. Sarah Kliff, "Sorry, Hillary, But Girls Already Rule," *Newsweee,* March 17, 2008.

27. "Persons of the Year," *Time magazine,* Dec. 30, 2002.

28. Michael Scherer, "The New Sheriffs of Wall Street," *Time magazine,* May 13, 2010.

29. Benchmarking Women's Leadership, Ibid.

Interviews:
- Kathleen Ligocki, August 17, 2007
- Lorraine Bolsinger, March 6, 2008
- Marie Wilson, January 21, 2009

- Scott Page, PhD, September 28, 2010

CHAPTER 2: THE PIONEERING INTERLOPERS

Notes:

1. "The Girl in Centerfield," documentary film about Carolyn King's historic, 1973 battle with the Little League, produced by: Brian Kruger and Buddy Moorehouse.

2. "Life After Citadel: Shannon Faulkner Reflects on Her Historic Battle With Elite Military College," ABC's Good Morning America, Dec. 8, 2009.

3. Katharine Dexter McCormick, National Women's Hall of Fame, *www.greatwomen.org*.

4. Leonard Pitts, Jr, Miami Herald, syndicated columnist

Interviews:

- Connie Morella, March 2008
- Barbara Whittaker, September 17, 2007
- Susan Davis, October 8, 2007
- Marjorie O'Connell, October 12, 2007
- Honorable Hilda Gage, July 7, 2007
- Anne Stevens, January 29, 2009
- Barbara Rom, September 20, 2007
- Carol Hollenshead, October 31, 2007
- Joan LeMahieu, September 8, 2007
- Beth DunCombe, November 28, 2007

CHAPTER 3: THE INFLUENTIAL INSIDERS

Notes:

1. "The Explosion of Female College Attendance," *Center for Advanced Human Resource Studies,* Cornell University, November, 16, 1990.

2. Families and Work Institute, "Generation & Gender in the Workplace," the American Business Collaboration, 2002.

3. Felice N. Schwartz, "Management Women and the New Facts of Life." *Harvard Business Review,* January/February, 1989.

4. Lisa Belkin, "The Opt Out Revolution," *New York Times magazine,* October 26, 2003. *www.nytimes.com.*

5. "Overview of Title IX of the Education Amendments of 1972," Civil Rights Division, U.S. Department of Justice, *www.justice.gov.*

6. Nan Robertson, *The Girls in the Balcony: Women, Men and the New York Times,* iUniverse.com, Inc, New York, 1992.

7. Mary Lou Butcher, *Michigan Journalism Hall of Fame, www.hof.jrn.msu.edu.*

8. A. C. Showers, "Rocking the Boat: Women Enter Military Academies." University of Colorado, April 22, 2008.

9. "Facts About Women in the Military," *Women's Research and Education Institute, www.feminism.eserver.org/workplace/professions/women-in-the-military.txt.*

Interviews:

- Commander General Maggie Woodward, February , 2008
- Kathleen Ligocki, August 17, 2007
- Sandy Pierce, October 25, 2007
- Brigadier General Barbara Faulkenberry, November 19, 2007.
- Karen John, August 9, 2007
- Betty Harragan, June, 1979.
- Colonel Dawn Dunlop, February 2008
- Charlene Begley, March 6, 2008
- Judith Mühlberg, March 20, 2009
- Miriam Muley, February 21, 2008

CHAPTER 4: THE I'LL-DO'IT-MY-WAY INNOVATORS

Notes:

1. "United States Presidential Election 2008," Wikapedia.

2. *Newsweeek magazine,* March 17, 2008, Ibid.

3. "Despite Talk of a Revolution, Generation Y Does Not Plan to Permanently Opt-Out of Workforce," Lifetime Television Women's Pulse Poll, December 13, 2006.

4. Nadira A. Hira, "Attracting the Twenty-Something Worker." *Fortune magazine,* May 15, 2007.

5. Lifetime Television Women's Pulse Poll, Ibid.

6. Linda Babcock and Sara Laschever, *Women Don't Ask: Negotiation and the Gender Divide,* Princeton University Press, 2003.

7. Sheryl Sandberg, speaking at TED Women conference, Washington, D.C., December 21, 2010, www.ted.com/talks/sherylsandberg.

Interviews

- Susan Peters, March 6, 2008
- Carol Hutchins, October 3, 2007
- Jane Kay Nugent, September 18, 2007
- Jessica Mendoza, August 11, 2007
- Nancy Schlichting, September 13, 2007
- Lorraine Bolsinger, March 6, 2008
- Judy Rosener, PhD, January 31, 2009

CHAPTER 5: WHY GIRLS DON'T RULE

Notes:

1. Rita Andrews, Anne Litwin, Mary Lou Michael, "Stand If You Ever."

2. Ruth Yopp-Edwards, "Internalized Collective Consciousness: A Tool for Black Women's Socialization." Academic Paper presented at the 34th Annual Meeting of the National Council for Black Studies, New Orleans, March 17, 2010.

3. Susan Douglas, PhD, *Enlightened Sexism: The Seductive Message That Feminism's Work is Done.* Times Books, Henry Holt & Company, New York, 2010.

4. Susan Shapiro Barash, *Tripping the Prom Queen: The Truth About Women and Rivalry.* St. Martin's Press, New York, March 2006.

5. "The Eight Female Tribes That Power the Global Economy," Harris Interactive and Pacific Ethnographic study commissioned in 2008 by G23, an all-women strategic agency of The Omnicom Group, New York.

6. "What Multi-Cultural Women Want: New Findings From Working Mother's Face-to-Face Instant Polling," report, *Working Mother* 2007 National Conference.

7. Ariel Zirulnick, "Global Gender Gap Index: Iceland tops, France drops and US breaks into top 20," *The Christian Science Monitor,* October 12, 2010.

8. Michael Kimmel, PhD, *The Gendered Society.* Oxford University Press, NY, 2000.

9. Miguel Helft, "Mark Zuckerberg's Most Valuable Friend," *The New York Times,* October 2, 2010.

10. Joann S. Lublin, "The Corner Office and a Family: Most Big Company Women CEOs are Mothers, Book Finds." *Wall Street Journal,* October 17, 2010.

11. Brian O'Keefe, "Meet the New Face of Business Leadership." *Fortune magazine,* March 2010.

12. Lynn Sherr, "The Most Powerful Woman in U.S. History. *More magazine,* Oct., 2010.

Interviews:

- Connie Morella, March 2008
- Leslie Desjardins, October 2008
- Deedee Corradini, July 2007
- Marie Wilson, January 21, 2009
- Dr. Sonya Friedman, August 20, 2008
- Lucy Doyle, July 15, 2010
- KahWalla, October 2008
- Kym Worthy, March 31, 2009
- Janet Riccio, July 31, 2008
- Shirley Stancato, October 26, 2007
- Anne Litwin, PhD., April 17, 2009
- Glenda Price, PhD, April 23, 2010
- Rianna Moore, April 20, 2009
- Maloni Goss, March 23, 2009
- Sandy Pierce, October 25, 2007

CHAPTER 6: WHAT DO MEN HAVE TO DO WITH IT?

Notes:

1. "Female Ref Banned From Boys Game," *ABC News, Good Morning America,* February, 18, 2008.
2. Linda Jean Carpenter, Ph.D. and J.D.R. Vivian Acosta, Ph.D., "Women in Inter-Collegiate Sport: A Longitudinal, National Study, Thirty-three Year Update (1977-2010)," 2010. *www.webpages.charter.net/womeninsport.*
3. Maria Liberia Peters, "Women Striving to Reach the Top," excerpt from *Politics Had Its Price: The Life and Times of Maria Liberia Peters.*
4. Christine Brennan, *The Best Seat in the House: A Father, a Daughter, a Journey Through Sports.* A Lisa Drew Book/Scribner, New York, 2006.
5. Michael McCarthy, "Jets Owner Apologizes to female TV reporter for treatment at practice," *USA Today,* September 14, 2010.
6. Adam Bryant, "Xerox's New Chief Tries to Redefine Its Culture," *New York Times,* February 20, 2010.
7. Kathleen DeBoer, *Gender and Competition: How Men and Women Approach Work and Play Differently,"* Coaches Choice, 2004.
8. "100 Leading Women in the North American Auto Industry," *Automotive News,* September 13, 2010. *www.autonews.com/section/leading_women.*
9. "Sandra Bullock, Jesse James Divorce Finalized, *USA Today,* June 29, 2010
10. G. Gordon Liddy comment during nationally syndicated radio broadcast, May 28, 2009, "Liddy Worried About Sotomayor Judging While Menstruating," *National Organization for Women Hall of Shame; www.now.org/issues/media/hallofshame.*
11. Hanna Rosin, "The End of Men," *Atlantic magazine,* July/August 2010, *www.theatlantic.com.*

Interviews:

- Carol Hutchins, October 13, 2007
- Christine Brennan, June 29, 2010
- Susan Peters, March 6, 2008
- Kathleen DeBoer, August 9, 2008
- Barbara Barrett, December 18, 2007
- Kim Casiano, July 8, 2008

CHAPTER 7: DISCOVER YOUR PURPOSE

Notes:

1. Patricia Sellers, "Melinda Gates Goes Public," *Fortune magazine,* January 7, 2008.

2. Marianne Williamson, speaking to audience during "Sister Giant Conference, Los Angeles, February 27, 2010.

3. Judy Rosener, PhD and M. Jordan, "The Ways Women Lead," *Harvard Business Review,* November/December 1990.

4. Dan Ackerman, "Tire Trouble: The Ford-Firestone Blowout." *Forbes.com,* June 20, 2001. *In 2000, terrible vehicle crashes and many deaths occurred when the treads on certain 15-inch Bridgestone Wilderness tires, most of them on Ford Explorer SUVs, separated from the rest of the tire at high speeds, particularly in very hot climates. The product safety disaster, which led to congressional hearings and the eventual recall of 6.5 million tires, is still studied today in business and journalism schools.*

5. Marissa Levin, "We're Just Getting Started: Women-Owned businesses to generate 5+ million new jobs by 2018. *Examiner.com,* January 1, 2010.

6. Malcolm Gladwell, *Outliers: The Story of Success.* Little, Brown and Company/ Hachette Book Group, New York, 2008.

7. Marcus Buckingham and Donald Clifton, PhD, *Now, Discover Your Strengths.* The Free Press, a Division of Simon & Schuster, New York, 2001.

8. Sheelagh Whitaker, "Women in Power," *The Globe and Mail,* November 1, 2010.

Interviews:

- Judy Rosener, PhD, January 31, 2009
- Dr. Sonya Friedman, August 22, 2008
- Leslie Murphy, January 11, 2008
- Miriam Muley, February 21, 2008
- Teri Takai, December 21, 2007
- Megan Grano, October 14, 2008
- Dottie Deremo, November 12, 2007
- Felisha Leggett-Jack, April 22, 2009.
- Christine Brennan, June 29, 2010.
- Michelle Fanroy, October 24, 2008
- Florine Mark, June 2008

CHAPTER 8: RAISE YOUR VOICE

Notes:

1. "CBS Fires Don Imus Over Racial Slur," *CBSNews.com,* April 12, 2007.

2. "Sexism Sells But We're Not Buying It," video compilation produced by *The Women's Media Center,* www.womensmediacenter.com. See YouTube: Sexism Sells But We're Not Buying It.

3. *Enlightened Sexism,* Ibid.

4. Herminia Ibarra and Otilia Obodaru, "Women and the Vision Thing." *Harvard Business Review,* January 2009.

5. Michael Scherer, "The New Sheriffs of Wall Street," *Time magazine,* May 13, 2010.

6. Dr. Louann Brizendine, *The Female Brain.* Doubleday Broadway Publishing Group, New York, 2006.

7. *Time magazine,* May 13, 2010, Ibid.

Interviews:

- Carol Jenkins, January 16, 2008
- Mary Petrovich, December 17, 2007
- Nicole Navratil, October 25, 2008
- Commander General Maggie Woodward, February 2008
- Terry Sullivan, PhD, January 16, 2008
- Nancy Badore, PhD, March 16, 2009
- Teri Takai, December 21, 2007

CHAPTER 9: BREAK THE RULES

Notes:

1. Roger Angell, The Sporting Scene, "SHARING THE BEAT," *The New Yorker,* April 9, 1979.

2. Richard Fry and D'Vera Cohn, "New Economics of Marriage: The Rise of Wives," Pew Research Center Publications, January 19, 2010, *www.pewresearch.org.*

Interviews:

- Nicole Marble, March 12, 2009

- Christine Brennan, June 29, 2010
- Sandy Pierce, October 25, 2007
- Miriam Muley, February 21, 2008
- Barbara Barrett, December 18, 2007
- Honorable Hilda Gage, July 7, 2007
- Rabecca Heithoff, June 11, 2010
- Patty DeDominic, May 14, 2008

CHAPTER 10: CLAIM POWER

Notes:

1. Dave Ashenfelter, "Plan For Revamping Office Won U.S. Attorney Post," *Detroit Free Press,* February 14, 2010
2. O's First Ever Power List, "THE POWER OF AMBITION, DONNA BRAZILE," *Oprah magazine,* August 11, 2009.
3. Linda Babcock and Sara Laschever, *Women Don't Ask: Negotiation and the Gender Divide,* Princeton University Press, Princeton, N.J., 2203.
4. James Dao, "First Woman Ascends to Top Drill Sergeant Spot," *New York Times,* September 21, 2009.
5. "THE POWER OF SELF PROGRAM," Marsha Clark & Associates, Frisco, Texas, *www.marshaClarkandAssociates.com.*
6. Rochelle Riley, columnist, *Detroit Free Press*
7. Shifra Bronznick and Didi Goldenhar, "21st Century Women's Leadership," New York University Research Center for Leadership in Action, The White House Project, New York, October 2008.
8. Nicholas Confessore and Danny Hakim, "Kennedy Drops Bid for Senate Seat, Citing Personal Reasons," *New York Times,* January 21, 2009.
9. Karen Tumulty, "Is Caroline Kennedy Ready for the Senate?" *Time magazine,* December 15, 2008.
10. Ella L.J. Edmondson Bell and Stella M. Nkomo, *Our Separate Ways: Black and White Women and the Struggle for Professional Identity,* Harvard Business Press, 2001.
11. Benchmarking Women's Leadership, Ibid.

Interviews:

- Right Honorable Kim Campbell, October 31, 2008
- Kathleen Ligocki, August 17, 2007
- Brigadier General Barbara Faulkenberry, November 19, 2007
- Beth Brooke, March 20, 2009
- Marsha Clark, July 1, 2010
- Deborah Wahl Meyer, July 21, 2008
- Beth DunCombe, November 28, 2007
- Edith Castillo, December 14, 2007
- Gina Davis, November 18, 2009
- Marie Wilson, January 21, 2009

CHAPTER 11: DRINK AT DANGEROUS WATERS

Notes:

1. Mary O'Hara-Devereaux, *Navigating the Badlands: Thriving in the Decade of Radical Transformation,* Jossey-Bass, San Francisco, 2004.

2. Howard E. Gardner, "Leading Minds: An Anatomy of Leadership," Basic Books, New York, 1996.

3. International Women's Forum, Washington, D.C., *www.iwforum.org.*

4. "Hispanic Americans by the Numbers," U.S. Census Bureau, *www.infoplease.com.*

5. "An Older and More Diverse Nation by Midcentury," U.S. Census Bureau press release, August, 14, 2008; *www.census.gov.*

6. Jessica Bennett & Jesse Ellison, "Women Will Rule the World," *Newsweek,* July 6, 2010

7. Jennifer Cheesman Day, "Population Profile of the United States," U.S. Census Bureau, POPULATION PROJECTIONS OF THE UNITED STATES BY AGE, SEX, RACE, AND HISPANIC ORIGIN: 1993-2050. *www.census.gov.*

8. Doron Levin, "The Visionaries of Detroit: Carol Goss," *Fortune magazine,* August, 2010.

9. "Groundbreakers: Ibid.

10. Scott E. Page, *The Difference: How the Power of Diversity Creates Better Groups, Firms, Schools and Societies,* Princeton University Press, 2007.

11. Charlie Savage, "A Judge's View of Judging is on the Record," *New York Times,* May 14, 2009.

12. "Buffett, Gates Persuade 40 Billionaires to Donate Half of Wealth, *Associated Press (AP),* August 4, 2010.

13. Joe Klein, "The State of Hillary: A Mixed Record on the Job," *Time magazine,* November 5, 2009.

14. "2009 Catalyst Census: Fortune 500 Women Board Directors," Catalyst, *www.catalyst.org/research.*

15. John Gallagher, "Free Press Wins Pulitzer for Coverage of Mayoral Scandal," *Detroit Free Press,*April 20, 2009.

16. M. L. Elrick, Tresa Baldas, David Ashenfelter, Jim Schaefer and Joe Swickard, "Feds: Kilpatrick Ran Crime Ring," *Detroit Free Press,* December 16, 2010.

17. The Optimist Creed, OPTIMIST INTERNATIONAL, *www.optimist.org.*

Interviews:

- Patty DeDominic, May 14, 2008
- Right Honorable Kim Campbell, October 31, 2008
- Reem Abu Hassan, August 26, 2008
- Ophelia Cheung, October 17, 2008
- Glenda Price, PhD, April 23, 2010
- Kim Casiano, July 8, 2008
- Maloni Goss, March 23, 2009
- Beth Brooke, March 20, 2009
- Sherron Watkins, March 30, 2009

CHAPTER 12: GET BACK IN THE SADDLE

Notes:

1. "An Associate of Jerry Brown Calls Meg Whitman a "Whore" Over Pension Reform," POLITICAL, *Los Angeles Times,* October 7, 2010.

2. Russell Goldman, "Krystal Ball's Image Problem: Racy Photos of Virginia Candidate," *ABC News,* October 8, 2010.

3. Krystal Ball, "The Next Glass Ceiling," *The Huffington Post,* October 11, 2010.

4. Susan Page, "Study: Sexist Insults Hurt Female Politicians," *USA Today,* September 23, 2010.

5. Linda Babcock and Sara Laschever, *Women Don't Ask: Negotiation and the Gender Divide,* Bantam Dell, New York, 2007.

6. Ibid.

7. "Sexism Sells But We're Not Buying It," WOMEN'S MEDIA CENTER, *YouTube,* May 23, 2008.

8. *Big Girls Don't Cry,* Ibid.

9. Adam Bryant, "New Xerox Chief Tries to Redefine Culture," *New York Times,* February 20, 2010.

10. Ibid.

11. Elizabeth Warren, "Building a Progressive Economic Vision," Speech to Netroots Nation Conference, July 24, 2010. *www.rooseveltinstitute.org/new-roosevelt/elizabeth-warren-netrootsnation.*

12. Billie Jean King, *Pressure is a Privilege: Lessons I've Learned from Life and the Battle of the Sexes;* Life Time Media, Inc, New York, 2008.

13. Sylvia Ann Hewlett, PhD, *Off-ramps and On-ramps: Keeping Talented Women on the Road to Success;* Harvard Business School Publishing, Boston, 2007.

14. Buddy Moorehouse and Brian Kruger, *The Girl in Centerfield,* film by Stunt3Multimedia, Detroit, 2010.

Interviews:

- Mary Petrovich, December 17, 2007
- Kym Worthy, March 31, 2009
- Thear Sy, April 22, 2010
- Nancy Badore, PhD, March 16, 2009
- Teri Takai, December 21, 2007
- Nicole Navratil, October 25, 2008
- Susan Peters, March 6, 2008
- Mary Kramer, December 12, 2007
- Kym Worthy, March 31, 2009
- Carol Hutchins, October 3, 2007
- Terry Barclay, January 23, 2007
- Glenda Price, PhD, April 23, 2010

CHAPTER 13: WOMANINITY—BEYOND THE GIRLS AND THE GUYS

Notes:

1. "Sexism Sells, But We're Not Buying It," *Women's Media Center,* 2008. *www.womensmediacenter.com/blog/2008*

2. *Enlightened Sexism,* Ibid.

3. Lynn Sherr, "The Most Powerful Woman in U.S. History," *More magazine,* October 2010.

4. Peninah Thomson, online video commentary, "Fifty Lessons," Harvard Business Publishing, *www.hbsp.fiftylessons.com.*

5. Tom Kirvan, "Gold Standard Retired Judged Served as Inspiration to All, Remembered as Trailblazer," *Detroit Legal News,* September 15, 2010.

6. Michael Kimmel, Ph.D., *Guyland: The Perilous World Where Boys Become Men;* HarperCollins, New York, 2008.

7. Miguel Helft, "Mark Zuckerberg's Most Valuable Friend," *New York Times,* October 2, 2010.

8. Alice Eagly, Ph.D. and Linda Carli, Ph.D., "Women and the Labyrinth of Leadership," *Harvard Business Review,* September 2007

9. Marianne Williamson, *A Woman's Worth,* Random House, New York, 1993.

10. Nicholas Kristof and Sheryl WuDunn, *Half the Sky: Turning Oppression into Opportunity for Women Worldwide,* Random House, New York, 2009.

11. Ellen Sirleaf Johnson, inaugural address, Liberia, January 16, 2006, www.allafrica.com/2006

Interviews:

- Terry Sullivan, PhD, January 16, 2008
- Kelly Schilling, April 7, 2010
- Carol Hutchins, October 13, 2007
- Kathleen Ligocki, August 17, 2007
- Barbara Whittaker, Septemer 17, 2007
- Christine Brennan, June 29, 2010
- Joan LeMahieu, September 28, 2007
- Cynthia Pasky, "Women Leaders" panel, April 22, 2010
- Leslie Murphy, January 11, 2008
- Lieutenant Colonel Dawn Dunlop, February 2008

- Susan Peters, March 6, 2008
- Mary Petrovich, December 17, 2007
- Honorable Hilda Gage, July 7, 2007
- Judith Muhlberg, March 20. 2009
- Charlene Begley, March 6, 2008
- Marie Wilson, January 21, 2009
- Marianne Williamson, May 8, 2009

EPILOGUE: ANSWERING THE CALL TO LEADERSHIP

Notes:

1. Alan Goldenbach, "Natalie Randolph Takes Reins at Coolidge High," *The Washington Post,* August 6, 2010.

2. Staff Sgt. J. G. Buzanowski, "WASPS Awarded Congressional Gold Medal," March 11, 2010, *www.af.mil/news*

Interviews:

- Susan Davis, October 8, 2007
- Reem Abu Hassan, August 26, 2008
- Felisha Legett-Jack, April 22, 2009

BIBLIOGRAPHY

Ailes, Roger. 1988. *You Are the Message*. New York: Doubleday.

Anderson, Joan. 2004. *A Walk on the Beach.* New York: Broadway Books, a Division of Random House, Inc.

Austin, Linda, M.D. 2000. *What's Holding You Back: Eight Critical Choices for Women's Success*. New York: Basic Books.

Babcock, Linda, and Laschever, Sarah. 2003. *Women Don't Ask: Negotiation and the Gender Divide*. Princeton: Princeton University Press.

Barkalow, Captain Carol. 1992. *In the Men's House*. New York: Berkeley Book published by arrangement with Poseidon Press.

Bell, Ella L.J. Edmondson, and Nkomo, Stella M, 2001. *Our Separate Ways: Black and White Women and the Struggle for Professional Identity.* Berkeley, CA: Third Woman Press.

Benko, Cathleen, and Weisberg, Anne. 2007. *Mass Career Customization: Aligning the Workplace with Today's Nontraditional Workforce*. Boston: Harvard Business School Publishing.

Bennis, Warren. 1989. *On Becoming a Leader.* Basic Books/Perseus Books Group; New York, 2009.

Bethel, Sheila Murray, PhD. 2009. *A New Breed of Leader*. New York: Berkley Publishing Group.

Black, Kathy, 2007. *Basic Black*. Three Rivers Press, New York.

Brizendine, Louann, Dr., *The Female Brain*, (2006) Broadway Books.

Brooks, Geraldine. 1995. *Nine Parts of Desire: The Hidden Life of Islamic Women.* Anchor Books, New York.

Buckingham, Marcus. 2007. *Go Put Your Strengths to Work*. New York: Free Press, a division of Simon & Schuster, Inc.

Buckingham, Marcus, and Clifton, Donald O., Ph.D. 2001. *Now, Discover Your Strengths*. New York: Free Press, a division of Simon & Schuster, Inc.

Collins, Jim, 2001. *Good to Great* HarperCollins, New York.

Condren, Debra, PhD, 2006. *am-BITCH-ous*, Morgan Road Books, New York.

Covey, Stephen R. 1989. *Seven Habits of Highly Effective People.* New York: Simon & Schuster, Inc.

Covey, Stephen R. 2004. *The 8th Habit: From Effectiveness to Greatness*. New York: Free Press, a division of Simon & Schuster, Inc.

Davis, Angela. 1981. *Women, Race & Class*. New York: Random House.

Dilenschneider, Robert L. 1994. *On Power*. New York: Harper Collins Books.

Dilenschneider, Robert L. 2000. *The Critical 2nd Phase of Your Professional Life*. New York: Citadel Press Books.

DeLuca, Joel R, Ph.D. 1999. *Political Savvy*. Berwyn, PA: EBG Publications.

Douglas, Susan J. 2010. *Enlightened Sexism: The Seductive Message that Feminism's Work is Done*. New York: Henry Holt & Company.

Fels, Anna. 2004. *Necessary Dreams: Ambition in Women's Changing Lives*. New York: First Anchor Books.

Fisher, Roger, Ury, William L, and Patton, Bruce. 1991. *Getting to Yes: Negotiating Agreement Without Giving In.* New York, Penguin Books.

Frankel, Dr. Lois, 2007. *See Jane Lead: 99 Ways for Women to Take Charge at Work, 2007* New York, Warner Business Books.

Friedan, Betty. 2001. *The Feminine Mystique.* New York, W.W. Norton & Company. First published in 1963.

Friedman, Stewart D. and Greenhaus, Jeffrey H. 2000. *Work and Family—Allies or Enemies: What Happens When Business Professionals Confront Life Choices.* New York: Oxford University Press.

Friedman, Thomas. 2005. *The World is Flat: A Brief History of the Twenty-First Century.* New York: Farrar, Strauss and Giroux.

Gilligan, Carol, 1982. *In A Different Voice,* Boston: Harvard University Press.

Goldsmith, Marshall and Reiter, Mark, 2007. *What Got You Here Won't Get You There,* New York: Hyperion Books.

Harragan, Betty Lehan, 1977. *Games Mother Never Taught You.* New York: Warner Books.

Hartman, Mary S. 1999. *Talking Leadership, Conversations with Powerful Women.* Rutgers University Press, New Jersey.

Harvard Business Review 1998 *What Makes a Leader*, 1998. Boston: Harvard Business School Publishing Group.

Heim, Patricia, and Golant, Susan K. 1993. *Hardball for Women: Winning at the Game of Business.* New York: The Penguin Group.

Hewlett, Sylvia Ann. 2007. *Off-Ramps and On-Ramps: Keeping Talented Women on the Road to Success.* Boston: Harvard Business School Press.

Huffinton, Arianna. 2006. *On Becoming Fearless . . . in Love, Work and Life.* New York: Hachette Book Group.

Ireland, Patricia. 1997. *What Women Want.* New York: Penguin Group.

Kanter, Rosabeth Moss. 1977. *Men and Women of the Corporation,* Boston: Harvard Press.

Kanter, Rosabeth Moss, and Stein, Barry. 1980. *A Tale of "O": On Being Different in an Organization.* New York: Harper & Row.

Kimmel, Michael. 2007. *The Gendered Society,* Oxford University Press. New York: Oxford University Press.

Kimmel, Michael, 2008. *Guyland: The Perilous World Where Boys Become Men.* New York: HarperCollins.

King, Billie Jean. 2008. *Pressure is a Privilege: Lessons I've Learned from Life and the Battle of the Sexes.* New York: LifeTime Media.

Klaus, Peggy. 2003. *Brag! The Art of Tooting Your Own Horn Without Blowing It.* New York: Time Warner Book Group.

Kouzes, James M. and Posner, Barry Z., 2002. *The Leadership Challenge.* San Francisco: Jossey-Bass.

Kristof, Nicholas D., and WuDunn, Sheryl. 2009. *Half the Sky: Turning Oppression into Opportunity for Women Worldwide.* New York: Alfred A. Knopf, a division of Random House, Inc.

Maloney, Congresswoman Carolyn B. 2008. *Rumors of Our Progress have Been Greatly Exaggerated.* New York: Rodale, Inc.

Monk, Sue, 1996. *The Dance of the Dissident Daughter.* New York: HarperCollins.

Myers, Dee Dee. 2008. *Why Women Should Rule the World.* New York: Harper Collins.

O'Hara-Devereaux, Mary. 2004. *Navigating the Badlands: Thriving in the Decade of Radical Transformation.* San Francisco: Jossey-Bass.

Patton, Bruce, Heen, Sheila, Fisher, Roger. 1999. *Difficult Conversations: How to Discuss what Matters Most.* Penguin Books. New York: Viking Penguin.

Peters, Thomas H. and Robert H. Waterman, Jr., 1982. *In Search of Excellence: Lessons from America's Best-Run Companies.* New York: Warner Books.

Schembechler, Bo, and Bacon, John U. 2007. *Bo's Lasting Lessons: The Legendary Coach Teaches the Timeless Fundamentals of Leadership.* New York: Business Plus, a division of Hachette Book Group.

Shipman, Claire, and Kay, Katty. 2009. *Womenomics: Write Your Own Rules for Success.* New York: HarperCollins Publishers.

Smith, Lillian. 1961. *Killers of the Dream,* New York: W.W. Norton,

Steinem, Gloria. 1992. *Revolution from Within.* Boston and Toronto: Little, Brown and Company 1949. First published, 1978, New York: W.W. Norton.

Tannen, Deborah. 1994. *Talking From Nine to Five: How Women's and Men's Conversational Styles Affect Who Gets Heard, Who Gets Credit, and What Gets Done at Work.* New York: William Morrow.

Tichy, Noel M. & Bennis, Warren. 2007. *Judgment . . . How Winning Leaders Make Great Calls.* New York: Penguin Book Group.

Tichy, Noel 2002, The *Leadership Engine: How Winning Companies Build Leaders at Every Level.* 2002. New York: Harper Collins.

Traister, Rebecca, 2010, *Big Girls Don't Cry: The Election That Changed Everything for American Women.* New York: Simon & Schuster.

Ulrich, Laurel Thatcher. 2007. *Well-Behaved Women Seldom Make History,* New York: Alfred A. Knopf.

Warner, Fara. 2006. *The Power of the Purse: How Smart Businesses Are Adapting to the World's Most Important Customers—Women.* New Jersey: Pearson Education Inc.

Wilkerson, Isabel, 2010. *The Warmth of Other Suns: The Epic Story of America's Great Migration.* New York: Random House.

Wilson, Marie C. 2004. *Closing the Leadership Gap: Add Women, Change Everything.* New York: Penguin Books.

Witt, Christopher, with Fetherling, Dale. 2009. *Real Leaders Don't Do Powerpoint: How to Sell Yourself and Your Ideas.* New York: Crown Business.

Wollstonecraft, Mary. 1792. *A Vindication of the Rights of Woman.* London: Joseph Johnson.

Williamson, Marianne. 1993. *A Woman's Worth.* New York: Ballantine Books.

Research studies:

A Paradox in Public Attitudes: Men or Women: Who's the Better Leader? A Social & Demographic Trends Report. PewResearch Center, Aug. 25, 2008.

The Shriver Report: A Woman's Nation Changes Everything *Shriver, Maria and Center for American Progress. 2010.*

Groundbreakers: Using the Strength of Women to Rebuild the World Economy. 2009. Ernst & Young.

Lang, Ilene. September 28, 2010. Targeting Inequity: The Gender Gap in U.S. Corporate Leadership. Testimony to U.S. Joint Economic Committee.

21st Century Women's Leadership, Bronznick, Shifra and Goldenhar, Didi. The White House Project and Research Center for Leadership in Action, Oct. 2008.

The White House Project Report: Benchmarking Women's Leadership. New York, 2009.

Women in Intercollegiate Sport: A Longitudinal, National Study Thirty Three Year Update: 1977-2010, Carpenter, Linda Jean, PhD and Acosta, J.D.R. Vivian, PhD. Feb. 4, 2010.

Articles:

A Female Midlife Crisis, by Nancy Gibbs. *Time* magazine, May 16, 2005

Gender, Diversity, and Organizational Change: The Boy Scouts vs. Girl Scouts of America. Arneil, Barbara. Perspectives on Politics, March 2010

Hear Her Roar: Gender, Class and Hillary Clinton, by Tina Brown, *Newsweek* magazine, March 17, 2008

How Women Lead: 20 of America's Most Powerful Women on Their Lives—and the Lessons They've Learned. *Newsweek* magazine, Oct. 24, 2005.

Terminated: Why Women of Wall Street are Disappearing by Anita Raghavan, Forbes. com, Feb. 25, 2009

The Corner Office and a Family, by Joann S. Lublin, *Wall Street Journal,* Oct. 18, 2010.

The Future of Work, *Time* magazine, May, 25 2009.

The One Hundred Billion Dollar Woman: Melinda Gates by Patricia Sellers. *Fortune* magazine, January 21, 2008.

The State of the American Woman by Nancy Gibbs. *Time* magazine, Oct, 26, 2009.

What's Holding Women Back? Sheila Wellington, Marcia Brumit Kropf, Paulette R. Gerkovich. *Harvard Business Review,* June 2003.

Women and Power: Do Women Really Lead Differently Than Men? Kantrowitz, Barbara, *Newsweek* magazine, Oct. 15, 2007.

Women In Power (Special week-long series), *Globe & Mail,* Montreal, Oct. 10-18, 2010.

Work and Life: The End of the Zero-Sum Game. Friedman, Stewart D., Christensen, Perry, DeGroot, Jessica, *Harvard Business Review,* 1998.

Japanese Women Shy from Dual Mommy Role, *Washington Post,* Aug. 28, 2008, Blaine Harden.

On Diversity, America Isn't Putting Its Money Where Its Mouth Is, *Wall Street Journal,* Carol Hymowitz, Feb. 25, 2008.

INDEX

D

E

F

G

N

O

P

R

S